AF473895

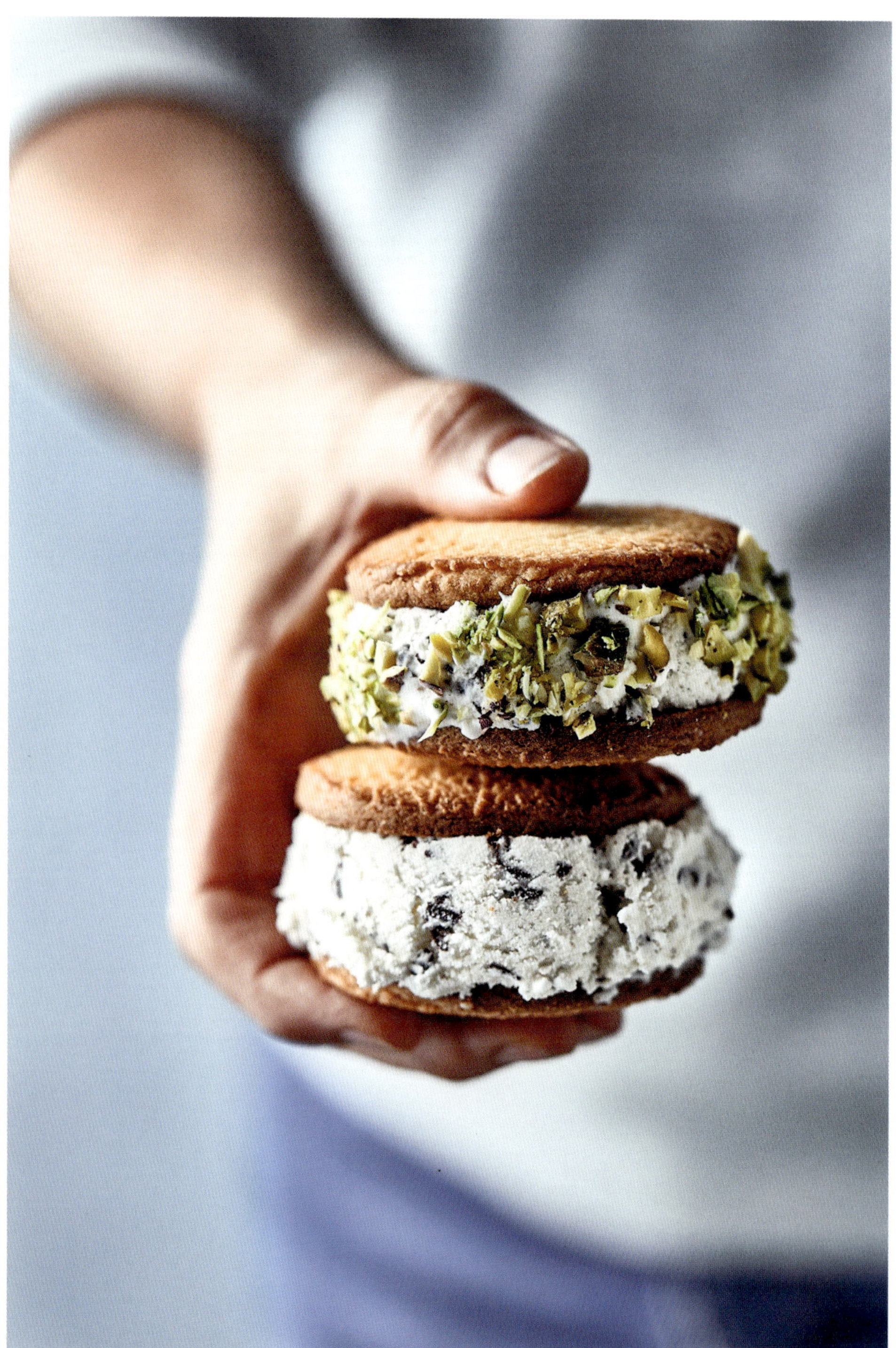

FOOD PHOTOS & STYLING

Make fabulous food photos with your camera and smartphone

Eveline Boone

Lannoo

THE SECRET OF LIGHT

IS IN ITS
SHADOW.

TABLE OF CONTENTS

122

4 FOOD STYLING

182

5 CASES

INTRODUCTION

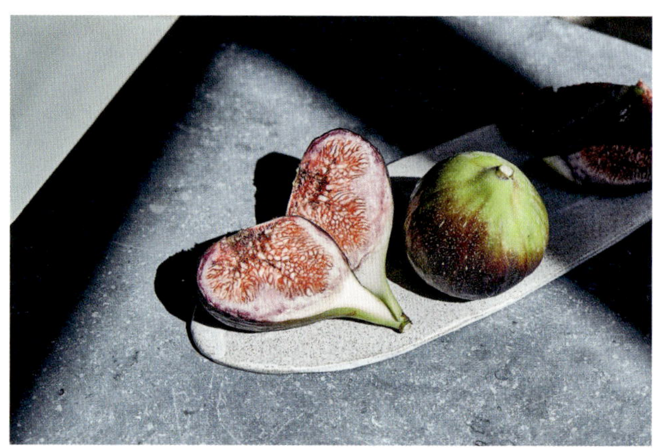

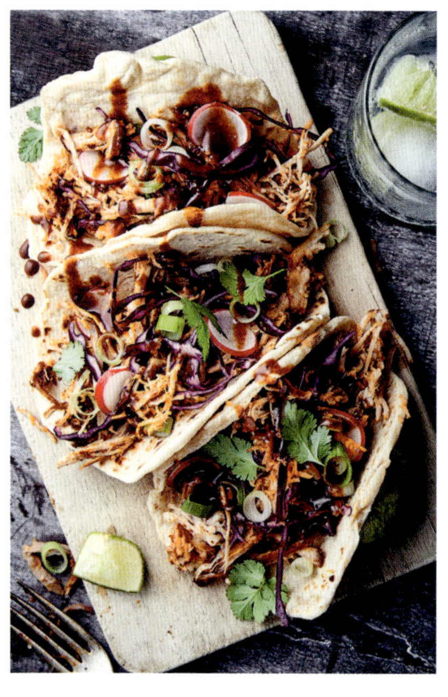

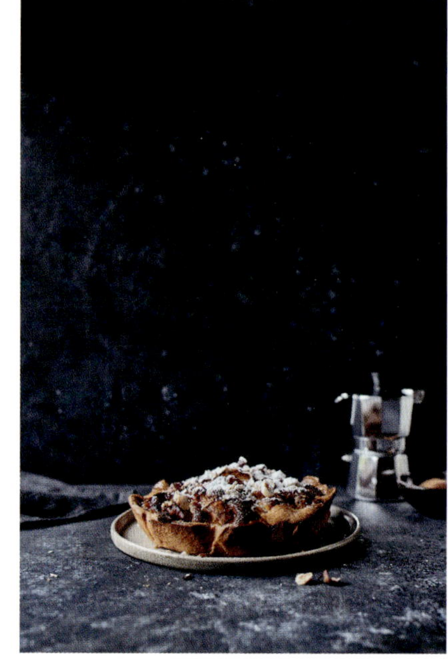

ABOUT THIS BOOK

You're stirring your pots and you think: this looks really delicious. You want to quickly take a picture of it, but the result you had in your head turns out completely different in the photo!

That's the hard thing about food photography. Smells, flavours and even sounds ensure that a dish comes across as delicious. But with a photo you have to be able to capture all those stimuli with just one of the five senses: sight.
This book will help you use a photo to get your audience excited about eating your dish, trying your recipe, buying your products or liking your post. We look more deeply at which elements make a good photo, provides some techniques for fashioning your own visual language and discusses extensively what food styling is and how you can style quickly. Because not everyone has plenty of time to fiddle with that one leaf of lettuce until it's perfect.

The book is based on my vision of food photography. With this she wants you to taste her love for photographing food. This book is written for beginners and advanced learners. You don't have to master all the elements at once. Think of it as a buffet, where you start with a little bit of each. Once you've digested that, you can come back for more, until you've tasted everything ...

ABOUT ME

I am passionate about photography. I often don't think about it, but I photograph with my eyes. My camera is no more than my medium to share the result with others.

That was not always the case. Freshly graduated from photography college, I saw no money in a life as a professional photographer. So I went on to study graphic design. I got my diploma, looked for work and got bored to death in our small apartment in Ledeberg, until I picked up my camera again and captured my boyfriend's culinary creations in the kitchen.

French Beans, the blog I started ten years ago, caught on immediately. Back then, food photography was not nearly as popular and Instagram was not yet on the map. After a quiet period which saw me glued to a screen with InDesign and Illustrator and with life as a self-employed beckoning, I said goodbye to my job as a graphic designer.

At the time I started as a food photographer, my dream was to run my own professional photo studio. In 2017 we fell in love with an old farmhouse in the Flemish Ardennes and decided to renovate the barn into a photo studio. The studio is now my home base for food photography and food styling.

My passion for food and drink is reflected both on set and in my everyday life. Whether it's trying out new restaurants, travelling or collecting beautiful cookbooks.

As a photographer working with food, I find the collaboration with food stylists, videographers, graphic designers, set builders and many other talented people inspiring because food photography isn't a one-man job.

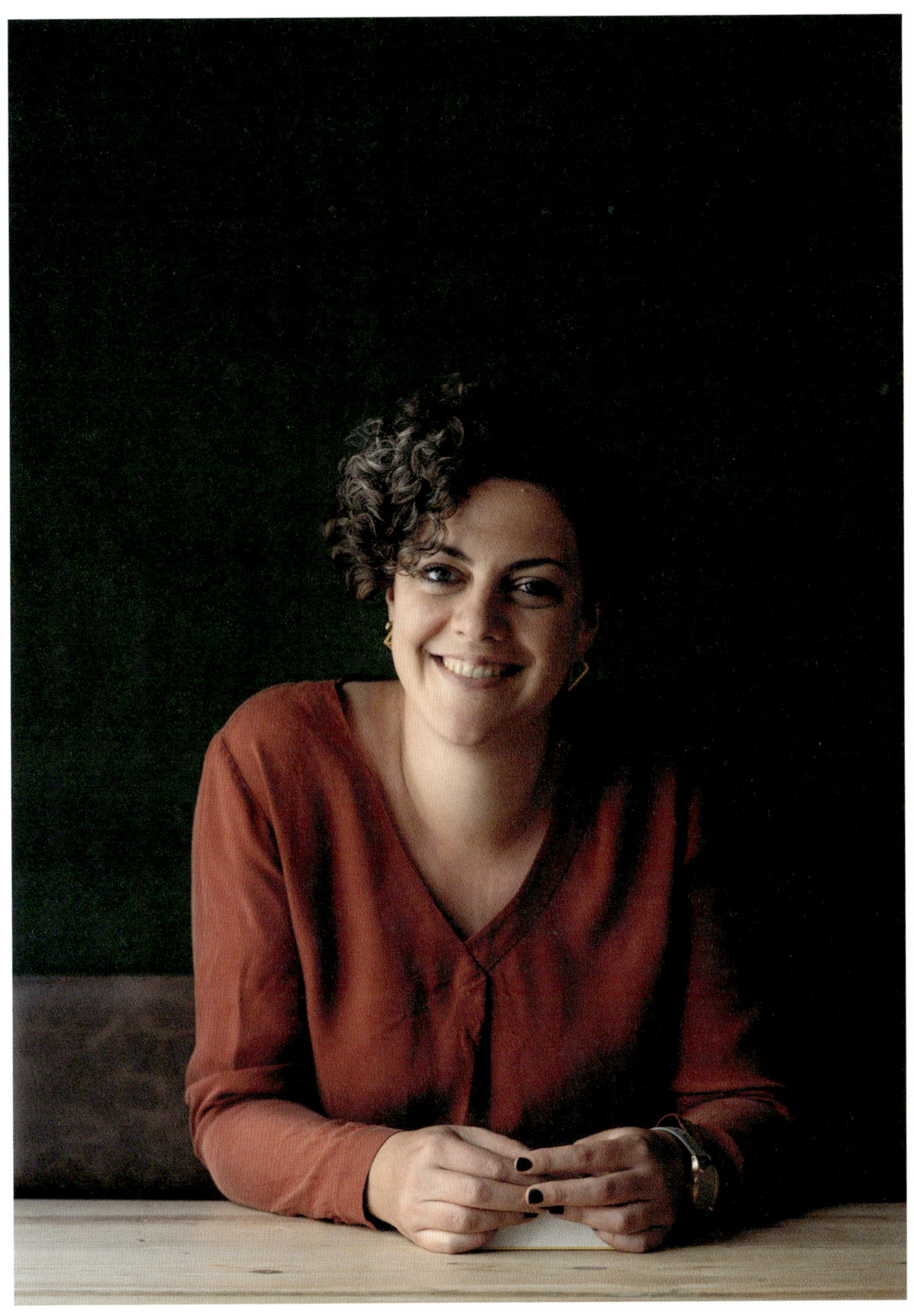

ABOUT FOOD PHOTOGRAPHY AND FOOD STYLING

Food is certainly not the easiest subject to photograph. Ten years ago, nobody saw food photography as a vocation. Food photographers were old men in dark studios (no offence, gentlemen) and food stylists were chefs or home makers. The profession certainly did not have the prestige it has today.

Since then digitization, with Instagram in the lead, has made food photography immensely popular. Place a poor photo of your delicious creations onto the web today and you'll get bad looks. Lost ten followers. Twenty percent fewer likes. The pressure is increasing.

Instagram and reality are not always one and the same. What I post are often things I'm proud of, situations that surprise me, moments I'm grateful for. As a result, I realize that my job can often seem like roses and moonshine. In fact, it's very often hard work, but I really enjoy doing it and can talk about it very passionately.

People are amazed when I say that my fridge contains ten kilograms of pot roast to be shown in a commercial for a mere 0.1 of a second.

Or when I spend four hours in the car to fetch a plate I need in that particular colour for the photo shoot. As a food stylist I've been referred to as a magician. Self-praise stinks, you might think, but then I point to my styling kit that opens up like a magic box. You're allowed to peep inside, but not to touch. For that reason I always bring extra croquettes to the set. Even before they're photographed, the crew has already run off with half a bag.

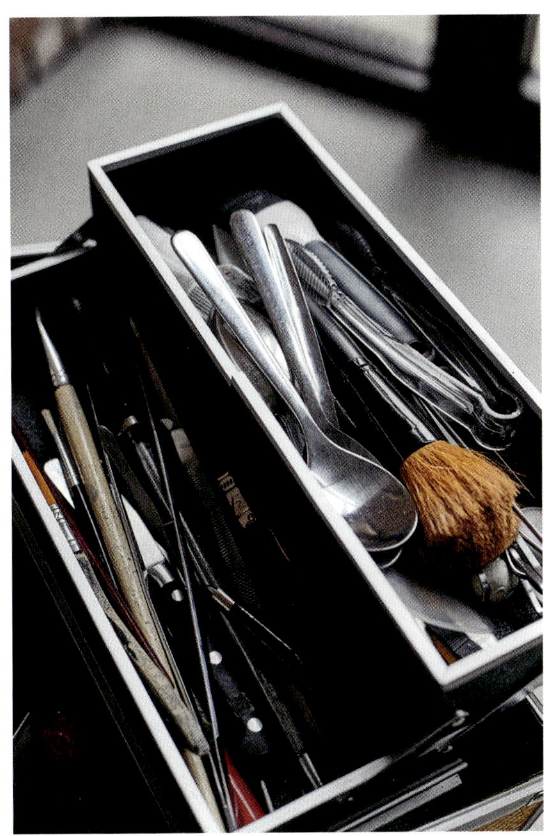

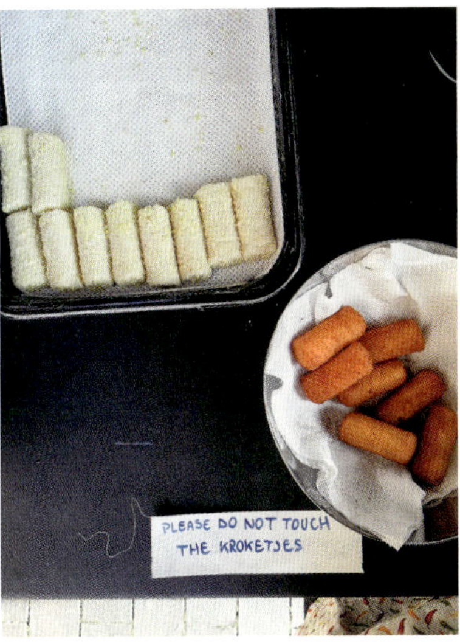

Taking a photo for a customer and seeing it appear online or printed in large format on an exhibition stand makes me happy. Helping people to present their product better and more beautifully, so that it really shows its superiority to the consumer, that's what it's all about for me.

And now to work!

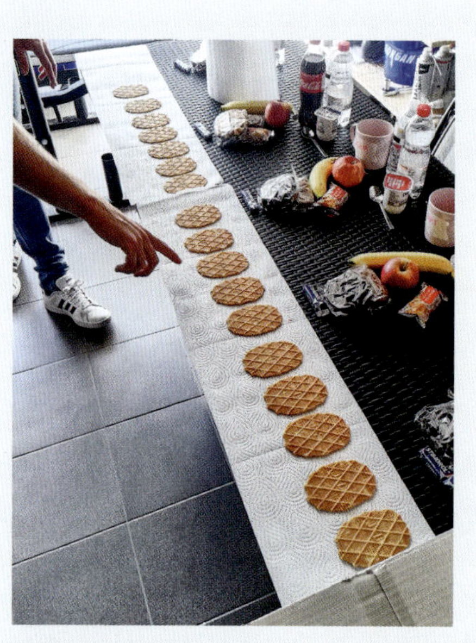

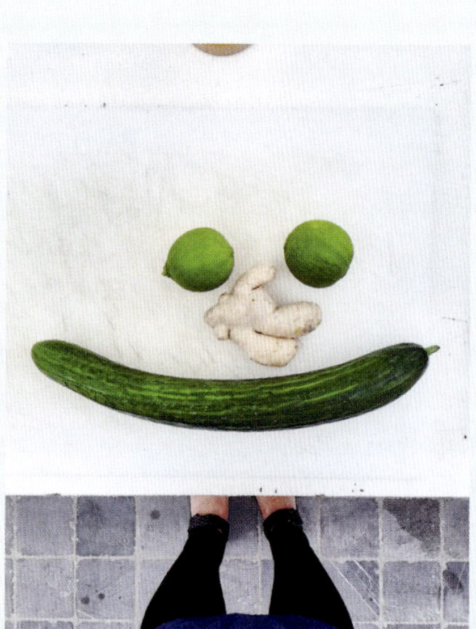

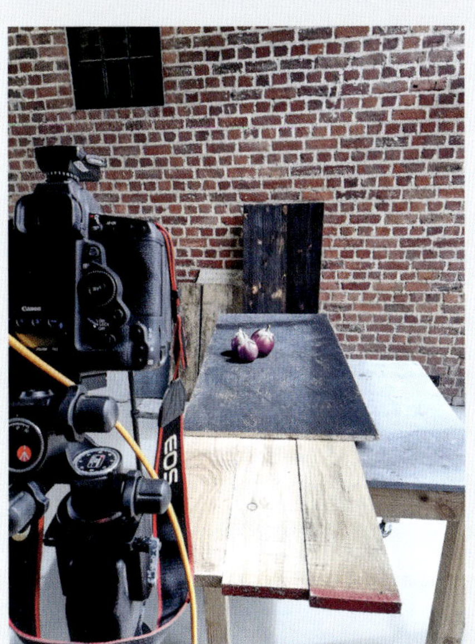
EOS

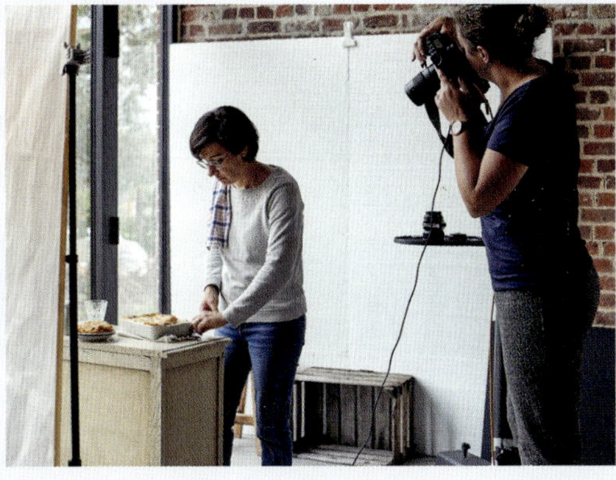

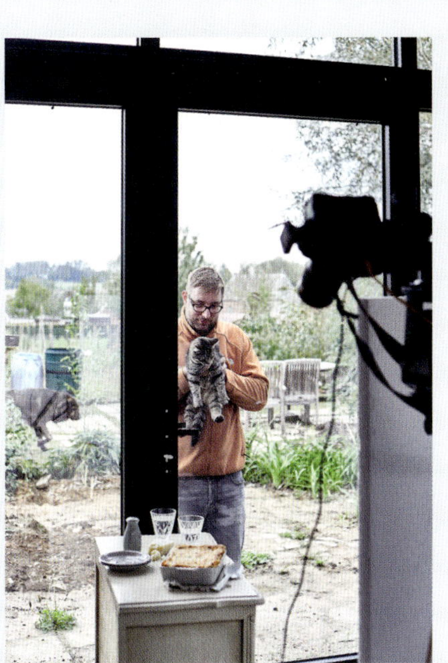

INSPIRATION

01

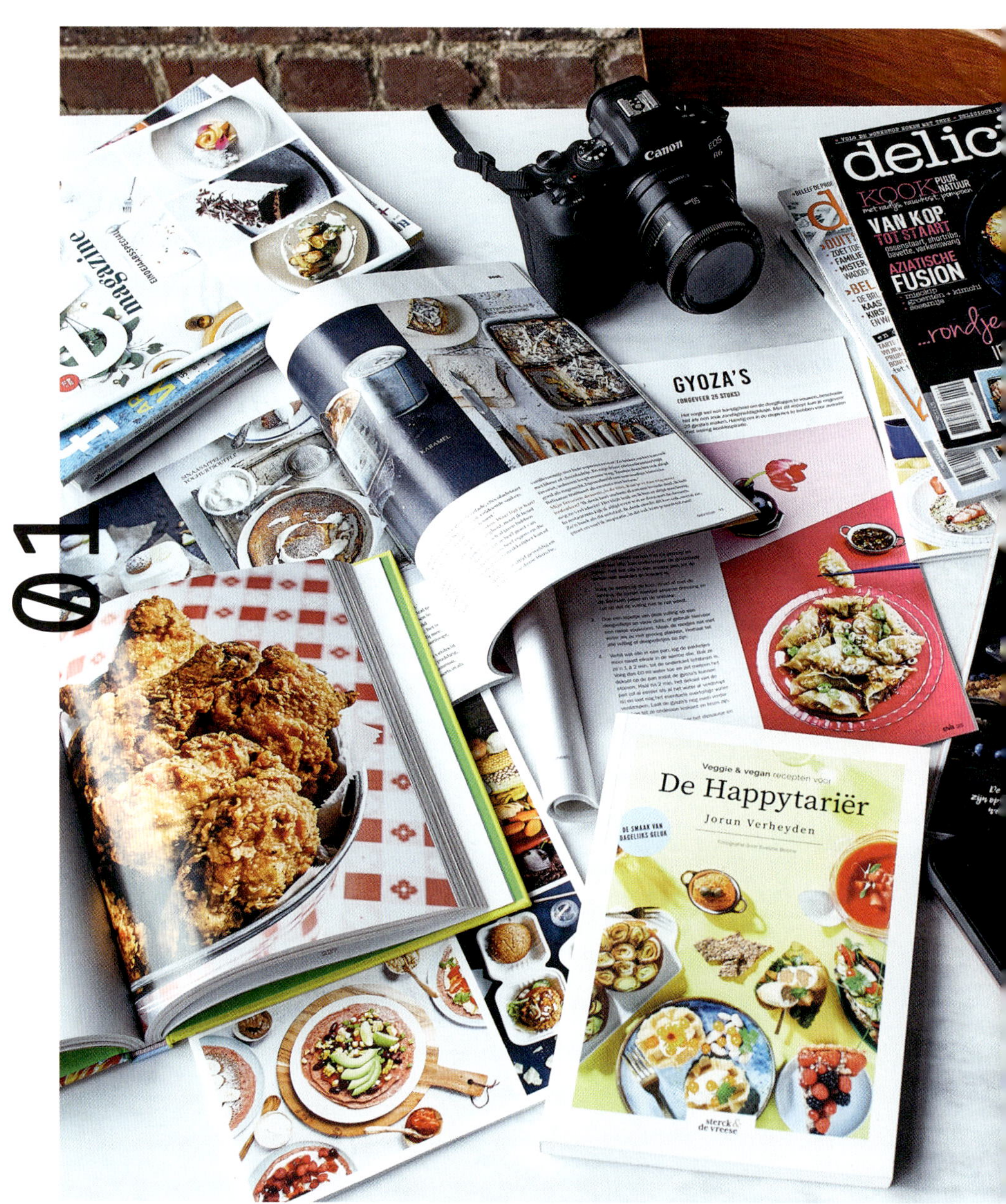

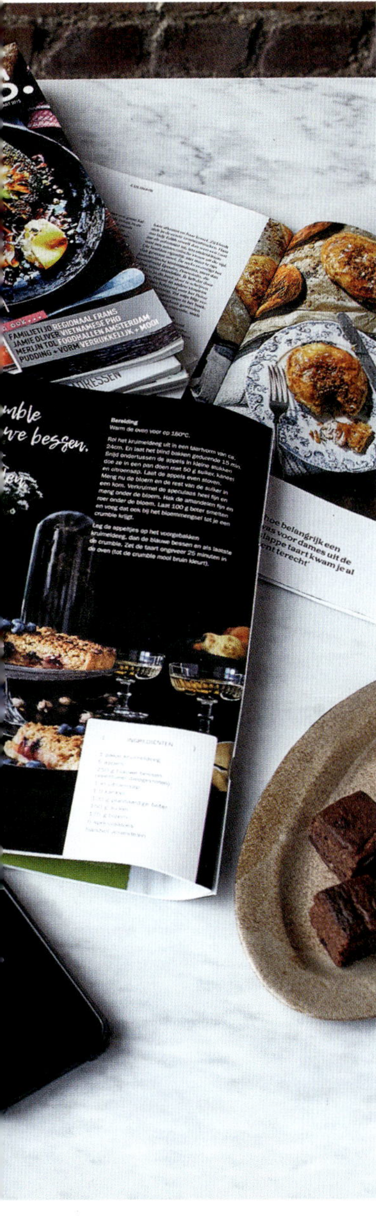

Everything starts with an idea. To create anything you need inspiration. That might be a photo from a cooking magazine, but it could just as well be a scene from everyday life. To put it somewhat simplistically: inspiration can lead to a 'theme' around which you work, or else start from something you're convinced of.

Inspiration can come suddenly, but can also develop gradually. I'm quite forgetful and always regret when I don't remember the name of a photographer or a book. For this reason I write everything down as soon as possible. Images I come across online go on Pinterest. I take photos of magazines that I find worth keeping or go looking for the photographer.

Among my favourite magazines are *Gourmet Traveller*, *Delicious* and *Bon Appétit*.

You can also learn a lot from painting. So step into a museum and look at the composition, colour, the light that the painter used.

An image lingers on your retina. It develops further in your head. The more images are added, the more they will stick together. Like oil drops on a water surface, they connect up to form something new. That's what inspiration is to me. The next step is to translate that image in your head into a photo.

MOOD BOARDS

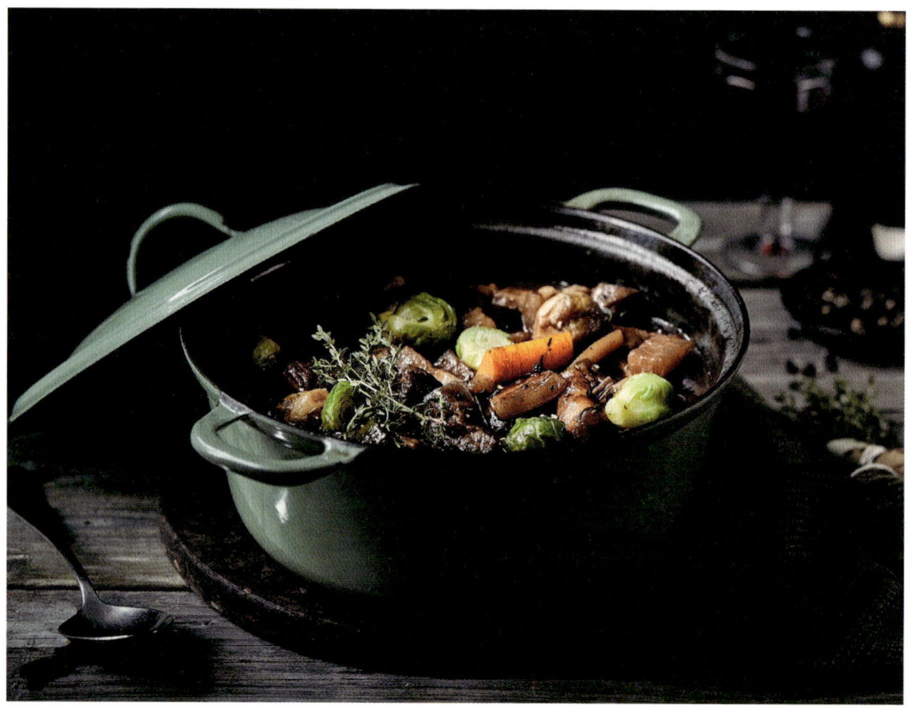

Before starting a photo shoot, take a moment to look for inspiration. The online offering is enormous. But there's also a lot to be found in printed matter. If you're going to photograph a goat's cheese salad, google 'salad goat's cheese photography' on Google Images.

When you start shooting later, leave the search results tab open. This way you can quickly take a look while you're on the job.

Save the images in a folder on your computer or on a Pinterest board. You can also print them and paste them together. Or create a collage with a program like Adobe Spark, Canva or InDesign.

WHAT IS A MOOD BOARD?

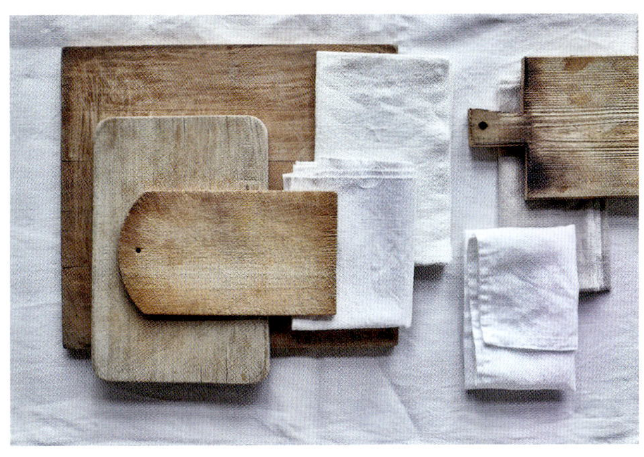

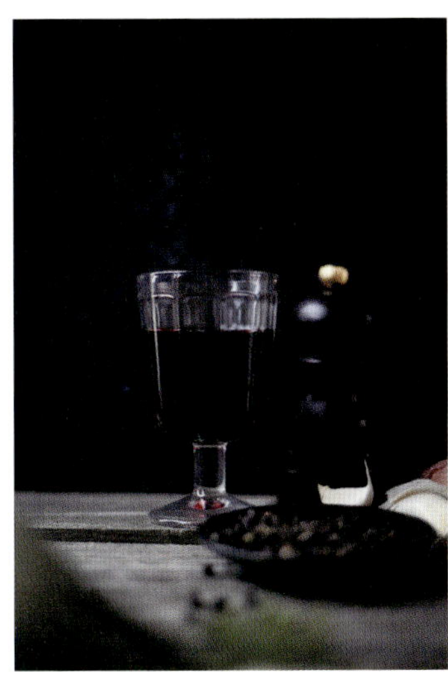

A mood board is a collection of images that together create an impression, represent an atmosphere, evoke a mood ... In short, a mood board shows you at a glance what any number of words cannot describe.

In addition to a general mood board, you can also create specific mood boards per recipe, theme or season, etc. It's a tool that can help us choose props. For example, a winter shoot of a delicious hearty stew can be supported by the use of wood structures, dark linen, soft textures. In that case, we put together a mood board with warm colours: dark red napkins, chocolate brown table linen, dark cork table mats, red wine, etc. In this way you get an idea of what your images can look like.

PUTTING TOGETHER A MOOD BOARD

ATMOSPHERE

An atmosphere can be rustic, urban, warm, rich in colour, natural, modern, as you want. An atmosphere is created through the use of materials, colours, textures and light.

USE OF COLOUR

The colour of the background and the props you use will in some cases largely determine how you use colour in the photo. If you like lighter photos, white and light-tinted props will be more suitable for you.
Bright, multi-coloured props attract attention. If you know what you're doing, you can create great compositions with them.

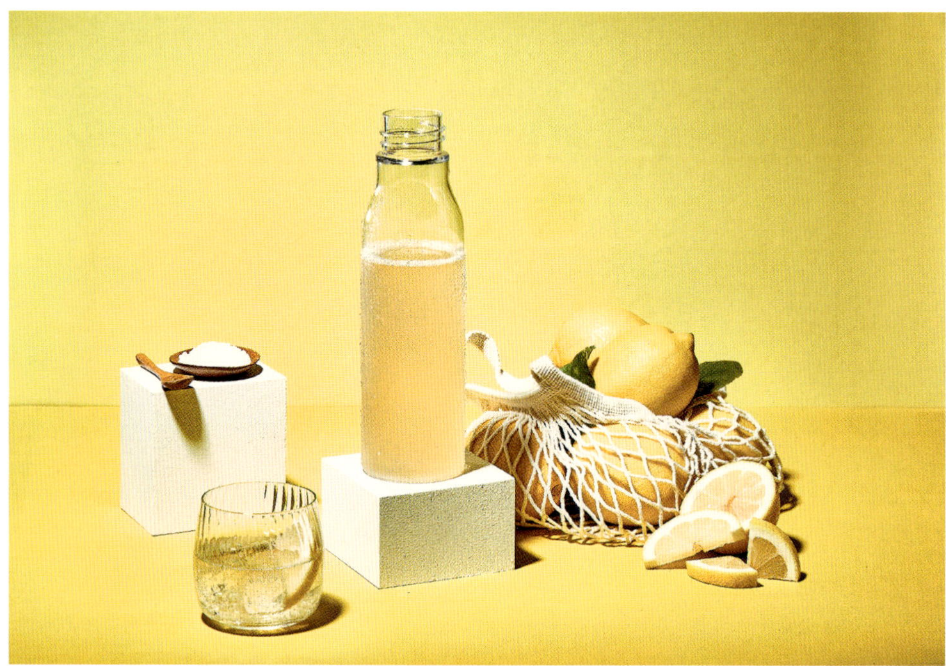

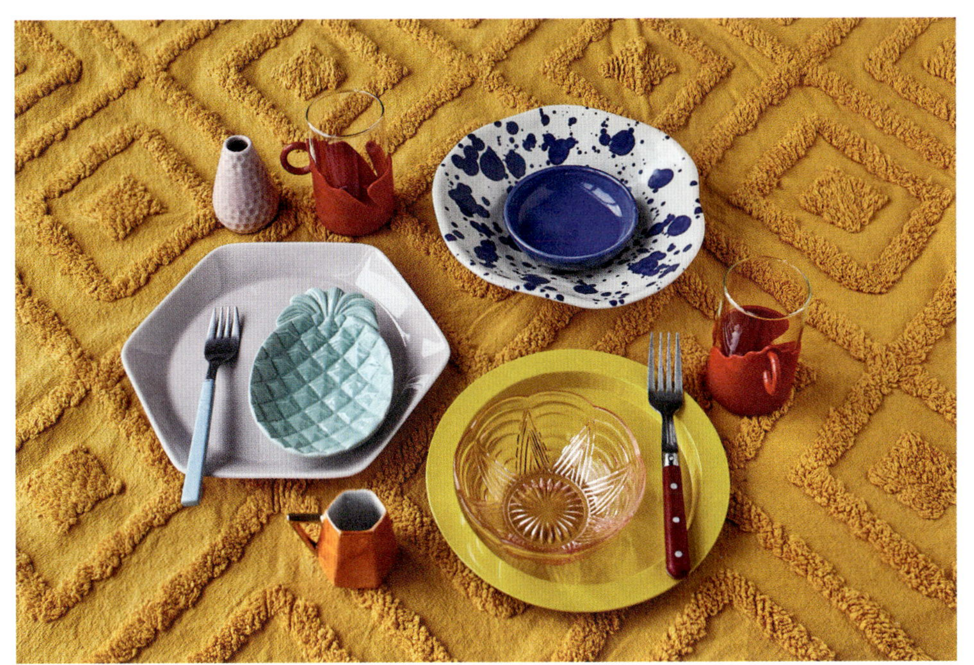

TEXTURES AND PATTERNS

Patterns such as flowers, lozenges and dots have the same effect. Many times they provide a vintage look. You can combine patterns and textures. Mismatching can also be fun.

COMBINING PHOTOS

Don't be afraid to cut out an element that appeals to you from a photo. It's often the combination of elements and photos that creates an overall impression.

Certain interior elements, a piece of clothing or type of location can also be part of your mood board. For example, combine a very modern table and chairs with a business outfit if you're going to photograph business lunches. The same business lunch tells a completely different story on a picnic bench by the water.

GRAPHIC ELEMENTS

Do you have your own logo? Or a specific branding? You can include these elements in your mood board. Shapes, lines and typography are also part of this. They ensure recognisability.

You can also repeat these graphic elements on your website, Instagram, Facebook and other social media for even greater recognition.

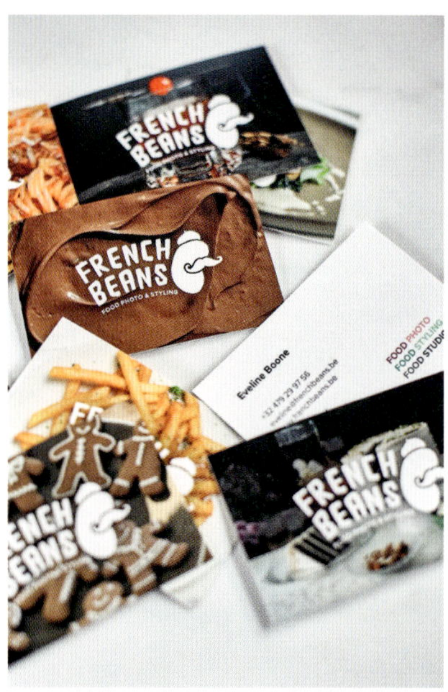

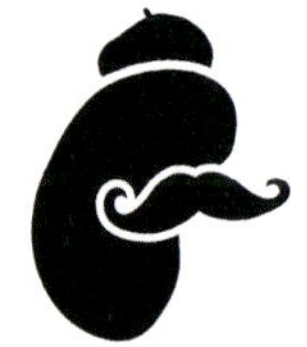

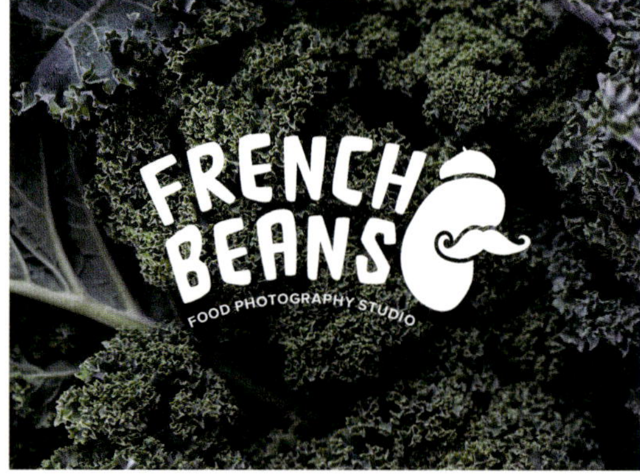

PEOPLE

You're the face behind your blog, Instagram or company. Don't be afraid to come into the picture yourself every now and then. It doesn't have to be an official portrait. A fun selfie, you holding a plate, or even just a hand in the picture, all lend a sense of humanity to your images.

To get into the picture yourself, you do need a tripod and self-timer (or someone who pushes the button for you). If you want to have more control, ask your other half, brother, sister, children or friends to pose for a while. Yes, even your grandmother can be photogenic.

Make sure that the people you portray are in line with your target audience or your story. If you like making authentic dishes, grandmother is certainly welcome. Hip smoothies may require a model from a different age category.

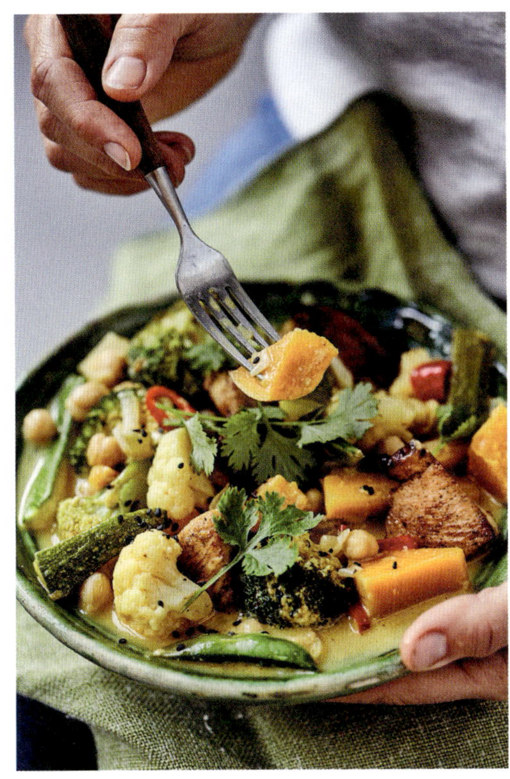

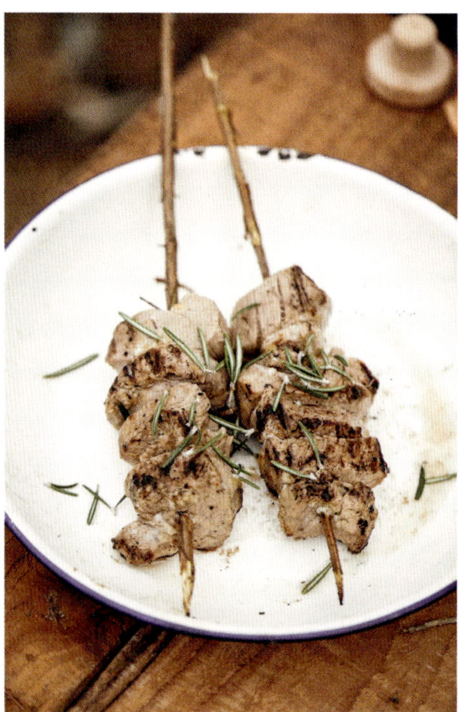

A sturdy winter barbecue could use a pint of beer in a sturdy male hand.

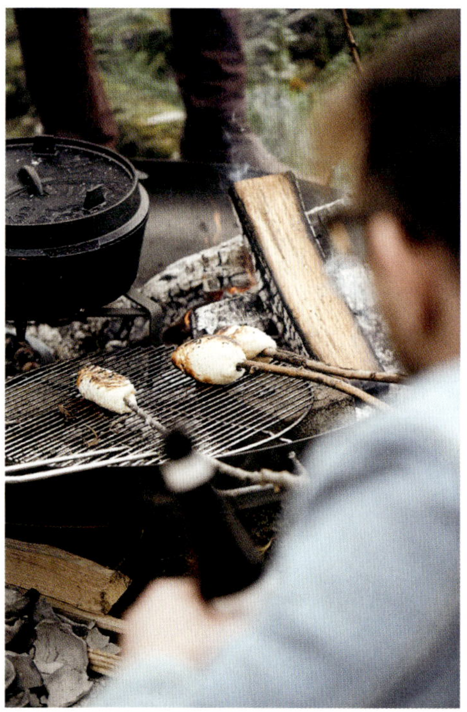

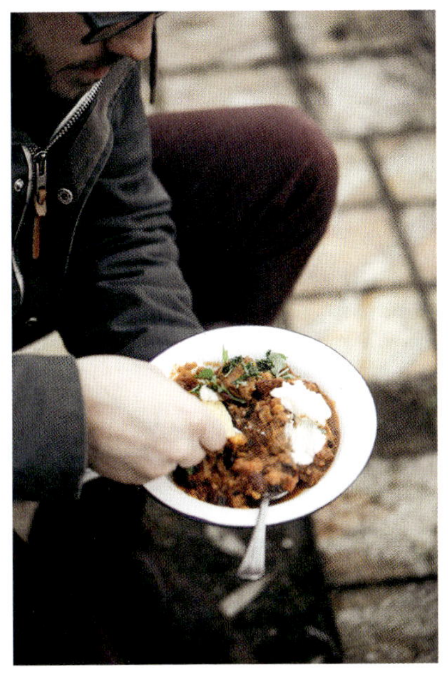

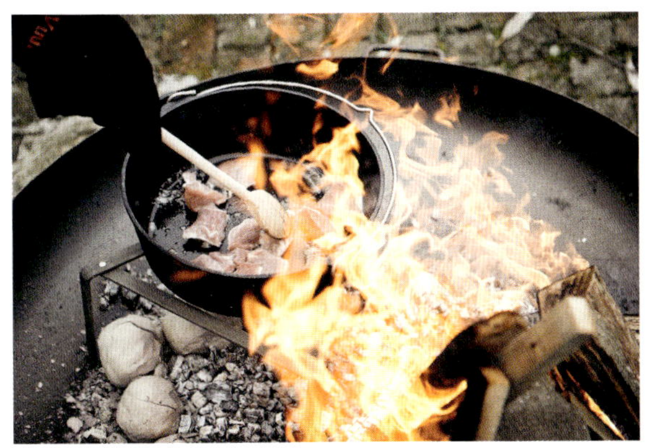

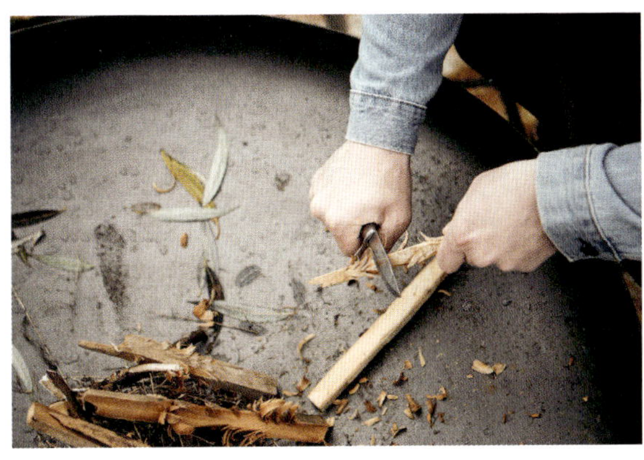

PHOTOGRAPHY

02

Photography uses visual language to convey a message. It has its own sort of grammar book, consisting of four elements: **technique (camera, lenses** and **other photographic tools), composition, lighting** and **content.**

These are your starting points, whichever way you go. You have to understand the basics of photography to take a good food photo. For me it makes little sense to throw haphazardly a heap of tips and tricks at you. Ultimately they all come back to the basics. Once you master these, you can apply them as you wish.

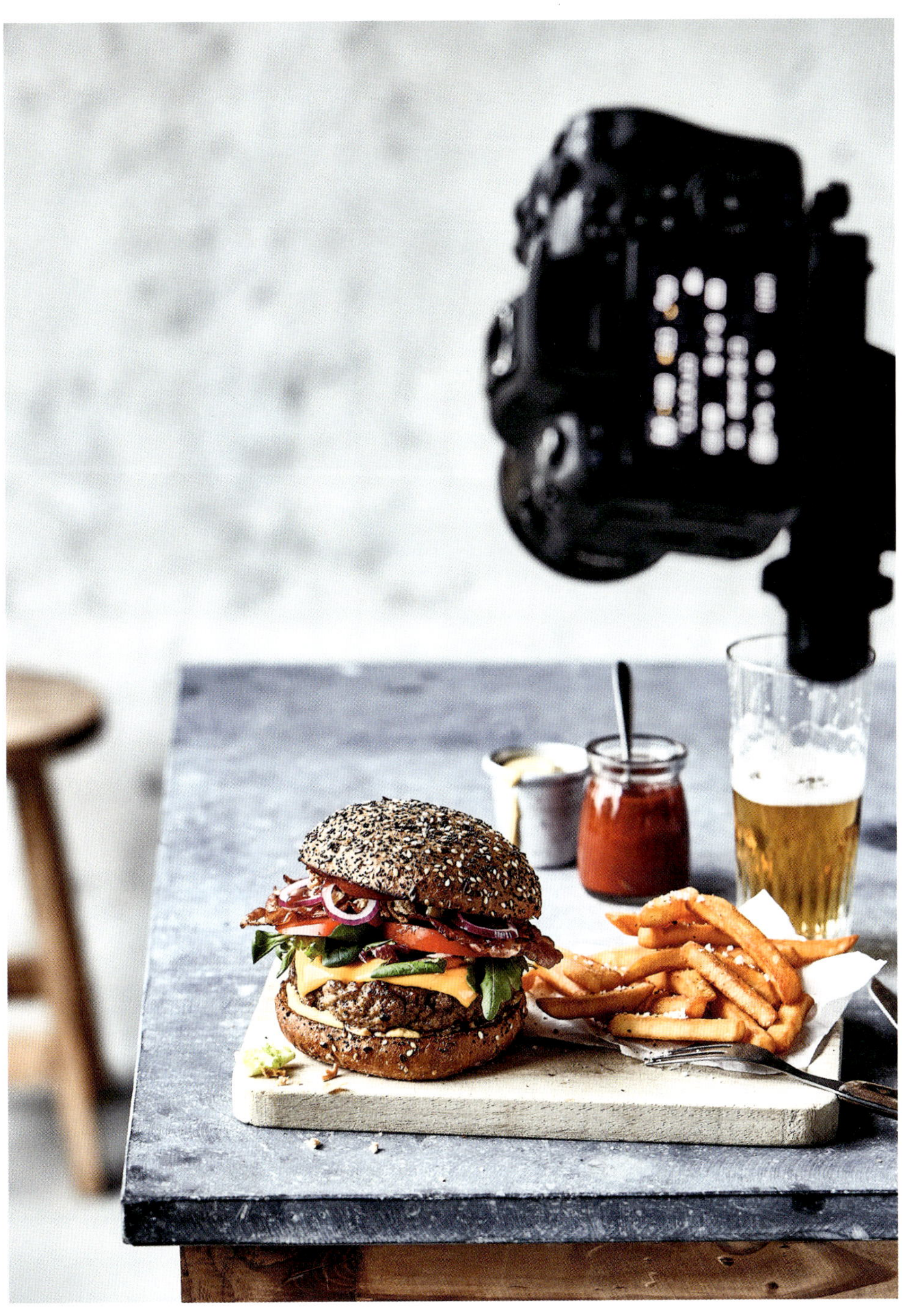

TECHNIQUE

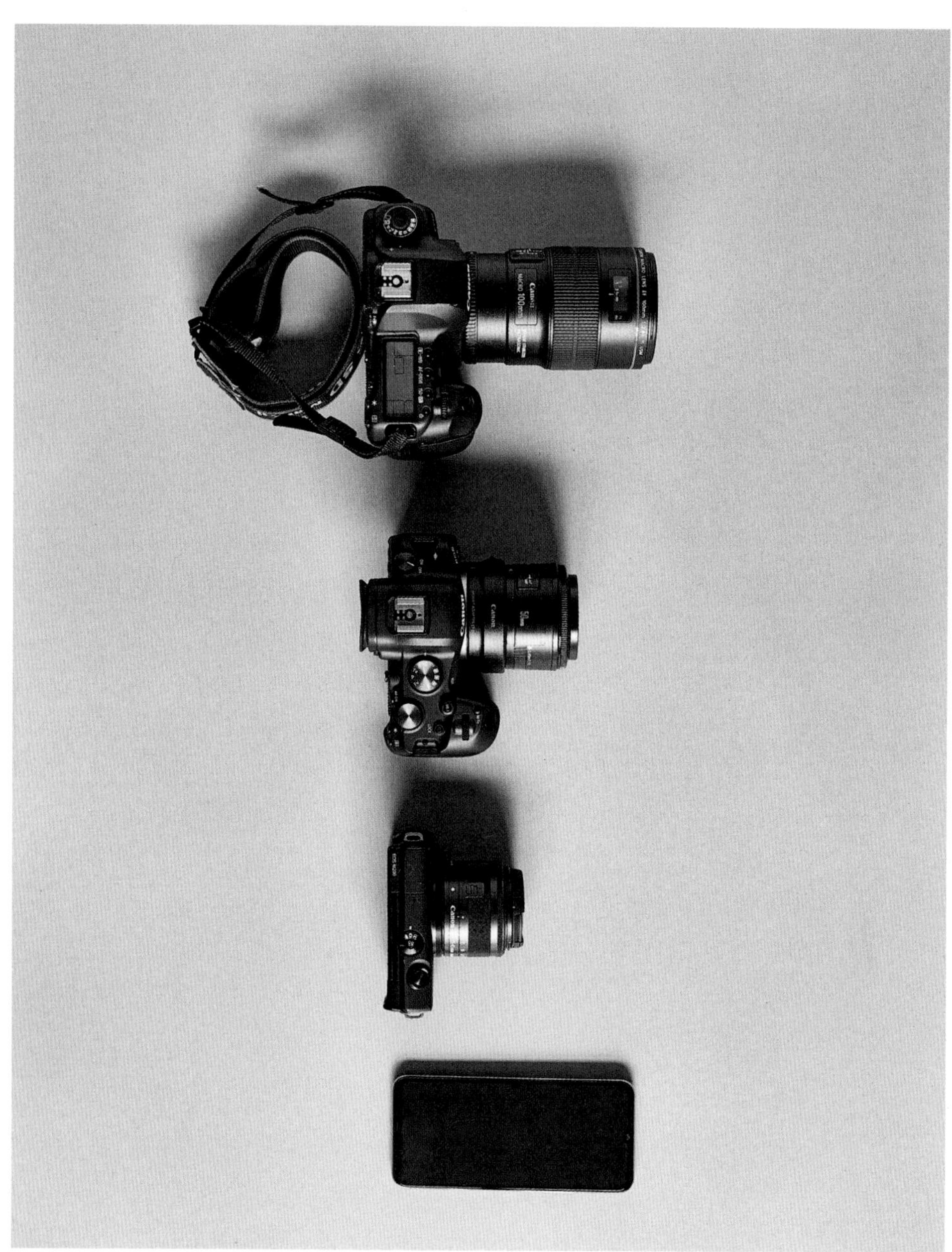

THE CAMERA

The best camera is the one you have with you. Whether it's a smartphone, a compact camera, a system camera, a digital SLR camera or an analogue version. You learn by taking pictures. The device you use for this is only a medium, albeit with small and large differences.

SMARTPHONE

A smartphone is by far the most practical camera owing to its size. Its biggest limitations are the lenses and quality. The latest smartphones have three lenses at the back: a standard lens, a telephoto lens and wide-angle lens. These lenses don't record images in the same resolution. The standard lens often has the highest resolution, the selfie lens on the front of the device often the lowest.

As yet, it's not possible to change smartphone lens. Clip-on lenses offer a solution to this, but you need to know that they only simulate an effect and will never give you the same results as a real lens.

Today, the quality (resolution) of photos you take with your smartphone is of sufficient quality to be shown on laptops, TVs and other screens, but also for making small prints. For this you have to set the resolution to maximum size in your settings (see 'Making prints'). The quality of smartphone sensors is often a lot lower than that of a camera. The sensor is very small and therefore compresses information to form the image.

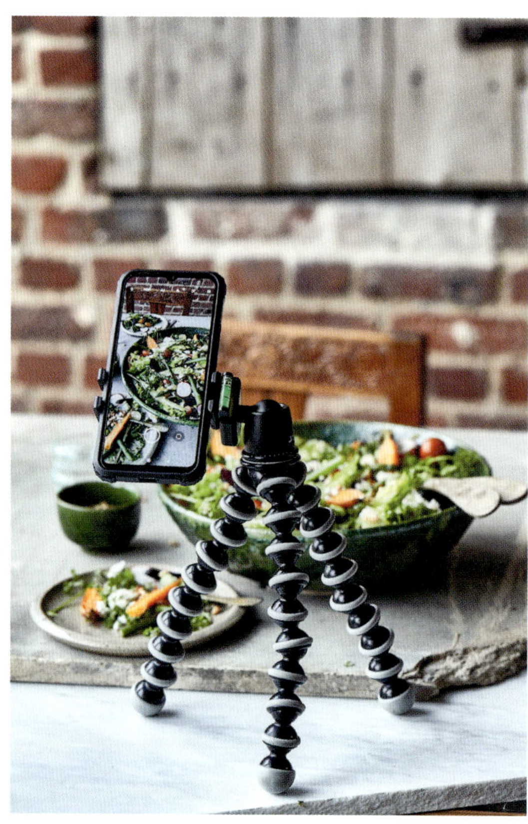

COMPACT CAMERA

People wanting to switch from a smartphone to a camera frequently opt for a compact camera. The optics (lens) and sensor are a lot better than in a smartphone. Many compact cameras allow you to send photos to your smartphone, allowing you to make some quick edits with certain apps and post to social media quickly.

Another advantage is the option of a tilt screen. Tilt the screen towards the set to see faster results, while arranging your props in a composition.

Some system cameras are, somewhat contradictorily, more compact than a compact camera. The Canon EOS M200, for example, is in principle a system camera, but is so small that it could be a compact camera.

If you choose a compact camera, be sure to look out for one with interchangeable lenses.

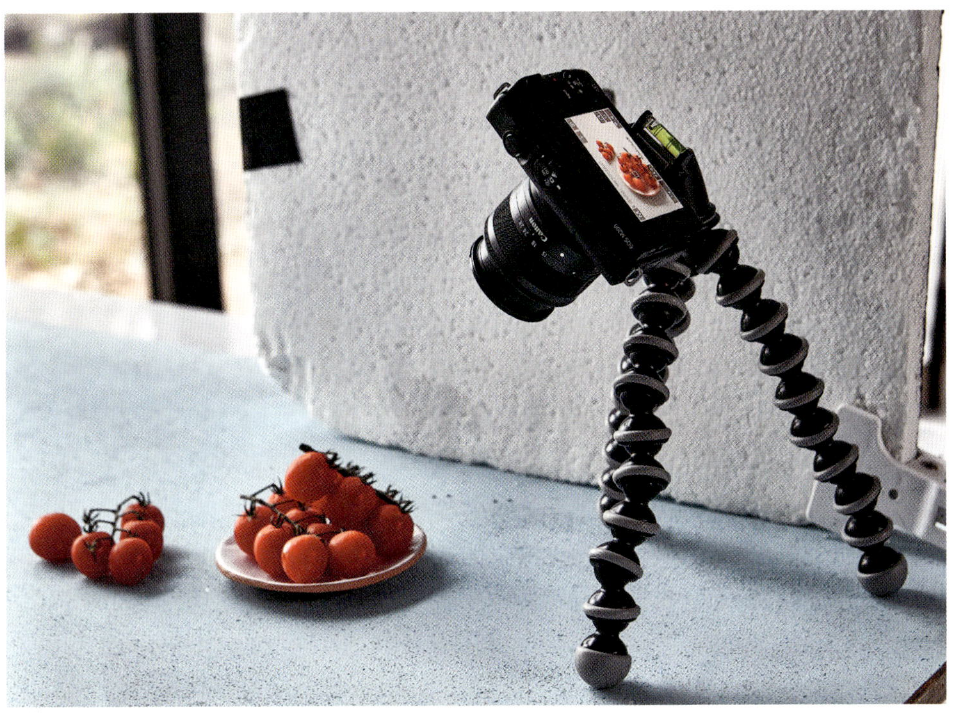

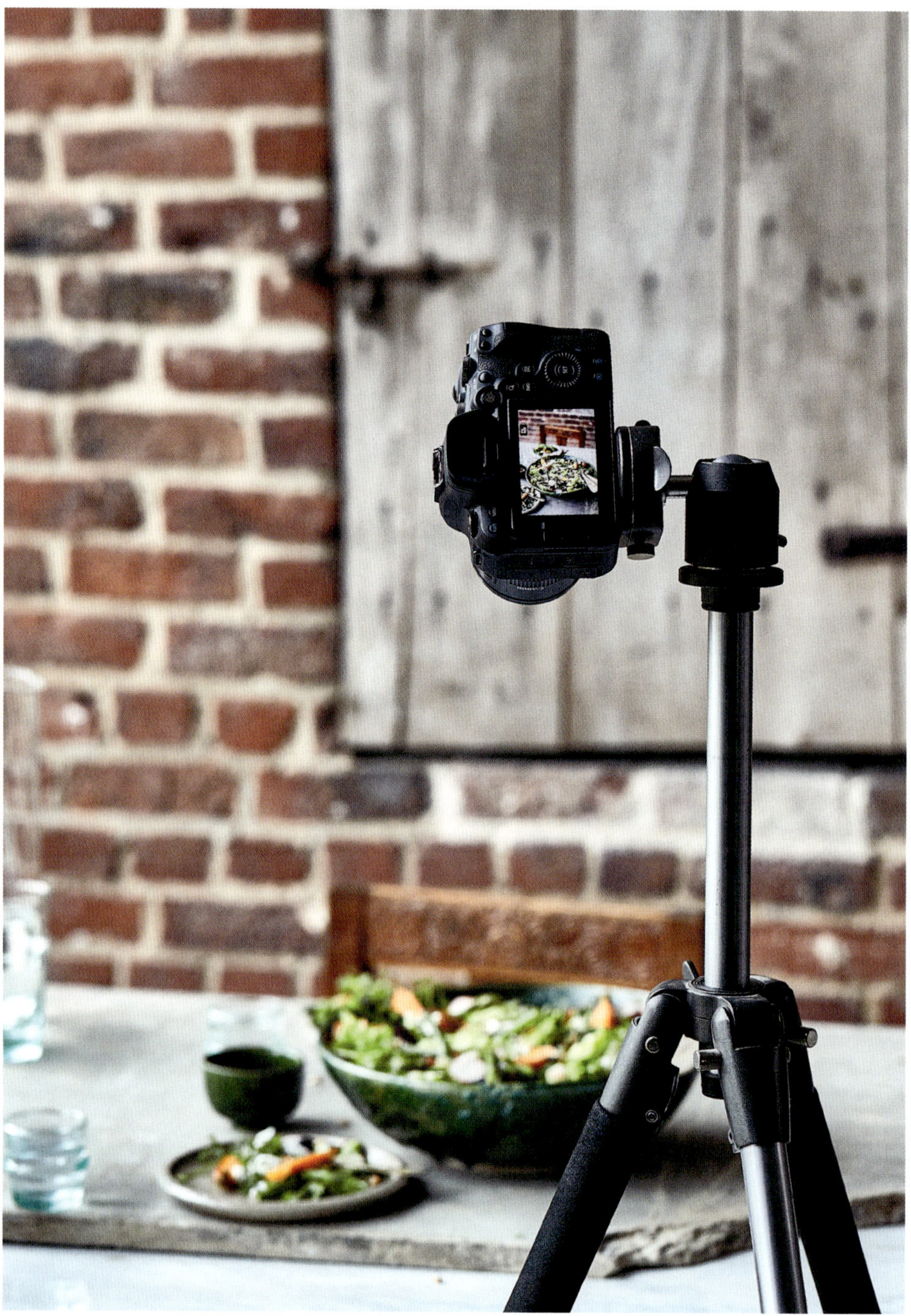

SYSTEM CAMERA

The system camera (also known as 'hybrid' or 'mirrorless') is the half-way stop on the way to an SLR camera. At least according to some. Others forsake their unwieldy SLR after years of service and go for mirrorless. I never thought I would be one of them, but now that mirrorless technology has become so good.

With system cameras you can shoot in manual mode, giving you complete control over the photo. But the biggest advantage is that you can see what you're shooting in real time on the LCD screen at the back of the camera. System cameras offer very good value for money.

For most mirrorless cameras you can buy all kinds of interchangeable lenses or even an adapter ring for lenses from an SLR camera, which broadens the possibilities. In this book I use my Canon EOS R6 system camera with one such adapter ring. Since I've been working with this brand for many years and have put together a collection of EF (electrofocus) lenses for their cameras, I can also use them on this device without any loss in image (quality).

Some system cameras, such as the Canon EOS R6, are equipped with a tilt screen and touchscreen. This is a huge advantage for food photography. That way you don't have to climb up and down a stepladder to see the effect in topshot of every adjustment you make to your composition. Time-saving and less hassle! If you still want to shoot by hand (not on a tripod), the internal image stabilization reduces the risk of motion blur at slow shutter speed (see Shutter speed p. 40).

SLR CAMERA

An SLR camera has a mirror that projects the image from your lens onto the viewfinder via a glass prism. The mirror pops up as soon as you press the shutter button, projecting the image onto the sensor behind the shutter.

In addition to countless interchangeable lenses, you also always have the option to photograph in manual mode. In this category of cameras, there are a handful of reference brands. Their lenses sometimes last for decades and are also constantly updated.

The great advantage in use is that the image through the viewfinder is a direct representation of reality. It's precisely because of this advantage that many photographers who have been working with an SLR camera for years cannot get used to a system camera. With a system camera, it's always a digital image that's shown through the viewfinder or screen.

The disadvantage is that SLR cameras are heavy and unwieldy.

However much the mirrorless camera also appeals to me, I still continue to use my Canon EOS 1DX Mark II. Call me old-fashioned.

SIDENOTE:

A war photographer told me that he once used his camera to defend himself when he got too close to his subject and showed me the dent in his camera. Fact or fiction, indestructible nonetheless.

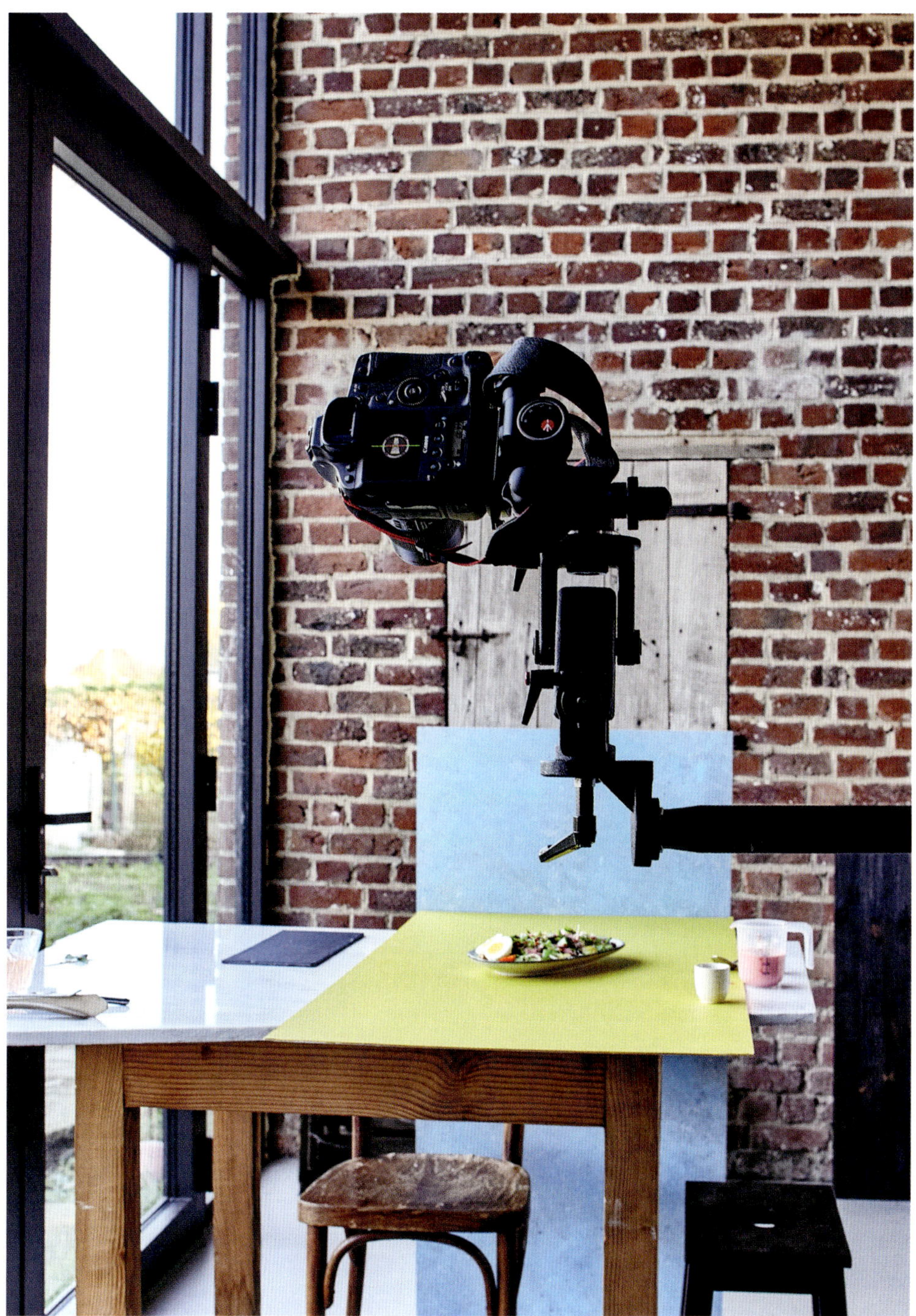

APERTURE - SHUTTER SPEED - ISO

Here it comes. The Holy Trinity of photography. With aperture, shutter speed and ISO value you can change the exposure and sharpness (depth of field) of the photo.

When you put the camera in auto mode, the combination will be made by your camera. In manual mode it's you who are in control! Once you've mastered the principles, manual control over these three elements gives you the creative freedom to put more individuality in your photos.

WHAT IS A WELL-EXPOSED PHOTO?

A smartphone will automatically take an average of the number of dark and light areas for light measurement. In this way, snow will be underexposed by default, because the light meter in your smartphone thinks: oops, too much white, I have to make that grey. A dark & moody photo is then overexposed, because your smartphone thinks: oops, so dark, I have to make that lighter, which is not what you intended!

You solve this by photographing in manual mode. You can enable spot metering on both the camera and smartphone. The light is then measured where you choose, usually where you focus. For a dark photo, choose the lightest point in your image; for a light photo, such as snow, choose the point in your image that's as close to 'medium grey' as possible.

With a camera you can also see a bar with a pointer on the screen. If the pointer is in the centre, the photo is correctly exposed. To the left it is underexposed, to the right it is overexposed.

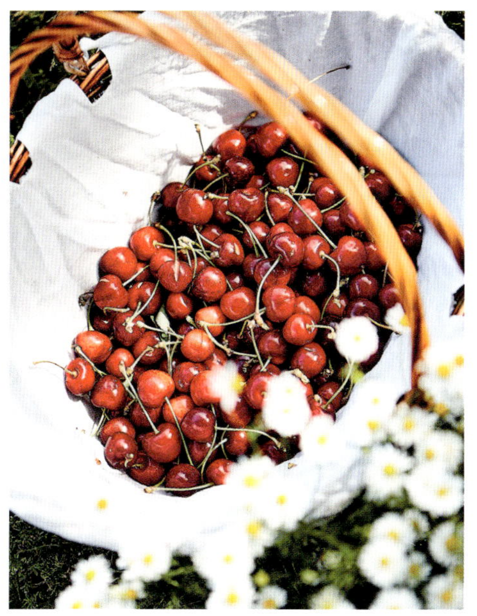

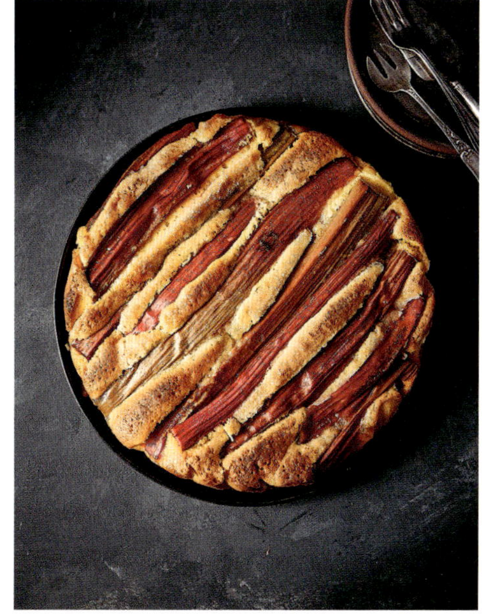

APERTURE

The aperture is located inside the lens (see Lenses p. 42). It is this aperture that determines how much light enters the sensor. A small opening lets in little light, and a large opening a lot. The maximum aperture values differ from one lens to another. A more expensive lens will have a larger maximum aperture. This allows you to take photos in poor light conditions without motion blur.

To make things even more confusing, a large aperture opening, resulting in a small depth of field (and therefore a lot of blur in front and behind your focus point), is indicated with a small number, for example f/1.4. Still following me?

The aperture thus affects the depth of field. A large aperture is very often used on purpose in food photography, precisely in order to give a blurred background.

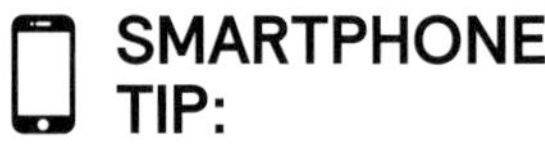

SMARTPHONE TIP:

On the smartphone the aperture is actually a simulation of the aperture. The amount of sharpness changes, but the exposure does not. In fact, your smartphone recognizes the object you want to have in focus, and applies a blurry filter to the background and foreground.

TIP:

Try photographing with a large depth of field, for example f/22. Here you cannot camouflage anything with background blur.

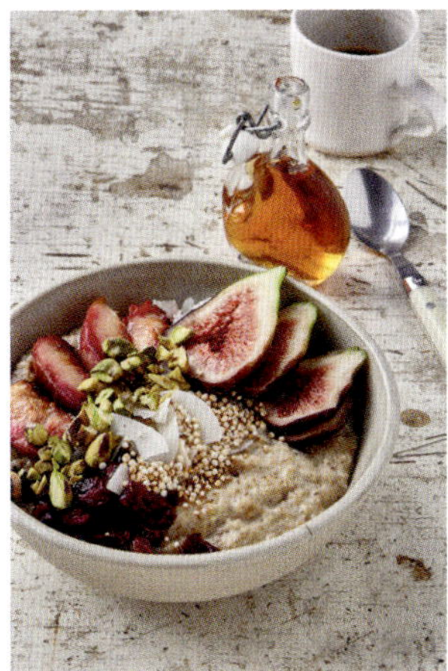

Aperture f/22

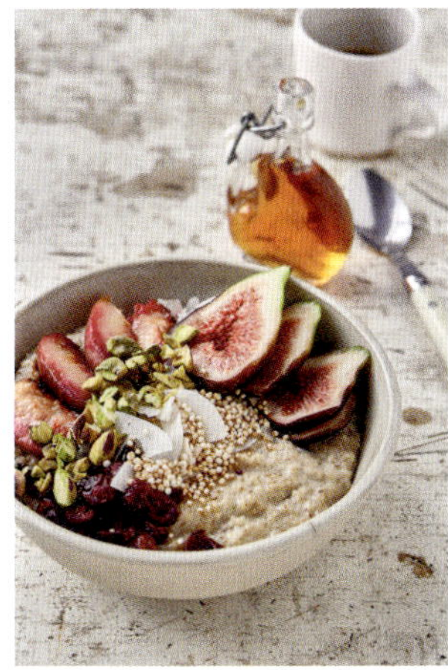

Aperture f/8

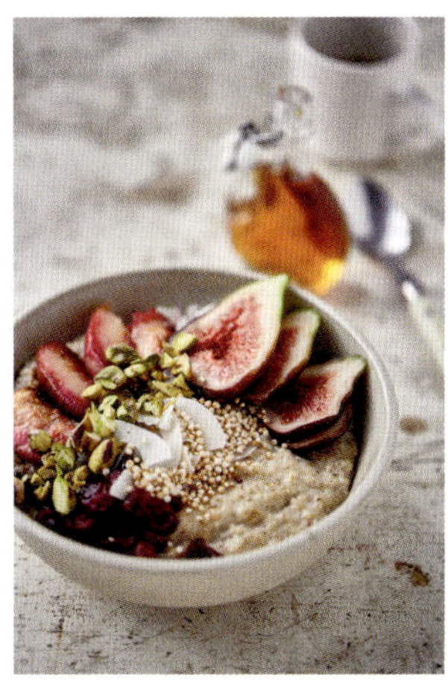

Aperture f/2.8

SHUTTER SPEED

The light falls on the image sensor, which in turn converts it into pixels. There is a shutter in front of that sensor. The amount of time the shutter remains open in front of the sensor is called - aha! - the shutter speed, or exposure. With a slow shutter speed, the incident light has plenty of time to

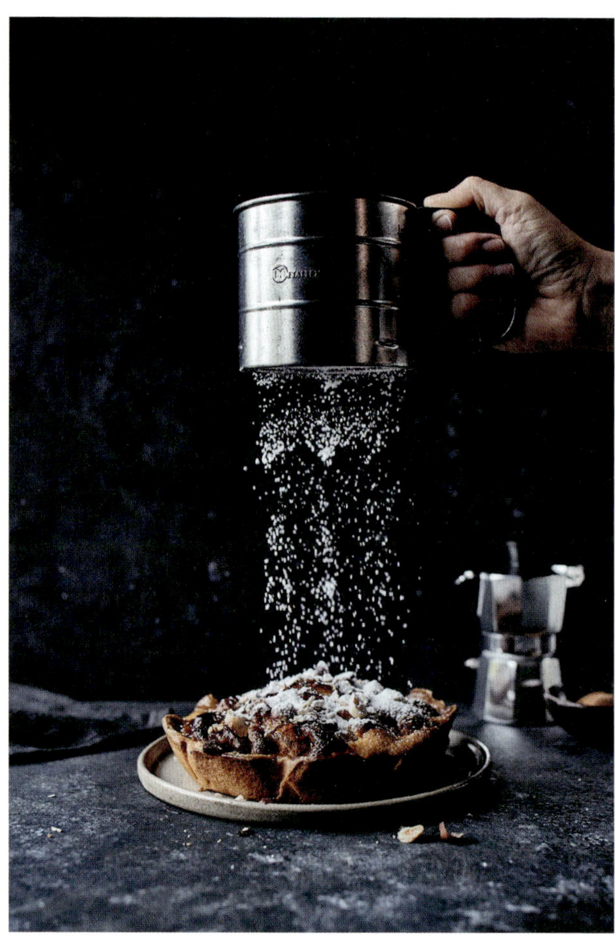

Shutter speed 1/500

TIP:

Do the test by sprinkling icing sugar through a sieve.

hit the sensor. If you don't hold your camera perfectly still, you'll have a blurred photo as a result. Place your camera on a tripod when shooting at slow shutter speed. With a fast shutter speed you let in less light. You give the sensor less time to record a movement, as it were. This allows you to photograph moving subjects sharply, for example.

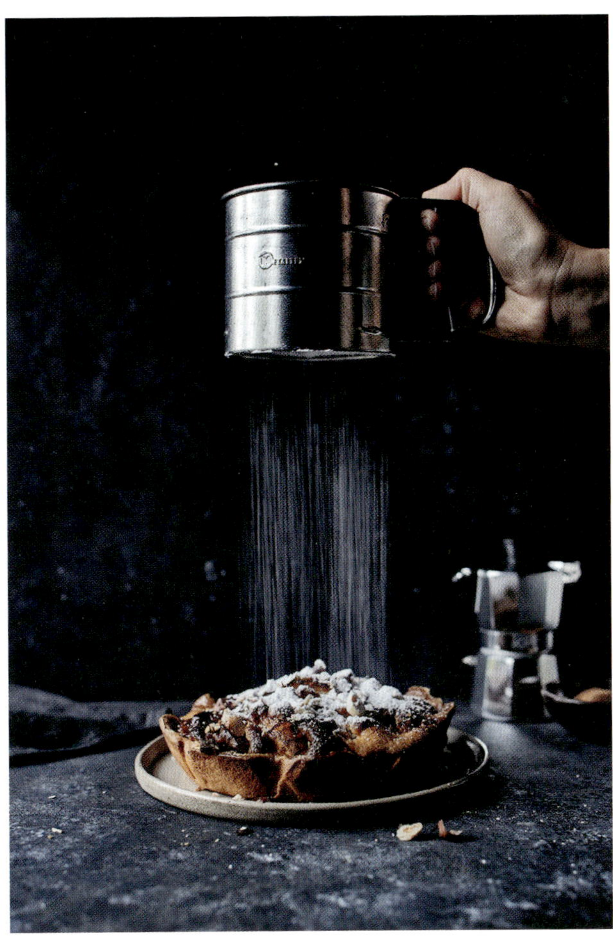

Shutter speed 1/15

ISO

This is the light sensitivity of the sensors. A low ISO value, for example 100, means that the sensor isn't very sensitive to incident light. With a high ISO, on the other hand, you can still take a correctly exposed photo in poor light conditions.

But please note that a higher ISO value gives more 'noise'. An underexposed photo, where you increase ('force') the exposure in post-editing can also produce noise. You can best compare noise with the 'graininess' of photos taken with roll film using an analogue camera. However, noise isn't aesthetically pleasing like grain used to be, but can often be very off-putting. It's like someone sprinkled a lot of sand over your photo in a perfect matrix. With an analogue camera and roll film this gives an artistic effect, but with digital devices and certainly for food photography, you'd be well advised to avoid this.

LENSES

Once you've chosen a camera brand, you can start building a collection of lenses. These are often brand-specific and even within the same brand you sometimes have different 'mounts', which makes it difficult to buy a different brand of camera afterwards.

LENSES ARE TO A PHOTOGRAPHER A BIT LIKE WHAT A TROUSSEAU USED TO BE FOR A NEWLY-WED COUPLE: THE START OF THE REST OF YOUR LIFE.

I'm dramatizing it a bit, but I have a love affair with my lenses. Whenever I buy a new one, it has always been carefully considered and researched.

TIP:

You can buy adapters for lenses that don't fit a particular camera.

Shutter speed

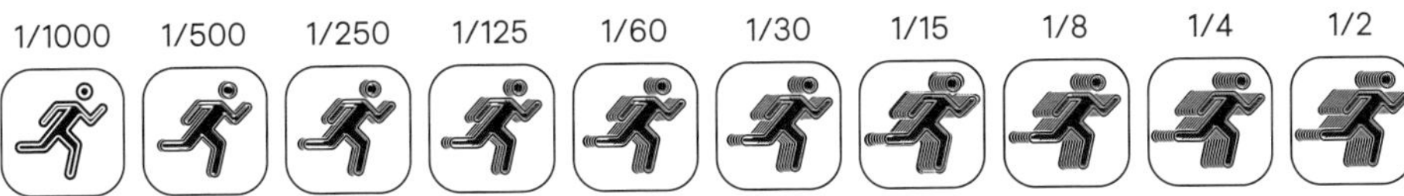

Aperture

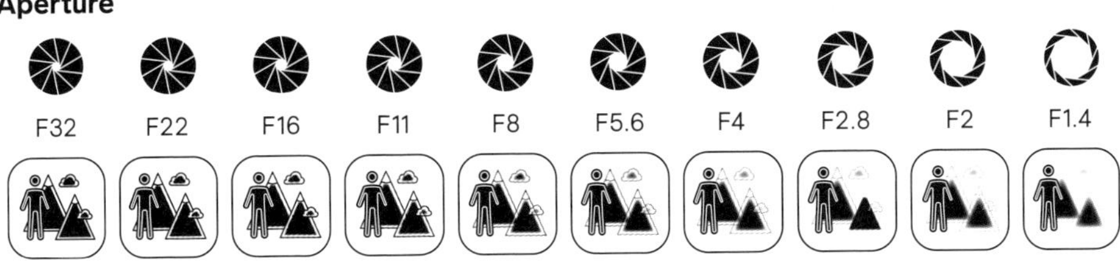

ISO

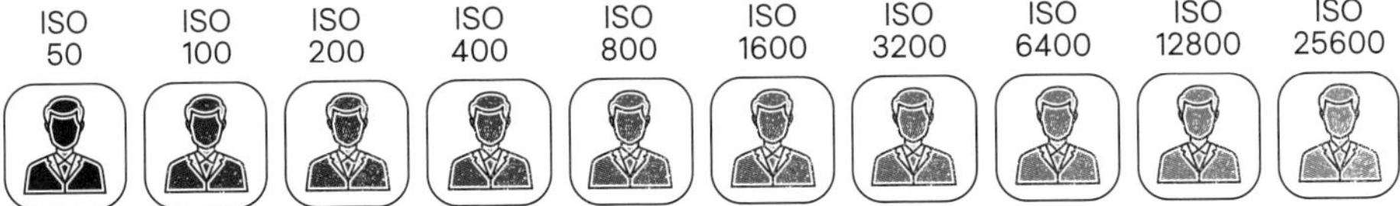

This illustration clarifies what happens to your image when you adjust shutter speed, aperture and ISO.

I'll explain the basics of lenses here.

What is a lens?

I use the term 'lens' here, even if a lens actually consists of several lenses. Lenses are glass elements placed one behind the other. The more of those elements in a lens, the higher the price tag. That's putting it a bit simply: the clarity and quality of the glass used for the lenses also plays a big role.

Focal length

There are zoom lenses and prime lenses. A prime lens has a fixed focal length, a zoom lens has a variable one. The point where the incident light rays intersect in the lens (after which they change direction) is the focal point. There is a certain distance between the focal point and the sensor: this is the focal length. The focal point is also the focus of the lens.

A lens with a short focal length, such as 14 mm, has a wide field of view, while one with a higher number, such as 200 mm, has a small field of view. A 14mm lens is also called a wide-angle lens, a 200mm lens is a telephoto lens.

A zoom lens has a variable focal length. By turning the lens, you zoom in or out and move the focal point. This has the great advantage that you don't have to move closer to your subject and that you don't have to change lenses if you want to get closer or further from your subject. Most cameras are sold with a kit lens (often an 18-55mm). This is a good start to master the basics.

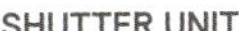
SHUTTER UNIT

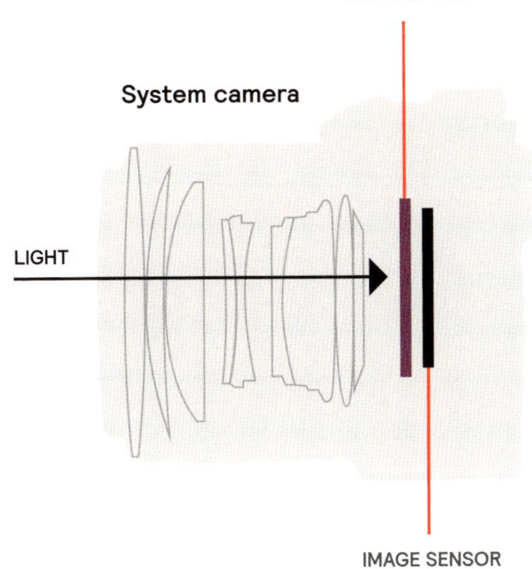
System camera
LIGHT
IMAGE SENSOR

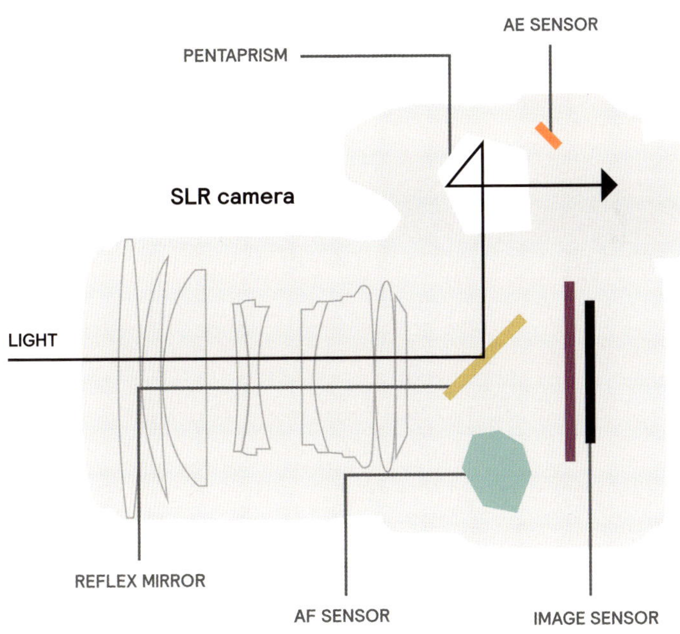
AE SENSOR
PENTAPRISM
SLR camera
LIGHT
REFLEX MIRROR
AF SENSOR
IMAGE SENSOR

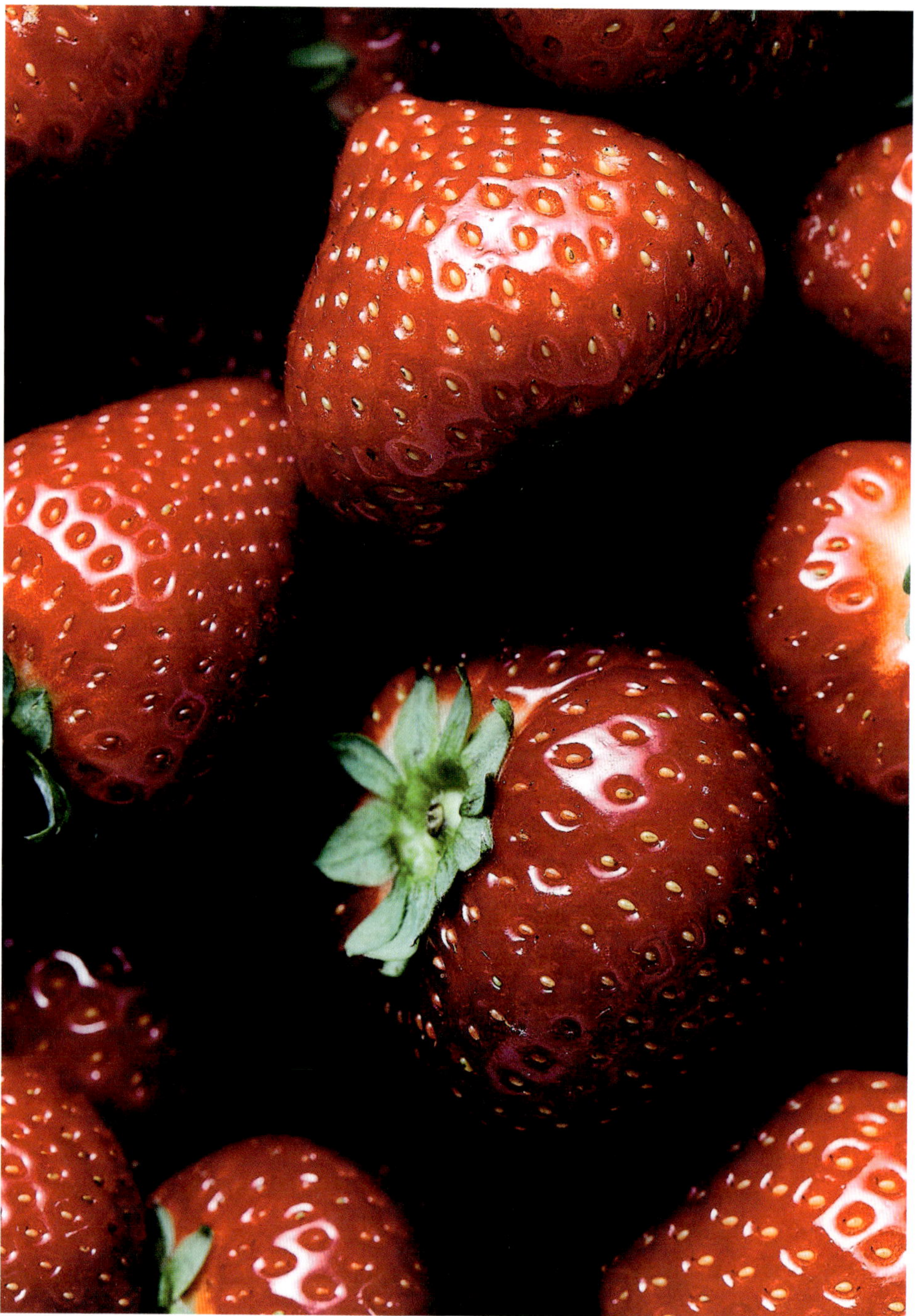

War photographer Robert Capa entered history books with this quote. By getting closer to your subject you can better capture the emotion. By moving closer to the plate of food you strengthen the bond the viewer has with the food on it. If you take a wider shot from further away, then that distance is tangible in your image. Close up or far away is a choice you make. A wider shot isn't necessarily wrong.

IF YOUR PHOTOGRAPHS AREN'T GOOD ENOUGH, YOU'RE NOT CLOSE ENOUGH.

— ROBERT CAPA

Full-frame vs. crop sensor

We talked above about your camera. The sensor in a full-frame camera has the same dimensions as a photo on a 35 mm film, namely 24 x 36 mm. The term crop sensor covers all types of sensors that are smaller than this standard 35mm size. It's important to bear in mind that if you photograph with a crop sensor camera (such as an APS-C or Micro 4/3 Sensor) with, for example, a 50mm lens, you won't get the same image as when using a camera with full frame sensor with that same 50mm lens. The angle of view will be much smaller.

Most compact cameras have a crop sensor. System and SLR cameras more often have a full-frame sensor.

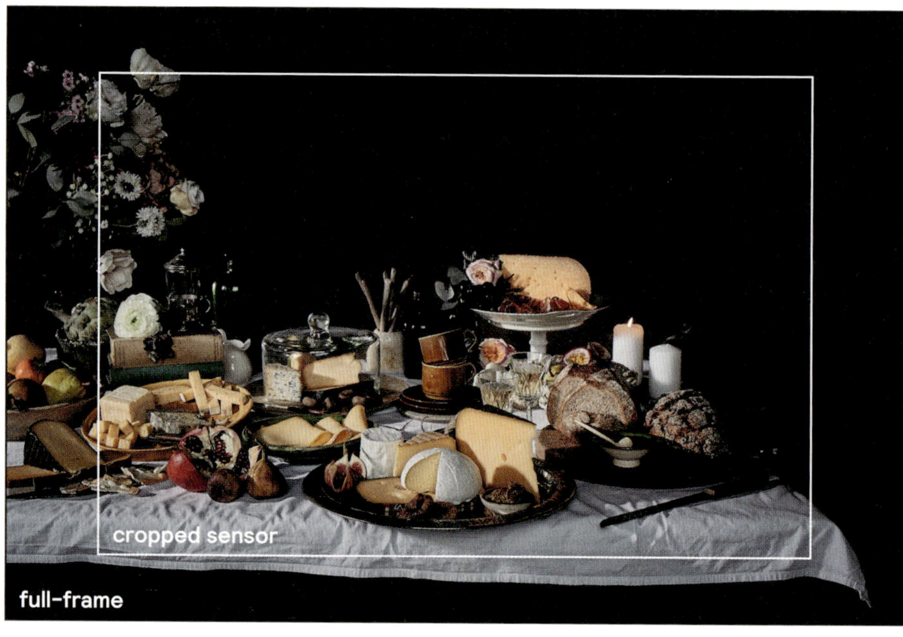

Then why choose a prime lens?

The answer to this is simple: quality. The elements in a prime lens are of much higher quality than in a zoom lens. Because a whole range of focal lengths is crammed into a zoom lens, you lose quality. Prime lenses therefore provide a sharper image than zoom lenses.

Another advantage of prime lenses is that they can have a larger maximum aperture opening. With a wider aperture, you can take photos in darker light conditions without motion blur and at the same time blur the background better than with a lens with a smaller maximum aperture. The wider the maximum aperture, the more expensive.

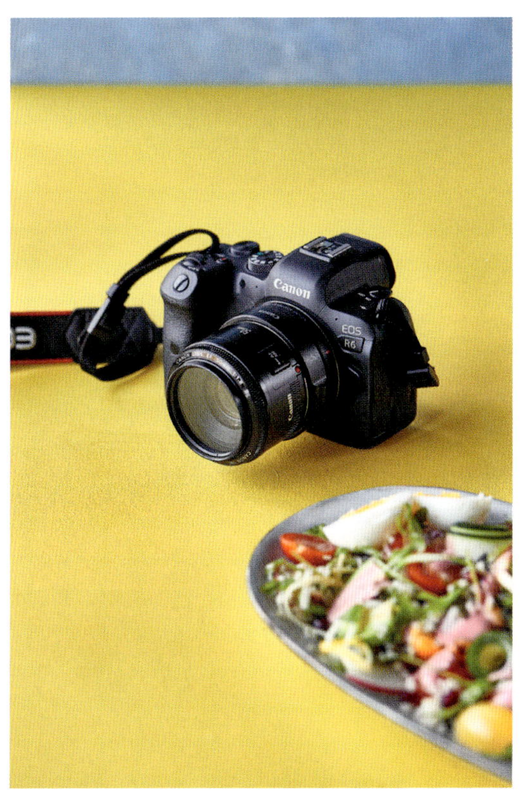

Which lens is best for food photography?
None. And all.

A telephoto lens gives little or no distortion at the edges of your image, a wide-angle lens gives a lot. Every situation requires its own approach. A wide-angle lens can be a conscious or necessary choice in order to tell a story. If you don't want distortion, use a lens with a long focal length.

Here you see some situations with different focal lengths.

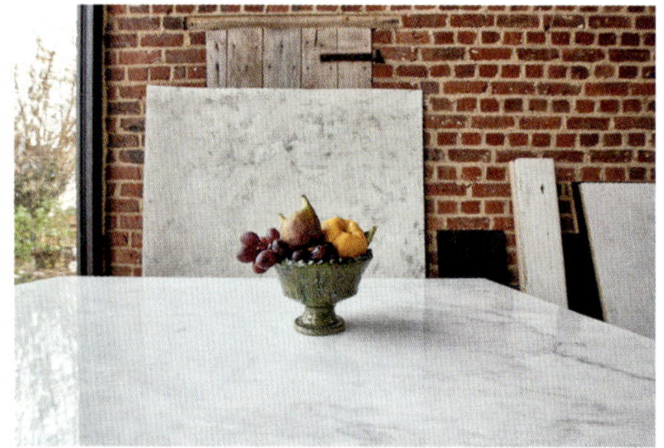

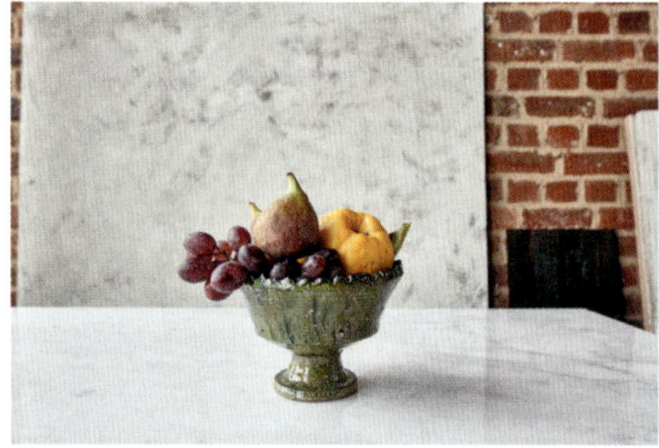

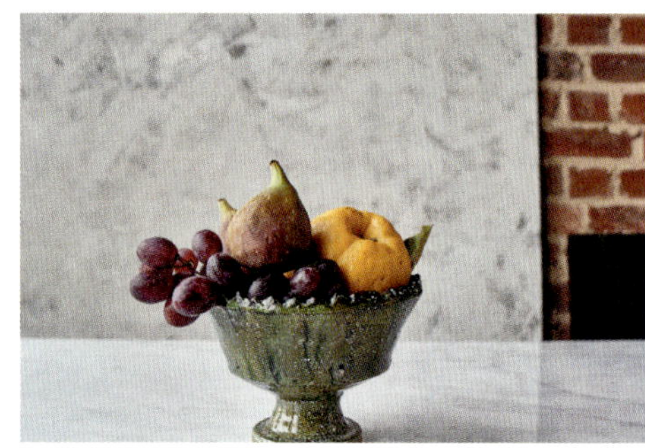

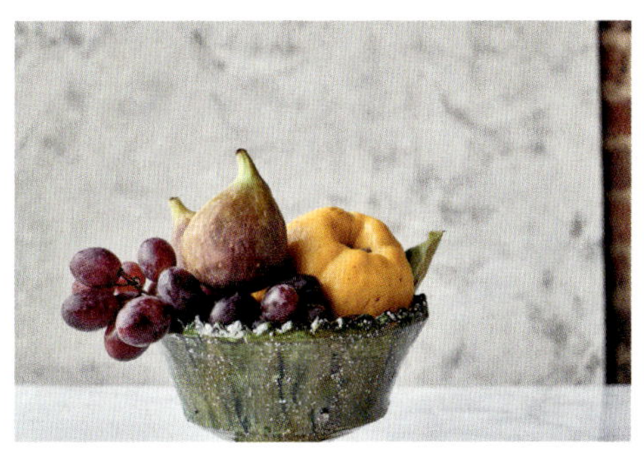

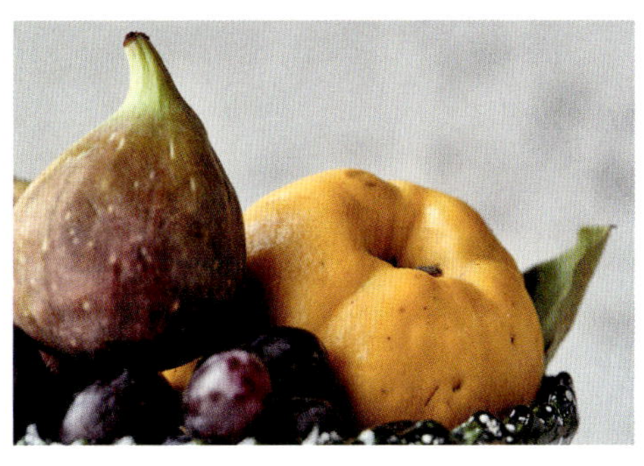

From l to r: Photo at focal length 17mm, 35mm, 50mm, 100mm and 200mm.

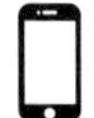

SMARTPHONE TIP: LENSES

Most new smartphone models have several built-in lenses: a standard, telephoto and wide-angle lens or sometimes a macro lens, with which you can get very close up to your subject and photograph the smallest details. The principles of these lenses remain the same as with detachable lenses for a regular camera, only the optics are pressed into a small, round lens. In technical terms they're therefore not as good. Smartphone lenses are less sharp, don't offer as attractive a contrast as detachable lenses and are less colour-true. Only you notice this less, because your smartphone digitally compensates for all this (and you also view the photos on a much smaller screen than when uploading photos from a camera to your computer).

If your smartphone has only a standard lens, you can opt for clip-on lenses. You can buy them for very little money, which makes them more of a gadget than a worthy alternative to a quality lens on a camera.

When buying a smartphone, pay attention to the number of times optical zoom. "Digital zoom" basically means that the photo is cropped, causing loss of pixels, so it has little value. With optical zoom, all the pixels are preserved.

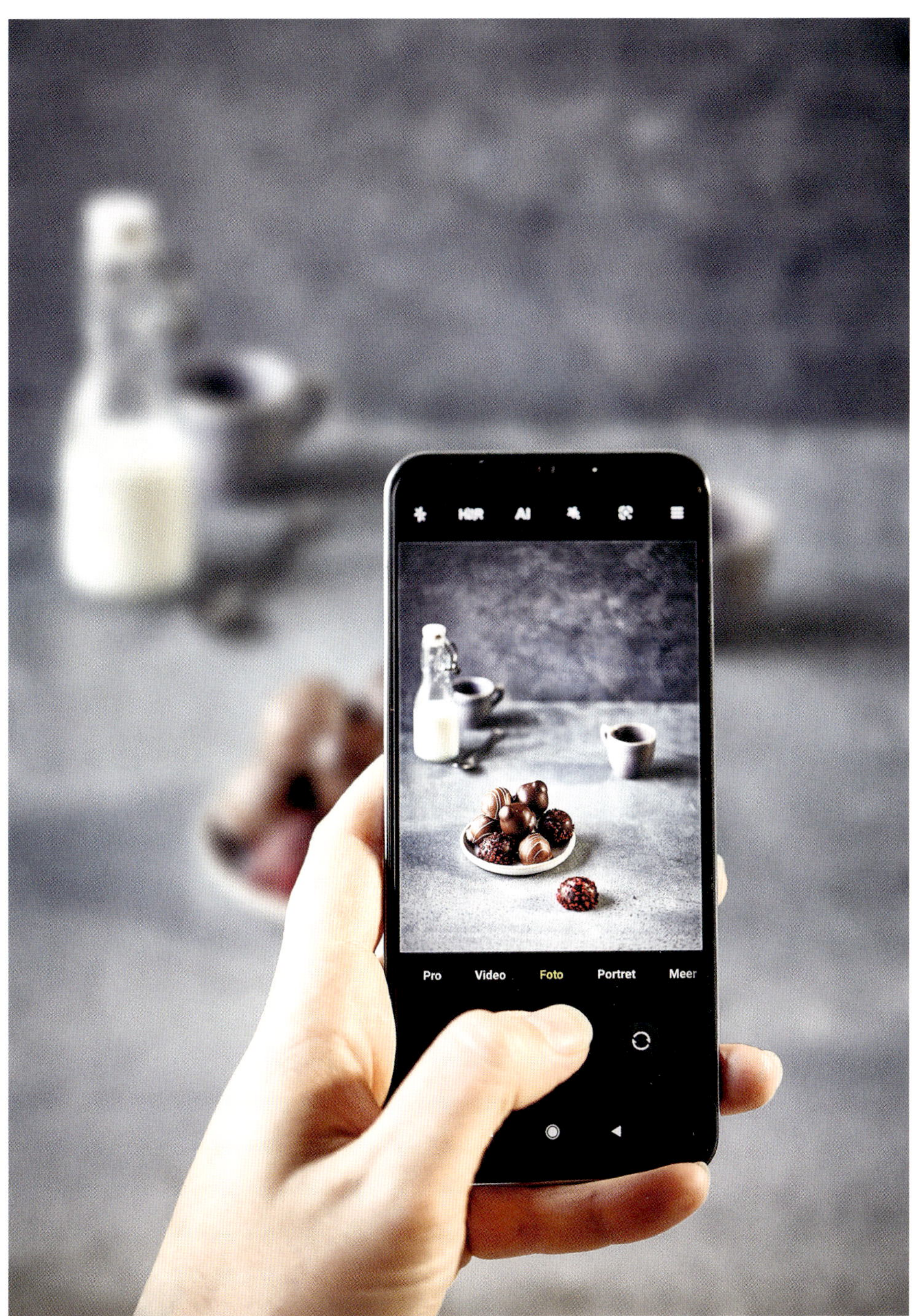
HDR
AI
Pro
Video
Foto
Portret
Meer

COMPOSITION

The added difficulty with food photography is that you not only have to ensure that the food looks good but is preferably compositionally balanced in itself. Everything "non-food" in the picture must also be in balance!

This makes for lots of things to take into account at the same time. And time isn't always on your side when photographing food. With the following 'ground rules' you can quickly create a balanced composition and save time, so that everyone can rapidly start eating that mouth-watering dish.

PERSPECTIVE

Topshot is 'easy' because there's only a single image plane. You have no background clutter to take into account.

But one subject type lends itself more to a side view and in another more to a top shot. For example, a pizza is better viewed in top view (unless you want to photograph a cheese pull, while a burger shows itself to best advantage side-on.

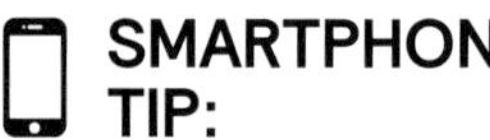

Purchase a smartphone holder that fits the screw thread of an ordinary tripod. This way you can 'hang' your smartphone high enough to get the entire composition in view, without having to hold the smartphone all the time.

Topshot
The camera is positioned horizontally above your subject and parallel to the surface, the lens is pointed down. Be sure to use a tripod to place your camera. This way you don't have to go up and down the stepladder every time you want to change something in your composition.

Flatlays are also made from this camera angle. To create a flatlay you place a few objects flat on a surface, often in a geometric composition, but also as if you were sitting at a table and looking down on it. The objects together tell a story, for example I am going on a trip and am taking with me: a vintage camera, a hat, a notebook, a world map, a compass... In short, all the essentials for the average city person to go into the jungle.

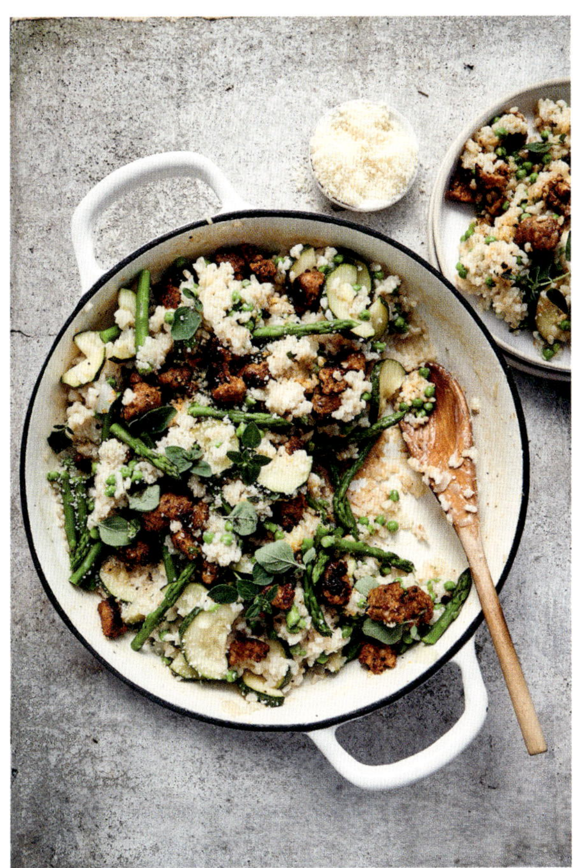

Bird's eye view

The camera is still high above the subject with the lens pointed almost vertically down. You can sometimes already see a piece of background or environment.

If you've set a nice table for dinner, you can sit on a chair between your guests and photograph them over their backs.

45 degrees

When you're sitting at table and a dish is presented to you, this is often done at an angle of about 45 degrees. That's why a photograph at this angle feels natural to the viewer. Don't get too close to your subject with the camera, otherwise you'll get distortion in the corners.

TIP:

Human presence in a food photo creates extra atmosphere and also tells a story.

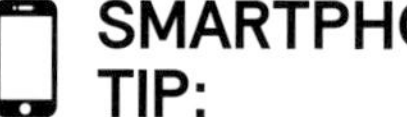

SMARTPHONE TIP:

The smartphone's standard lens will give a lot of distortion from this angle. Select the telephoto lens to avoid this and take a step back to get everything in view.

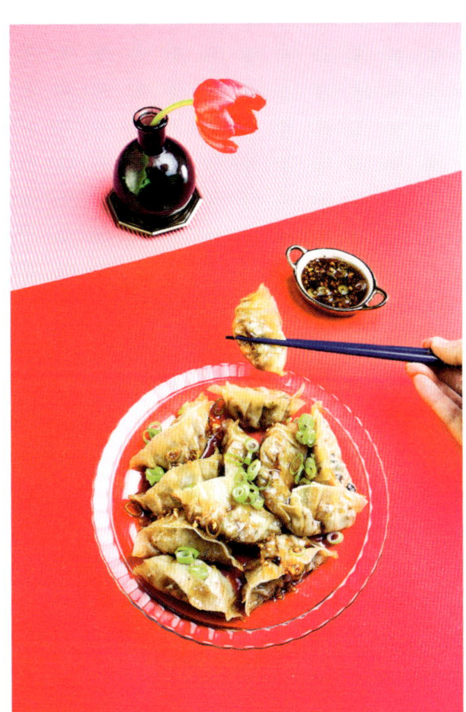

Bird's eye view

45 degrees

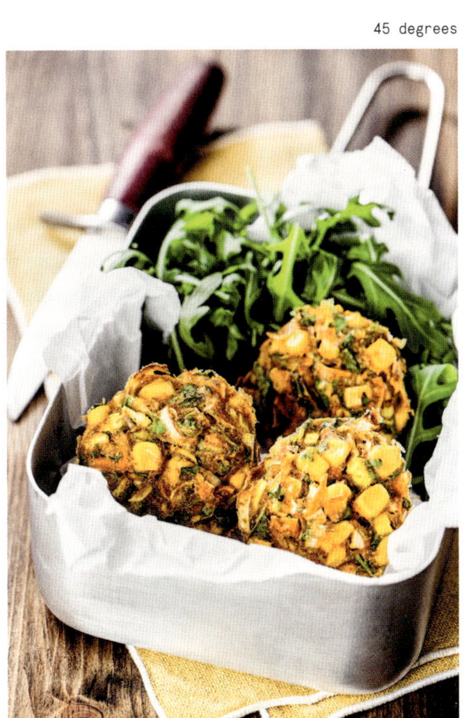

Side view
Dishes built up in layers lend themselves well to photos in side view. Show clearly what lies between the layers of a hamburger or club sandwich or how a lasagne is structured! A stack of pancakes looks so high from a side view.

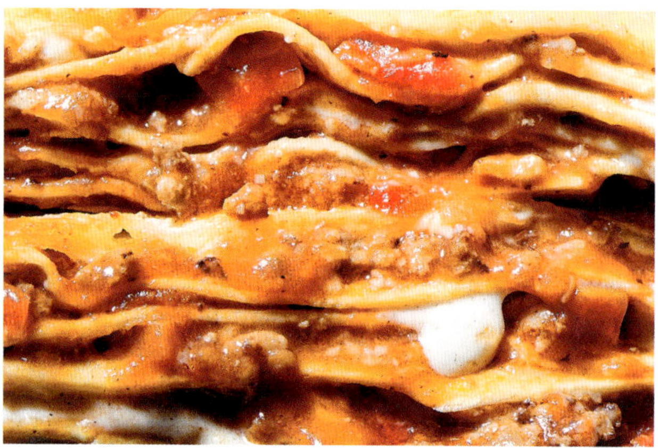

Frog perspective
Sweets and guilty pleasures take on hero status when shot from a very low viewpoint. It's like you're looking through the eyes of a child who is smaller than the table and is ogling that magnificent chocolate cake.

TIP:
Don't always choose the easy way out, but challenge yourself and try a different perspective.

SMARTPHONE TIP:

Do your photos look good only in topshot? This is because of the lens distortion that occurs when you move in very close to the subject in 45° or side view with your smartphone. In topshot, this distortion isn't always noticeable. Select the telephoto lens on your smartphone for less distortion.

Frog perspective

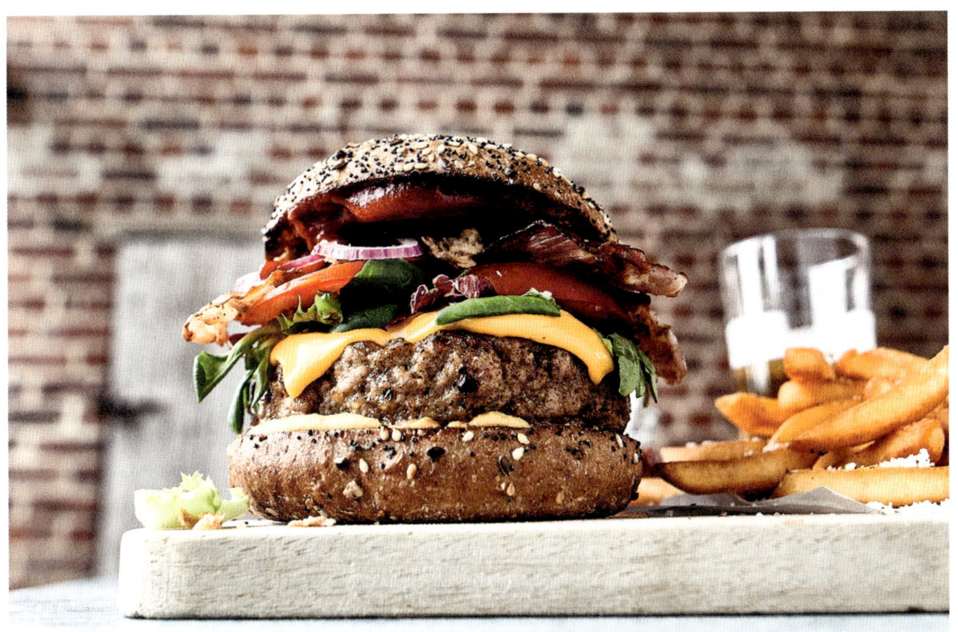

DEPTH

A photo that lacks depth is not so good as attracting the attention of the viewer, who would like to be sucked into the image, to move to another world. Without a sense of depth, it's more difficult for the viewer to step into the image.

There are many ways to create depth. Use lines, visible and invisible, to guide the eye through the image. By placing props (see Props p. 148) in a certain way you can create connection points. A triangle, a zigzag movement, even a circle.

Colour and its repetition lead the eye through the image.

By placing the bowl and the glass further back, you're not only sucked into the image, they also become less sharp. The background separates from the subject, which 'calms' the image. The focus is now more on the plate of spaghetti.

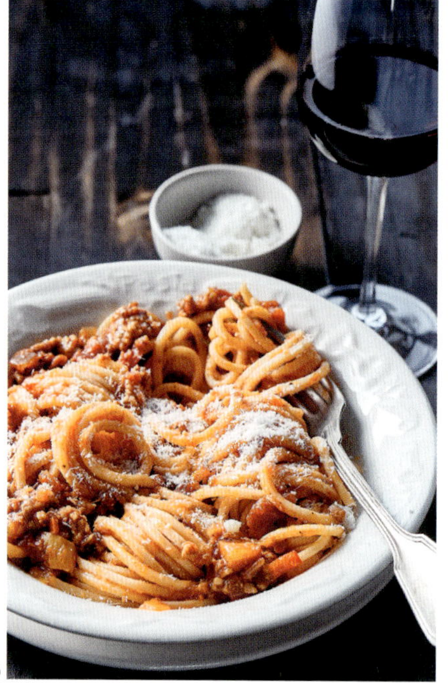

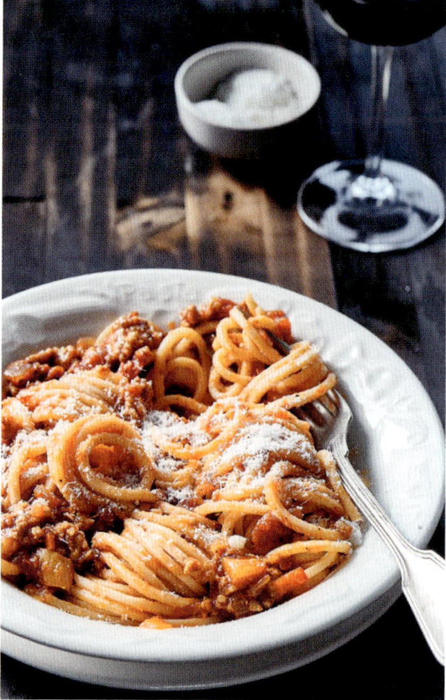

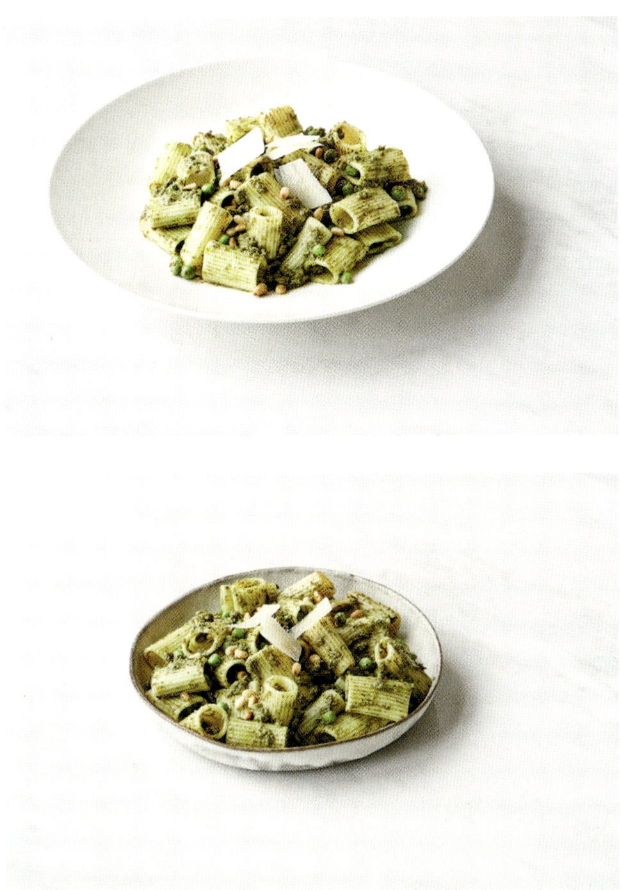

The large plate appears less full and therefore comes across as more 'chic' than the small, full plate.

FRAMING

Scale

When making a composition, it's not always easy to estimate the size of a particular object. Add an element that clarifies this by providing a comparison: a glass, a hand, someone holding a bowl ...

You can also manipulate the scale. For example, a small plate appears fuller with the same amount of food than a large plate.

White space

Just about the most important thing in a balanced composition is white space or negative space. Don't fill everything, but consciously leave some emptiness to bring some peace into the photo. Too little or no white space and you don't know where to look first. This diverts attention from the subject.

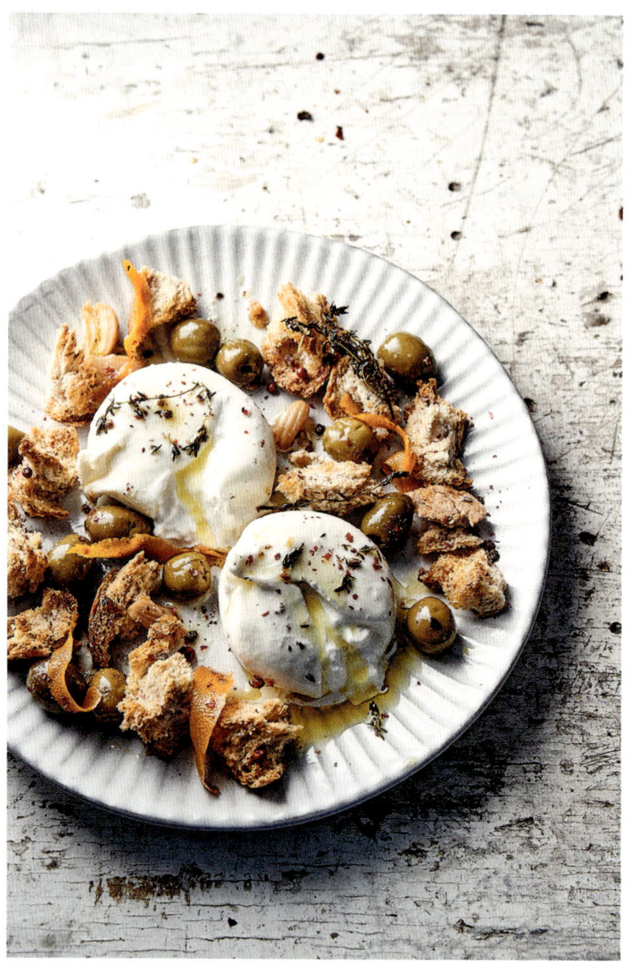

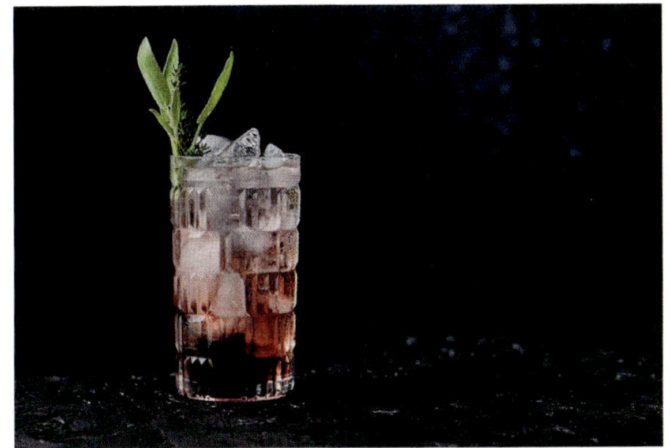

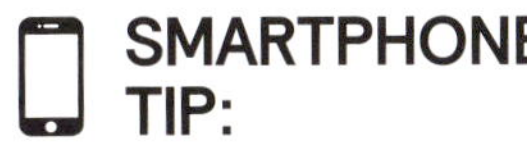

SMARTPHONE TIP:

Enable the 'Rule of Thirds' grid on your smartphone. This way you can immediately see on your screen whether your subject is at such an intersection.

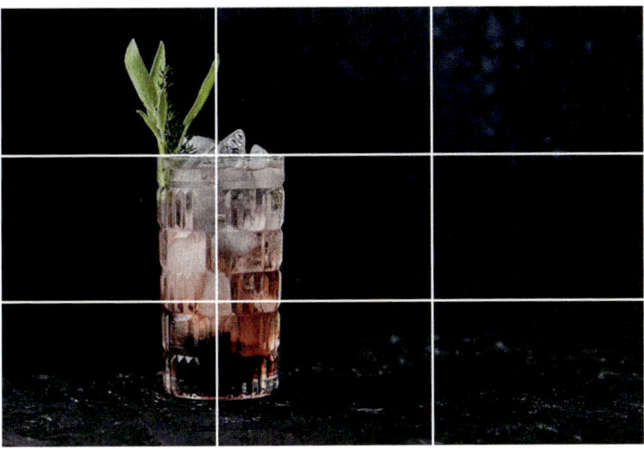

Rule of thirds

The best known and most easily applicable rule of composition is the rule of thirds. This states that a photo is divided into three equal parts over its width and length. If your subject is on one of the dividing lines between those planes, your eye will be guided there. This attraction is even stronger when your subject is at the intersection of two such dividing lines.

Symmetry

Symmetry can create strong tension in a photo. A small element that falls outside this immediately attracts attention.

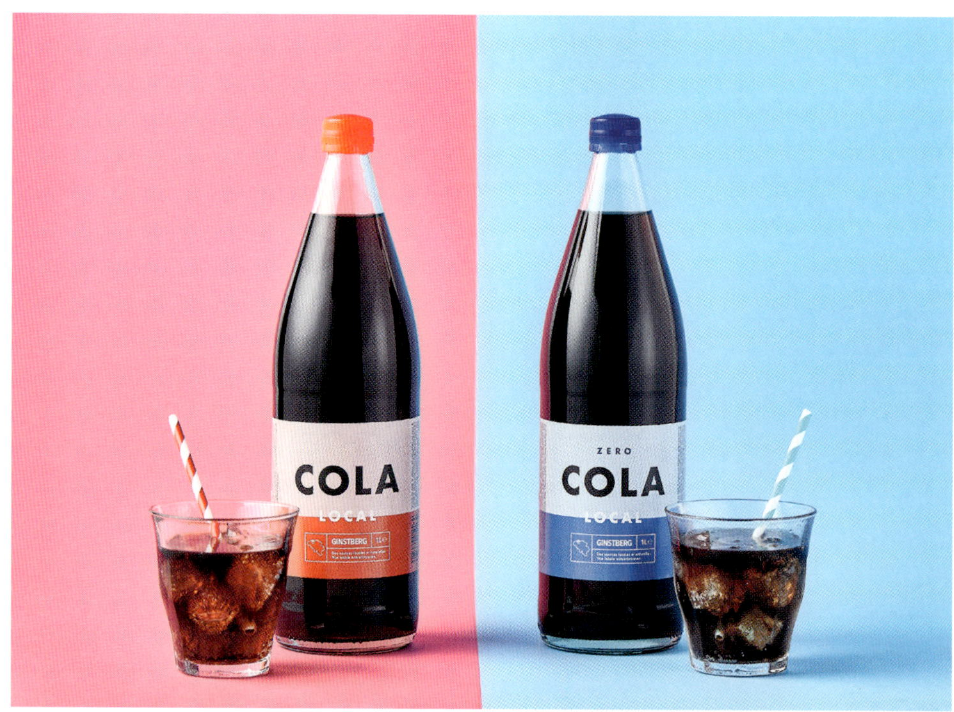

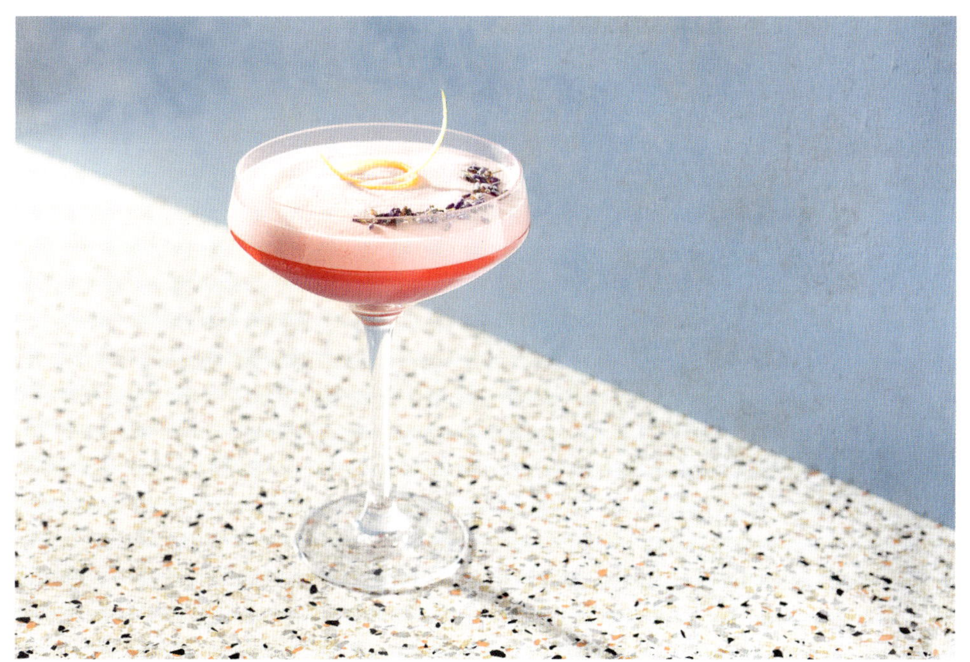

Play of lines
Diagonals, perspective lines, curves and geometric shapes all lead the eye to a certain point or even through the image.

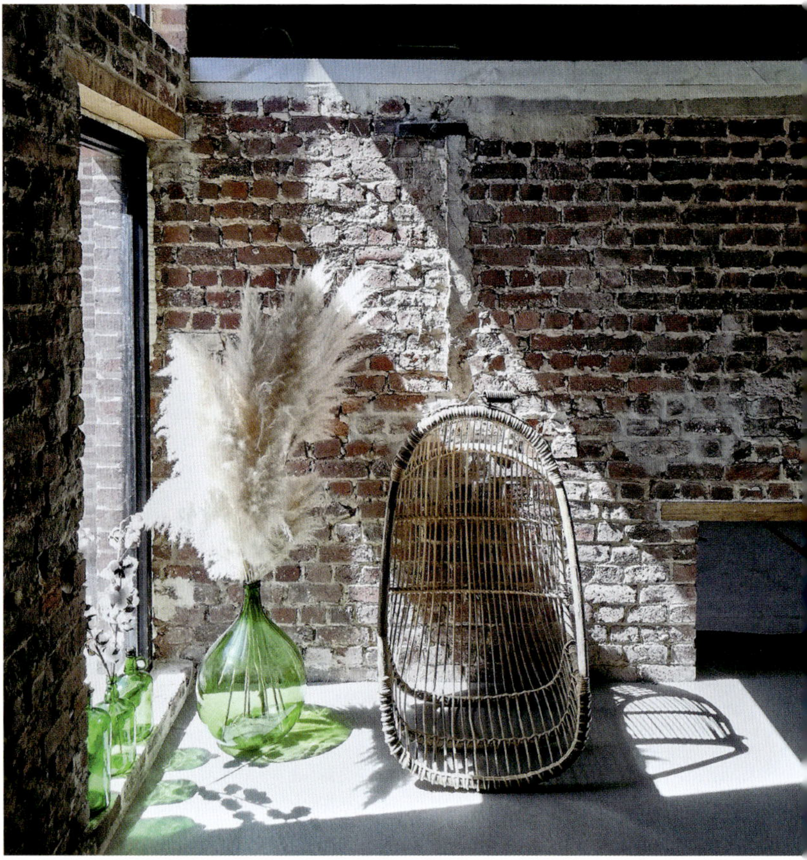

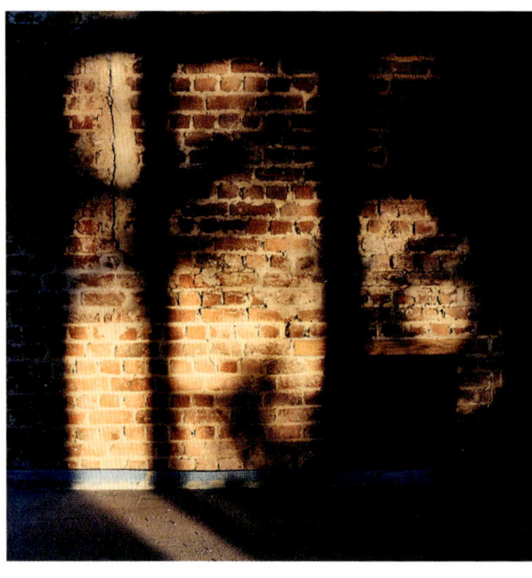

THE LIGHT

Photography literally means 'writing with light'.

The most important thing for a good photo is the light. When you pay attention to it, you'll begin to recognize attractive light. The trick is to capture it.

When you photograph at home, you can get to know the light. Find out where the sun rises and at what times of day the light comes through the window. It rises in the east and sets in the west. Even if there's no bright sunlight through a window, for example on the north side of your house, you can still 'catch' attractive light at that window. In fact, a north-facing window is ideal for food photography because it lets in soft daylight. Be sure to read further in this chapter why soft daylight is ideal!

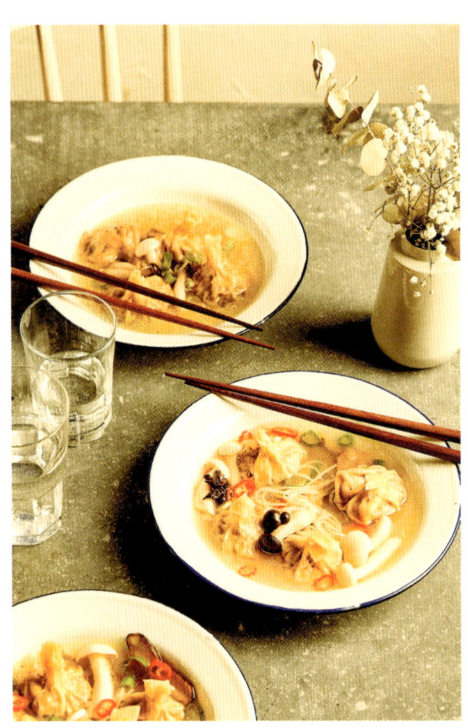

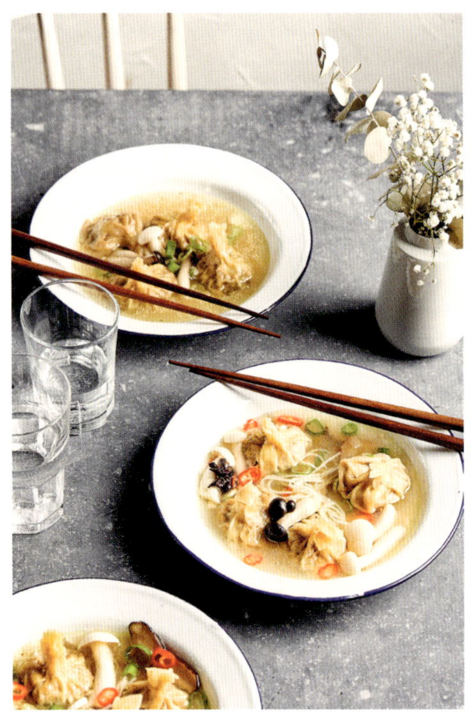

WHITE BALANCE - COLOUR TEMPERATURE

You can set white balance in your camera itself, but I prefer to use the automatic white balance. The reason for this is that the lighting situation in which you photograph often changes, especially when working with daylight. The automatic white balance will partly compensate for these changes. When clouds come in front of the sun, the colour temperature drops. This temperature is expressed in degrees Kelvin (K) and together with the hue (green-magenta) determines your white balance. A high colour temperature, for example 7000 K (K = Kelvin), has a bluer colour and is colder than a low colour temperature of 3000 K, which is in the warm red-yellow colours.

Correct white balance is important. If the white balance is already correct during the recording, it's easier to make small adjustments in post-editing. A photo with incorrect white balance at the time of shooting is much more difficult to correct afterwards.

Colour Temperatures in the Kelvin Scale

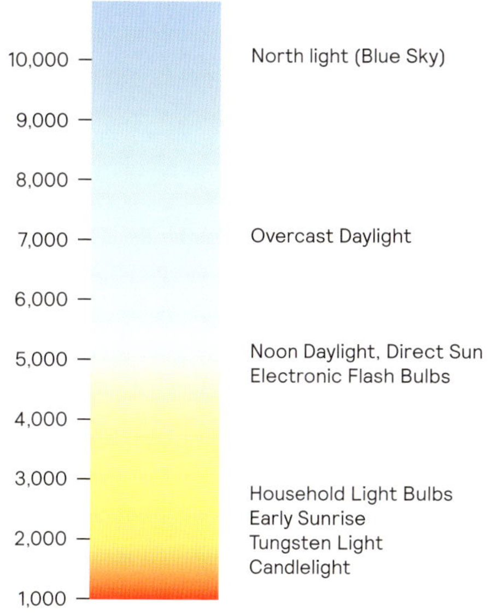

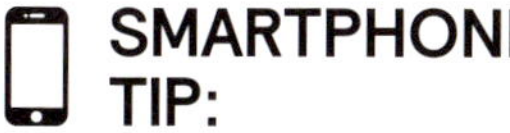

SMARTPHONE TIP:

You can manually choose shutter speed, aperture, ISO value and white balance. On Android devices you will find these functions in the Pro or manual option of your photo app. On iPhone you need to install an app such as VSCO to use manual white balance.

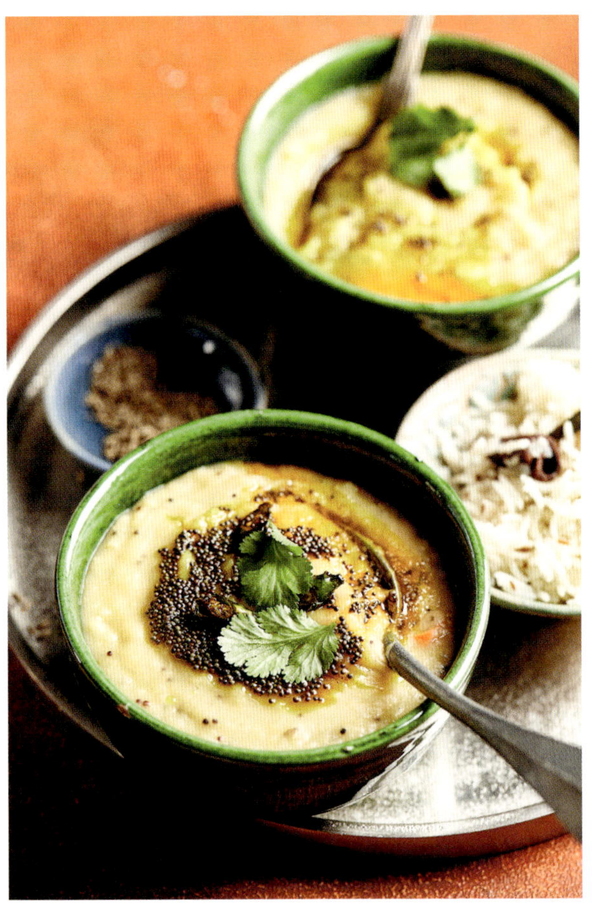

Play with the white balance to create a certain mood or feeling. A low colour temperature of 3000 K, for example, will give the impression of a sunny, warm environment, while a high colour temperature of 8000 K, for example, will create the feeling of a winter atmosphere.

Then there is such a thing as colour temperature. In dark winter months, when the number of hours of sunlight is limited, light bulbs are turned on more often. Dinner won't be eaten in daylight, but lit at most by a yellow light bulb.

Warm light

Incandescent lamps provide warm light. They have a low colour temperature between 1200 and 2800 K. This includes candlelight and halogen light. In this kind of warm light, food will look yellowish. This can be partly solved by correcting the white balance, but the shadows typical of this type of light are anything but flattering for dishes. This is all the more so when several light sources fall on the dish. You end up with a cacophony of shadows and your food looks anything but natural.

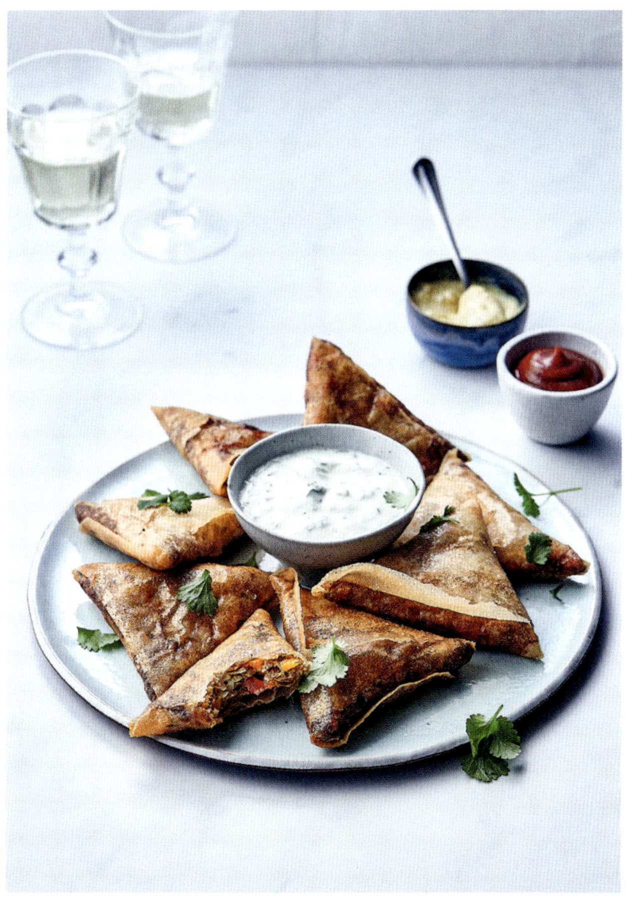

Cold light

Today there are LED lamps with warmer colour temperatures, but with the first LEDs there was no choice. It was cold light. Blue, that is. Light sources with a Kelvin value between 5600 and 10000 are very blue, which makes your food appear cold. Cold light in a living room can feel quite uncomfortable. Your television, computer and smartphone screen also emit a blue glow.

Anyone working in a restaurant kitchen and who has already tried to take a photo of his creations knows that such a kitchen isn't the ideal place to do that. Not only do you often have to bend over backwards to prevent your own shadow from falling on the dish, it also looks greenish-yellow! That's because many restaurant kitchens have fluorescent lights. They give a lot of light and use little energy, but boy, the colour of that light ... Run, while you still can...

But the natural light of a clear sky also has a blue glow. The colour temperature is 10000 K!

Neutral light

Your light is neutral white around 5000 K. Flash light is 5500 K. This ensures that the colours in the photo are displayed as you see them with the naked eye, because the eye automatically adjusts the perception of a warm or cold colour temperature. It has a kind of built-in automatic white balance, as it were. In this way we are not aware of a deviating colour temperature.

Daylight on a slightly cloudy day comes pretty close to this.

TIP:

If you want to purchase a light source, for example for dark winter evenings, you can buy LED lamps or spotlights of around 5500 K. Those are available in a wide price range.

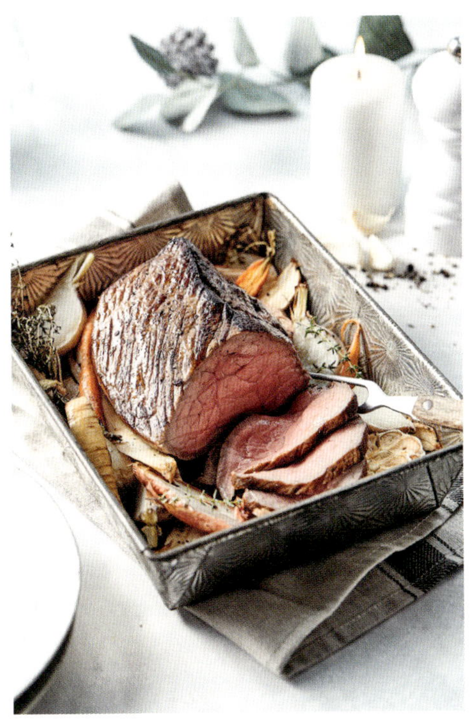

This roast beef looks anything but tasty in the warm kitchen light (3000 K). With daylight at the window on a sunny day (about 6000 K) and a candle in the background, it looks juicy and festive.

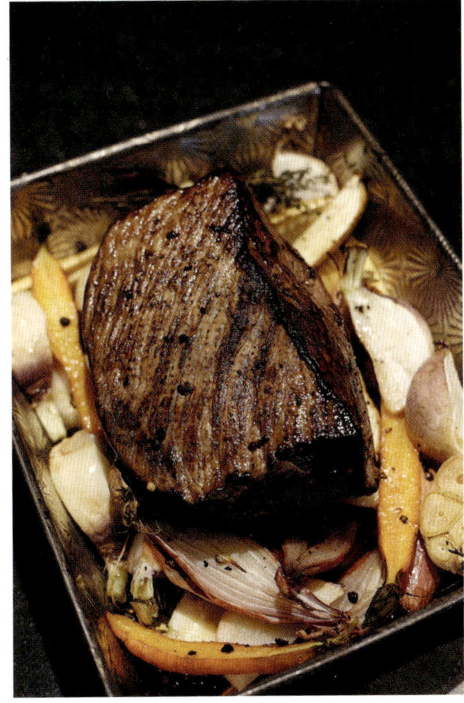

FLASHLIGHT

There are two types of flash: on-camera and off-camera. Everything that is on-camera (the flash built into your camera or smartphone) we throw overboard in food photography. You can hardly manipulate such a flash at all, and it gives a very harsh ugly shadow on your subject.

Off-camera flash is everything that concerns speedlite (attachment flash for system and SLR cameras) and studio flash. We won't elaborate on flash technology in this book for the simple reason that this is material for a book in itself.

CONTINUOUS LIGHT

The solution for dark winter evenings is continuous light. Just like flash, there's a lot one could say here, but the advantage of continuous light is that you can immediately see what it's doing to your subject, which isn't the case with flash light.

Continuous light has long been used for video recording. In the past there were only halogen lamps, which became very hot (and made the ice cream you want to photograph melt like snow in the sun). In addition, halogen light is not colour temperature-neutral, which already complicates things for food photography.

TIP:

For both continuous light (for example LED) and flash light, I recommend starting with a single light source. Once you've got the hang of that, you can use a second and third light source.

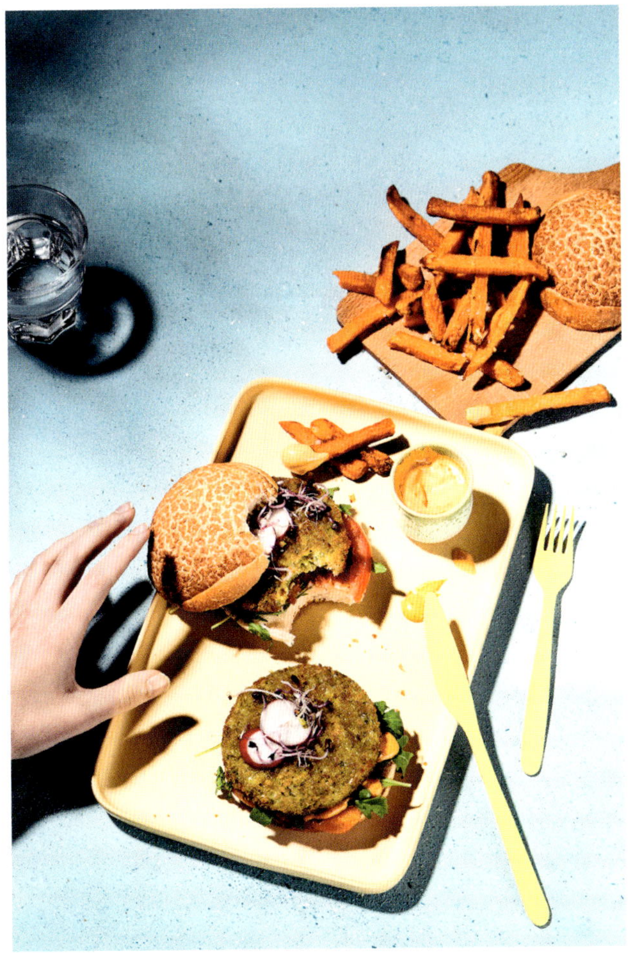

The harsh shadow of the flash light has been deliberately chosen here to enhance the dramatic effect.

DAYLIGHT

The holy grail of food photography. The great thing about daylight is that it's difficult to control, and that's also its weakness. There's only one light source, the sun, which we cannot turn up or down. Or make warmer or colder. Or?

Soft light

If you're just starting with food photography, I recommend starting with soft light. You can recognize soft light by the shadows that your subject casts on the background. They're not sharply defined.
A window on the north side of your home will let in soft light because you don't get direct sunlight on this side.

On a cloudy day you get very soft light. Sometimes even too soft. When there are no more points of light on ingredients that naturally shine, the photo becomes 'flat'. There's little contrast between points of light (highlights) and shadows. In this case, in post-production, you can raise the highlights and darken the shadows. In the chapter 'Editing photos' I explain how to do that.

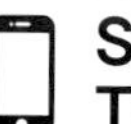

SMARTPHONE TIP:

Is your photo over or underexposed when you shoot in strong sunlight? That's because your smartphone averages all highlights and shadows to calculate the exposure for the photo. Tap your smartphone screen on the sunny side of your subject to meter the light there. Take the picture. You can still lighten up the shadows a bit in post-editing. On the other hand, it's impossible to darken an overexposed photo.

Hard light

Direct sunlight throws harsh shadows. Strong light gives your subject a sleek look, but also casts very strong shadows on one side of your subject.

Does that mean you shouldn't ever photograph in direct sunlight? Absolutely not. Are you sitting on a terrace in the first spring sun enjoying a fresh aperitif? Then direct sunlight is an indispensable element of the photo to convey your story.

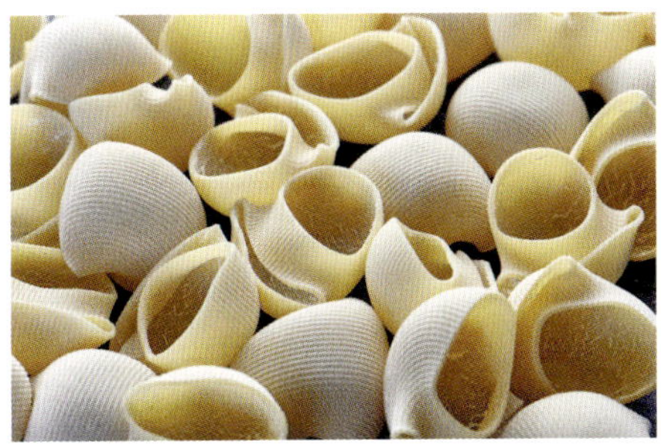

Pasta in cloudy conditions.

Note that the colour temperature is very different between the picture with clouds and the one with sunlight!

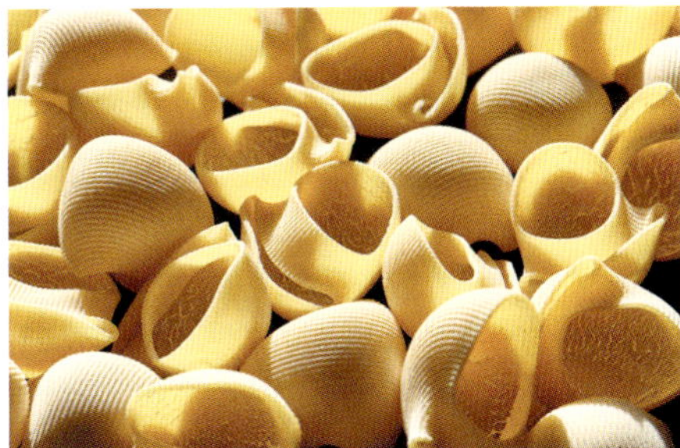

Pasta in full sun.

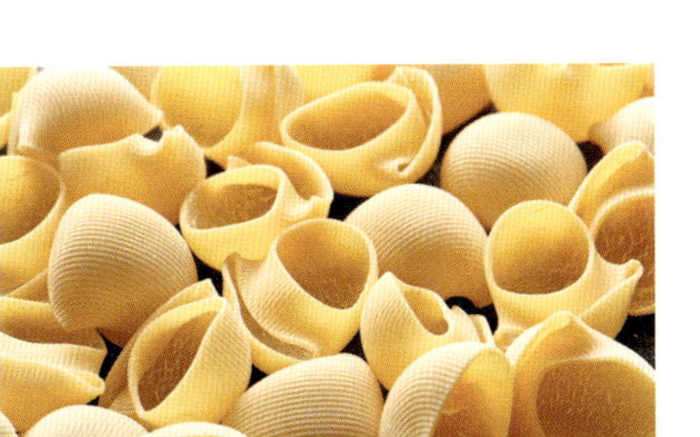

Pasta in sunlight with diffuser screen.

MANIPULATING LIGHT

Softening hard light

Stick a large piece of tracing paper or a very thin white fabric to your window when it's sunny. In this way you 'break' the hard light and you get soft shadows. But note that you'll need a higher exposure, because tracing paper blocks light.

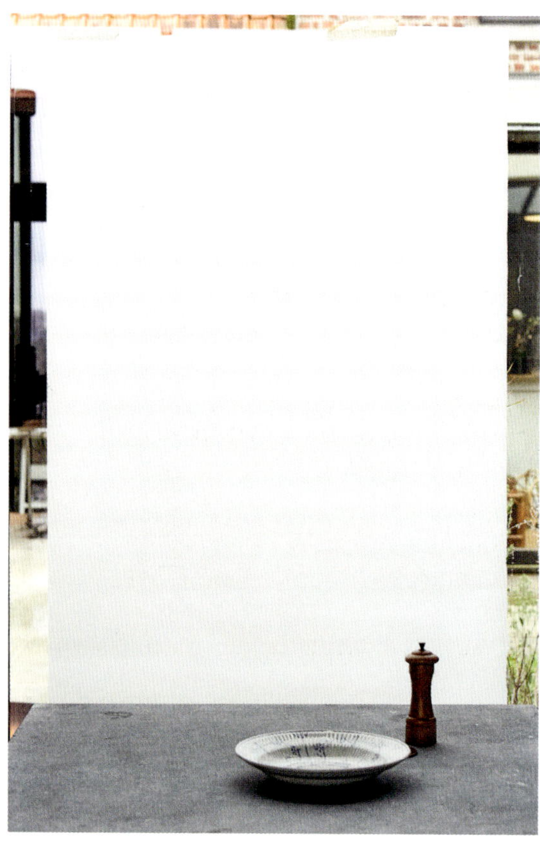

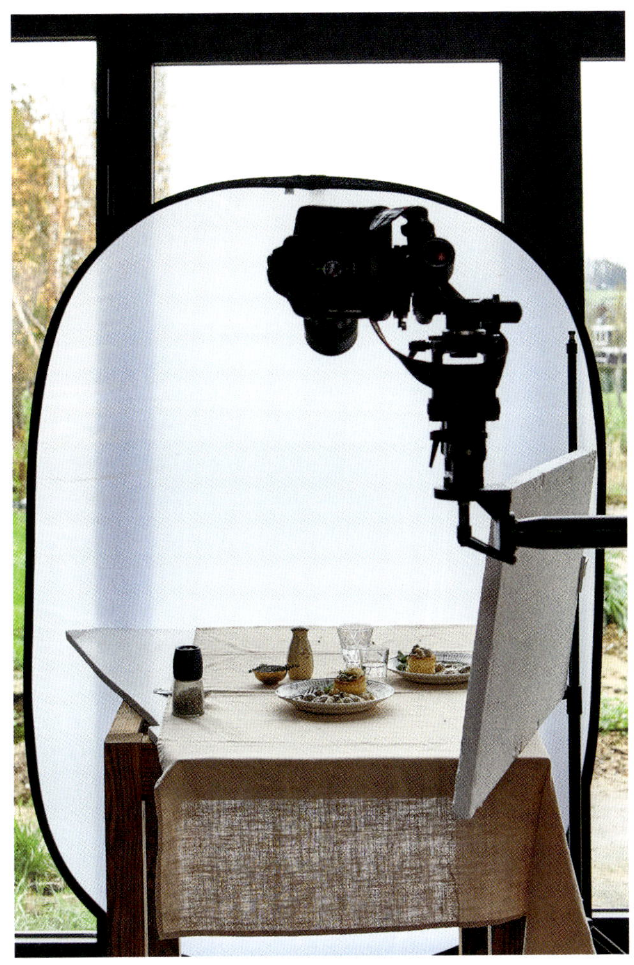

TIP:

You can buy a reflector panel, also called a reflection screen, as a package with a gold and silver or black cover over a diffuser screen. Remove the cover and use the diffuser screen to soften your light. Handy, because the metal frame ensures that your reflection screen remains in place.

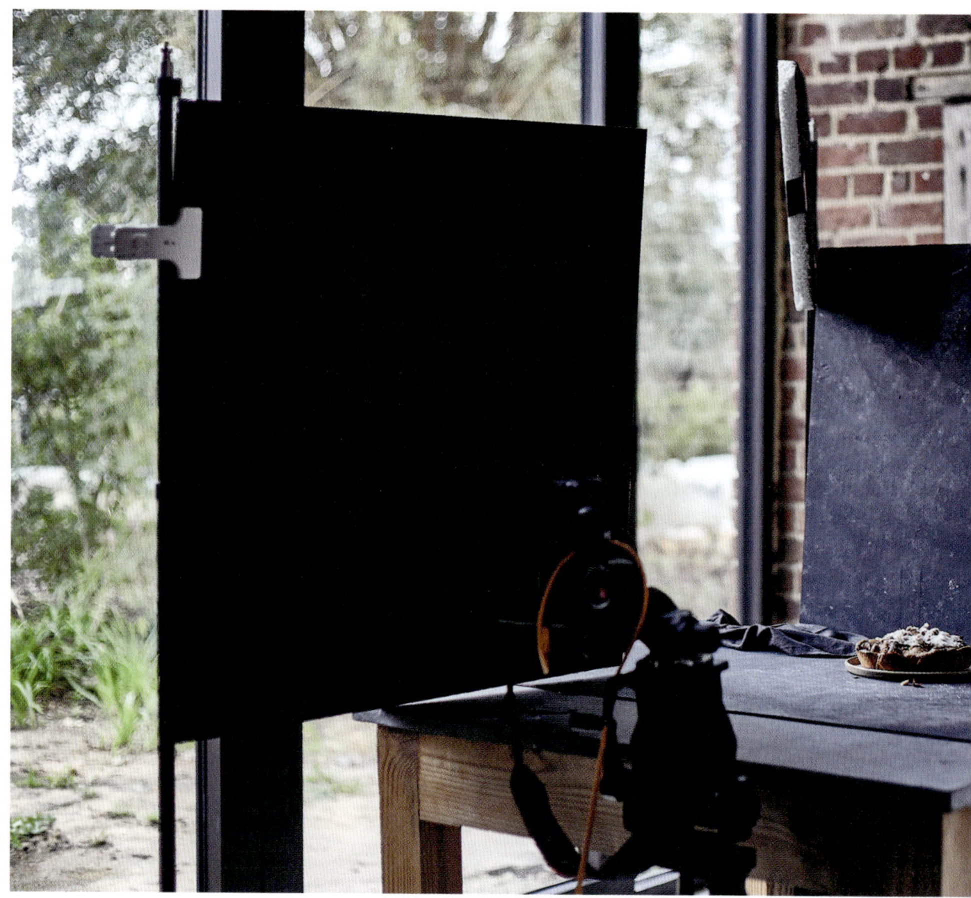

Darkening

Dark photos can be very atmospheric. By blocking the light locally, you can correctly illuminate the subject with a dark, atmospheric background. For this use black paper or cardboard. A board painted black can also serve here, as long as you've used matte paint. Glossy surfaces will cause unwanted reflections in your photo.

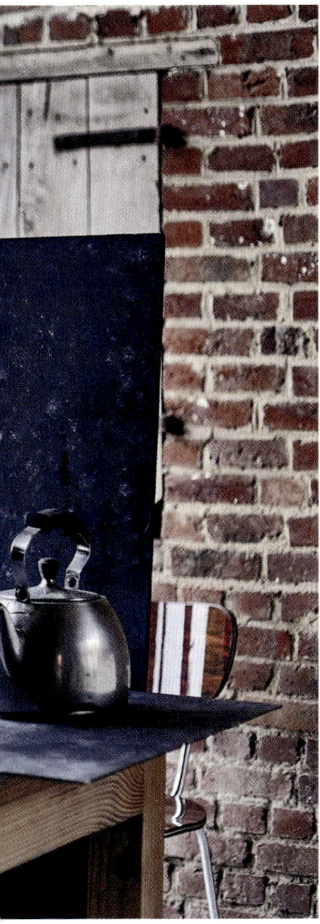

SIDENOTE:

In May 2020 - you know, when we all had to stay at home - I was commissioned by a jam brand to take product photos. My garden, with a chestnut fence and some large trees in the background, was the perfect setting for this shoot. The customer could attend the meeting online, thanks to a 75-metre internet cable, right up to the back of the garden. The diffuser screen I'd ordered did not get to me in time due to covid delivery problems, so I got creative with tracing paper and electrical tubes. I myself sat under a fishing umbrella to protect myself from the scorching sun.

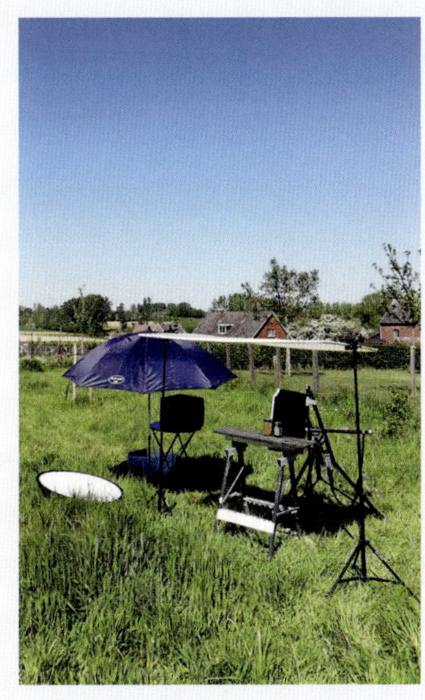

Lightening

When shooting in backlight, in hard light or even in soft daylight, the shadow side of your subject can turn out quite dark. In this case you need a reflector panel. Use a white piece of cardboard, styrofoam, paper, a white board... whatever is flat and white.

You can of course also buy reflector panels. They often have a white, gold, silver and black side.

Place the reflector panel parallel to the window or your light source and always along the shadow side of your subject.

Experiment with the position of your reflector panel. The closer you place it to your subject, the more it will light it up. The further away, the less.

Reflecting

You lighten something by reflecting light. With white panels, as described above, you refract the light before it's reflected. What is reflected on your subject is diffused light. With gold and silver panels, or even with a mirror, you bundle the light rays and get a hard reflection.

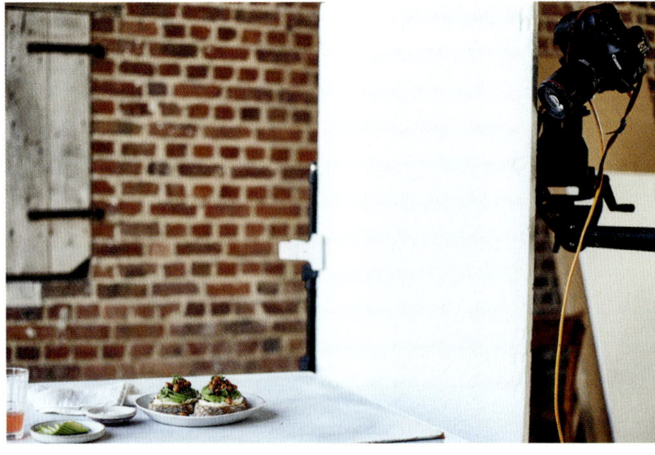

THE SECRET OF LIGHT IS IN ITS SHADOW

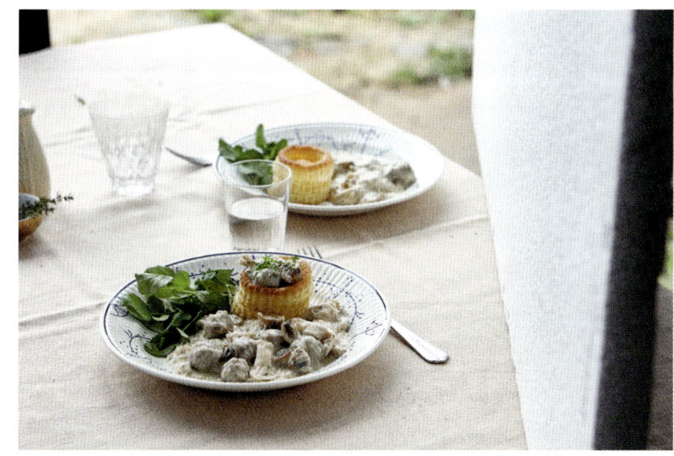

Photo above:
reflector panel close
by the subject.

Photo below:
reflector panel further
away from the subject.

Pay close attention to the
shadow side of the vol-au
vent in these two photos.

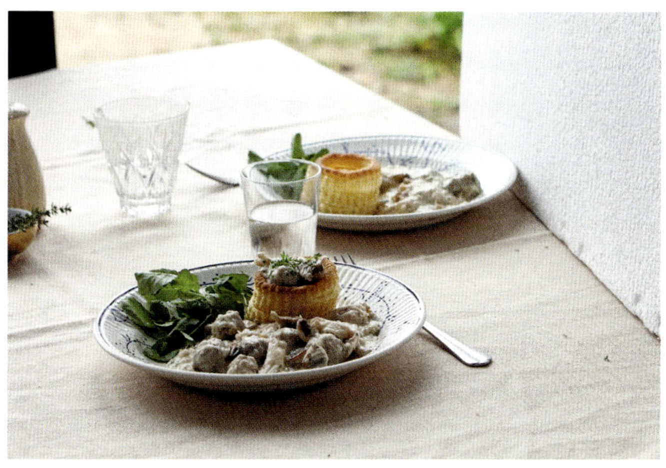

The direction of the light

You can't move the sun, of course, but you can change the direction in which you shoot.

FRONTAL LIGHT

The light comes from the same direction as where the camera is located. The window will therefore be behind (or above) the camera. This is not ideal because you or the camera are in front of the light source and therefore block the light.

SIDE LIGHT

Side-on light is the most popular for food. For this, place the direction of the lens parallel to the window.

BACKLIGHT

With backlighting you shoot into the light. Backlighting looks very fresh; especially with drinks that transmit light, this can give a very attractive effect.

LOW VS. HIGH LIGHT

At sunrise and at sunset you get a warm glow on your subject. You can use that in your photography! A cosy breakfast is even more convincing in the low morning light. But your time frame is limited: the sun rotates quickly and the light changes with it!

THE BEST LIGHT IS BACKLIGHT.

— MICHIEL HENDRYCKX

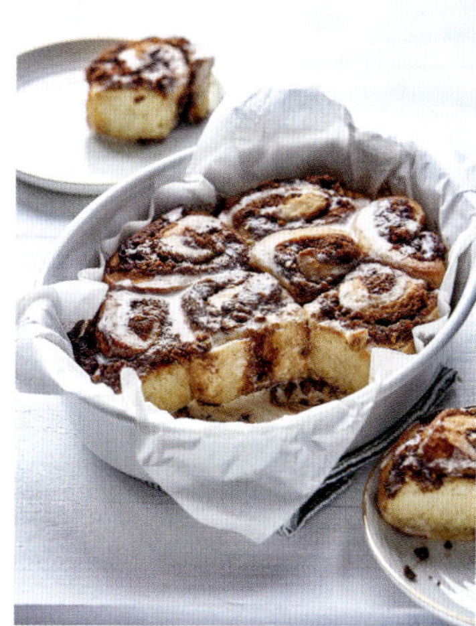

Backlight

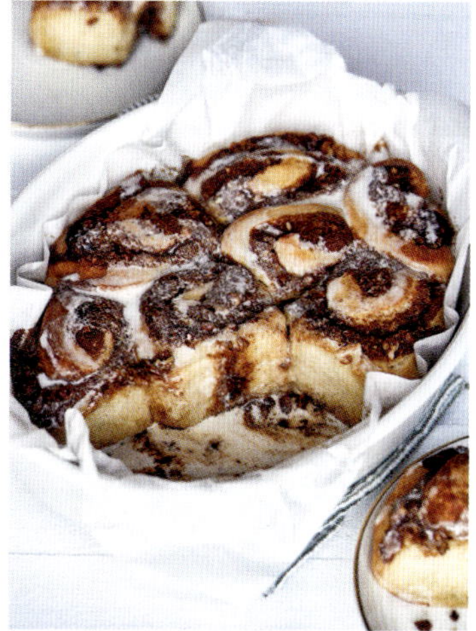

Frontal light

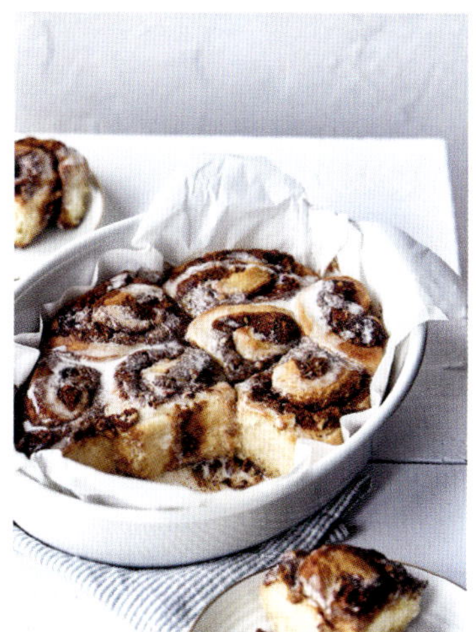

Side light

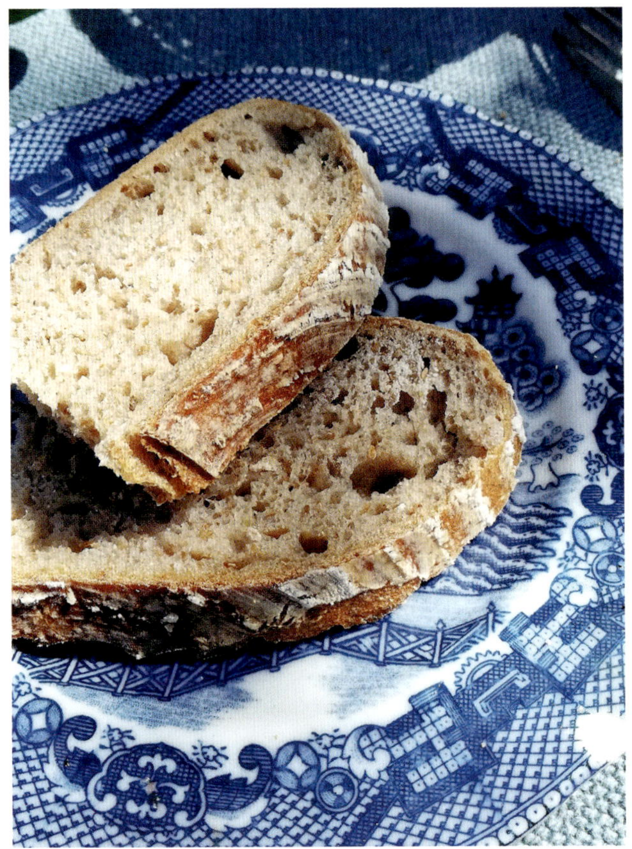

You can see from the shadow to the left of the bread that the sun is still low and therefore gives long shadows.

The best time to shoot

Once the sun sets or it's too dark indoors to take a sharp photo, then there's not enough daylight. This can sometimes happen on rainy winter days.

Try to organize yourself so that you can take pictures while there's plenty of daylight. Is it already dark when you come home after work and you'd like to take a picture of your meal? Then prepare an extra portion and photograph it at the weekend or on another day, while it's still light. But sometimes it's not possible to wait for daylight. In that case you can purchase a continuous light source and a diffuser so as to still have enough soft light for your photo (see Continuous light p. 74).

AS LONG AS THERE'S DAYLIGHT, YOU'RE FINE.

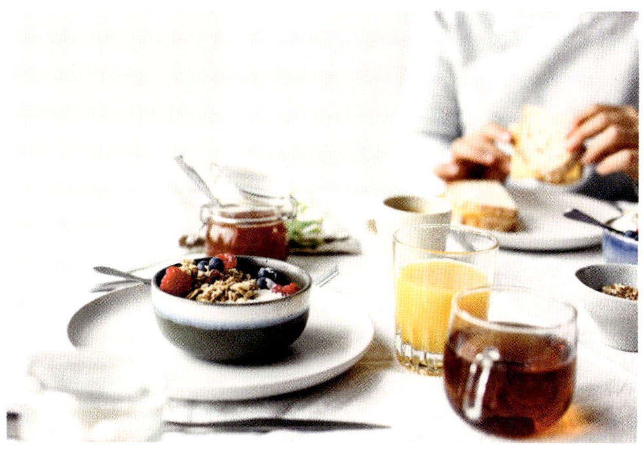

CONTENTS

Photography is more than just technical gadgets. Good equipment is not unimportant, but that alone does not make a good photo. Don't let big guns discourage you. First learn to 'look'.

LEARNING TO LOOK

Don't just photograph your plate of food. Take your camera outside with you. Notice things when walking down the street. Pay attention to shadows, how the light falls on a certain shape, on a particular grouping of objects, special coincidences ... It will provide inspiration and experience for when you need it.

Street photography is a great way to learn to photograph what is out there without being able to manipulate it. The place from which you choose to take the photo, whether you bend down or stand on a bench when pressing the camera button, what framing or depth of field you use... These are all factors that determine your view. It makes your photo of a subject different from someone else's.

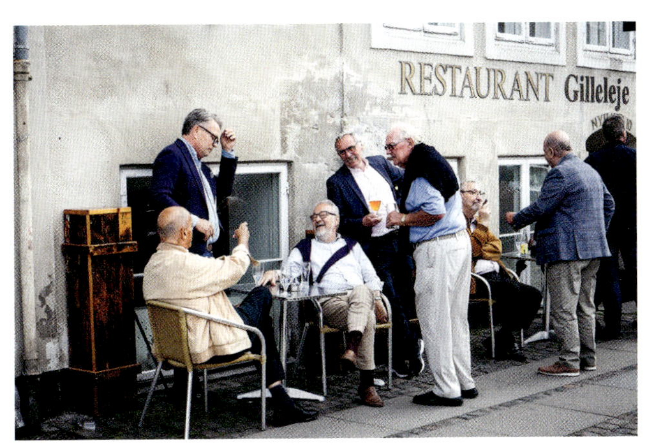
RESTAURANT Gilleleje

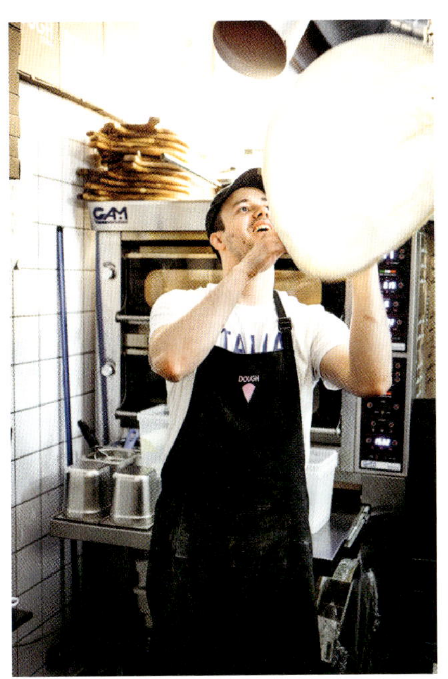
DOUGH

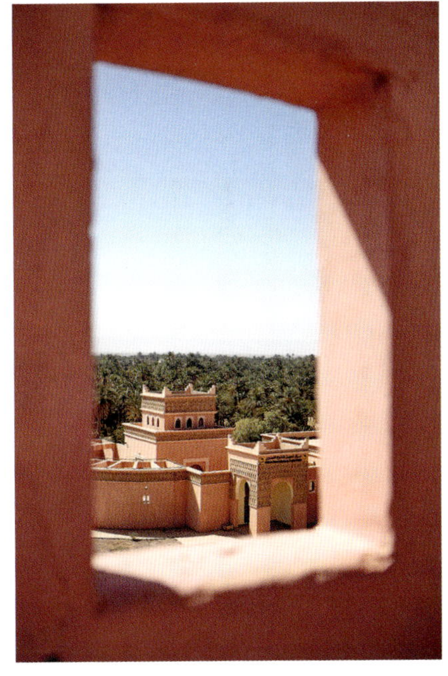

THE STORY

What story do you want to tell with your photos? Do you want to show others what you're doing? Or who you are? What are the values that are important for you?

Photography is a medium with which you can tell a whole story in a single photo.

LAYERING IS SOMETHING THAT DISTINGUISHES A SNAPSHOT FROM A GOOD PHOTO.

There's not always much 'happening' in the image, but small details can reveal a lot.

Therefore, think carefully about the light, composition and what props you use. Don't always make it simply good to look at, but try to give it meaning.

The trick isn't to tell a story with as many elements as possible, but to appeal to the imagination with a minimum of props, light and technology.

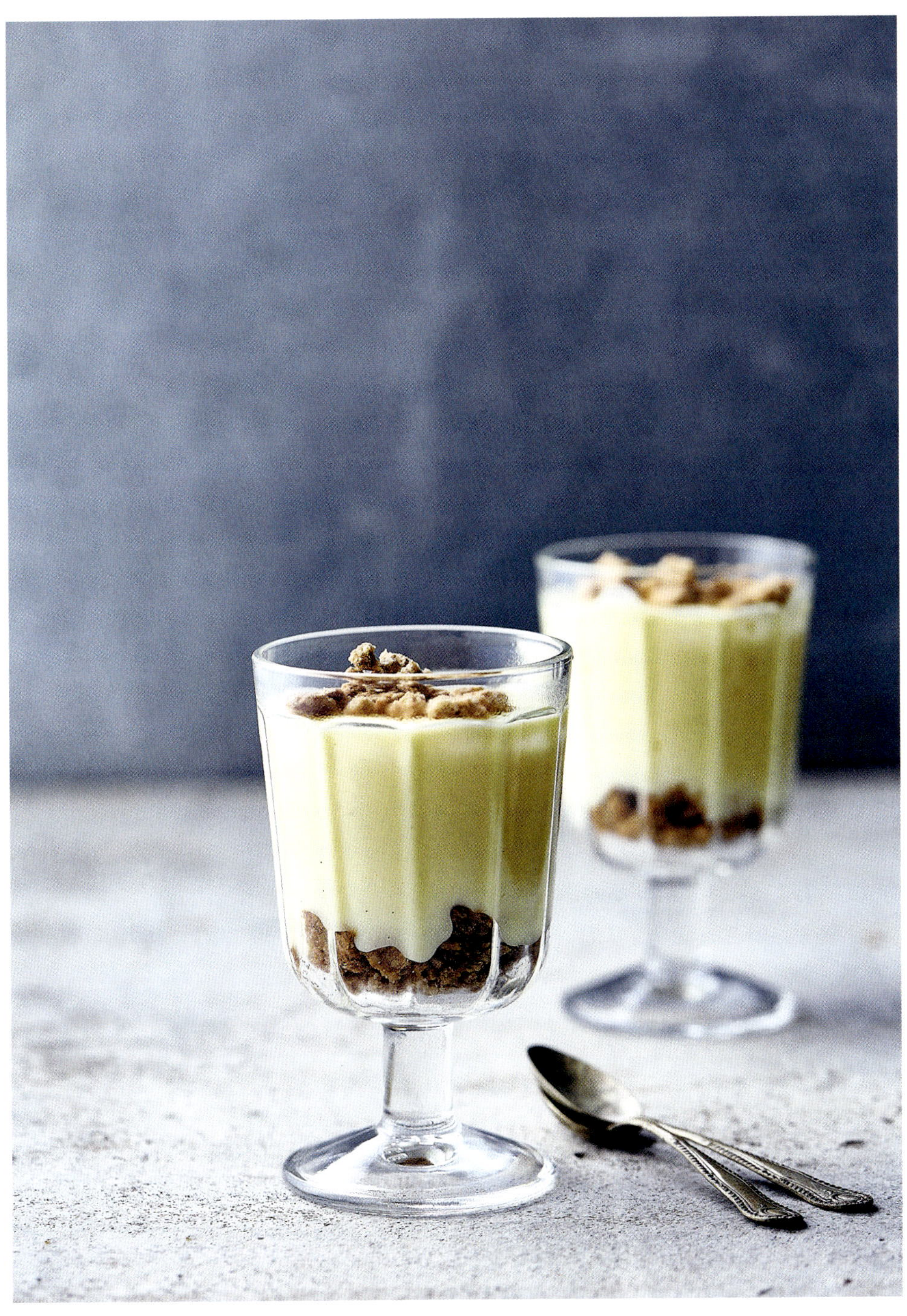

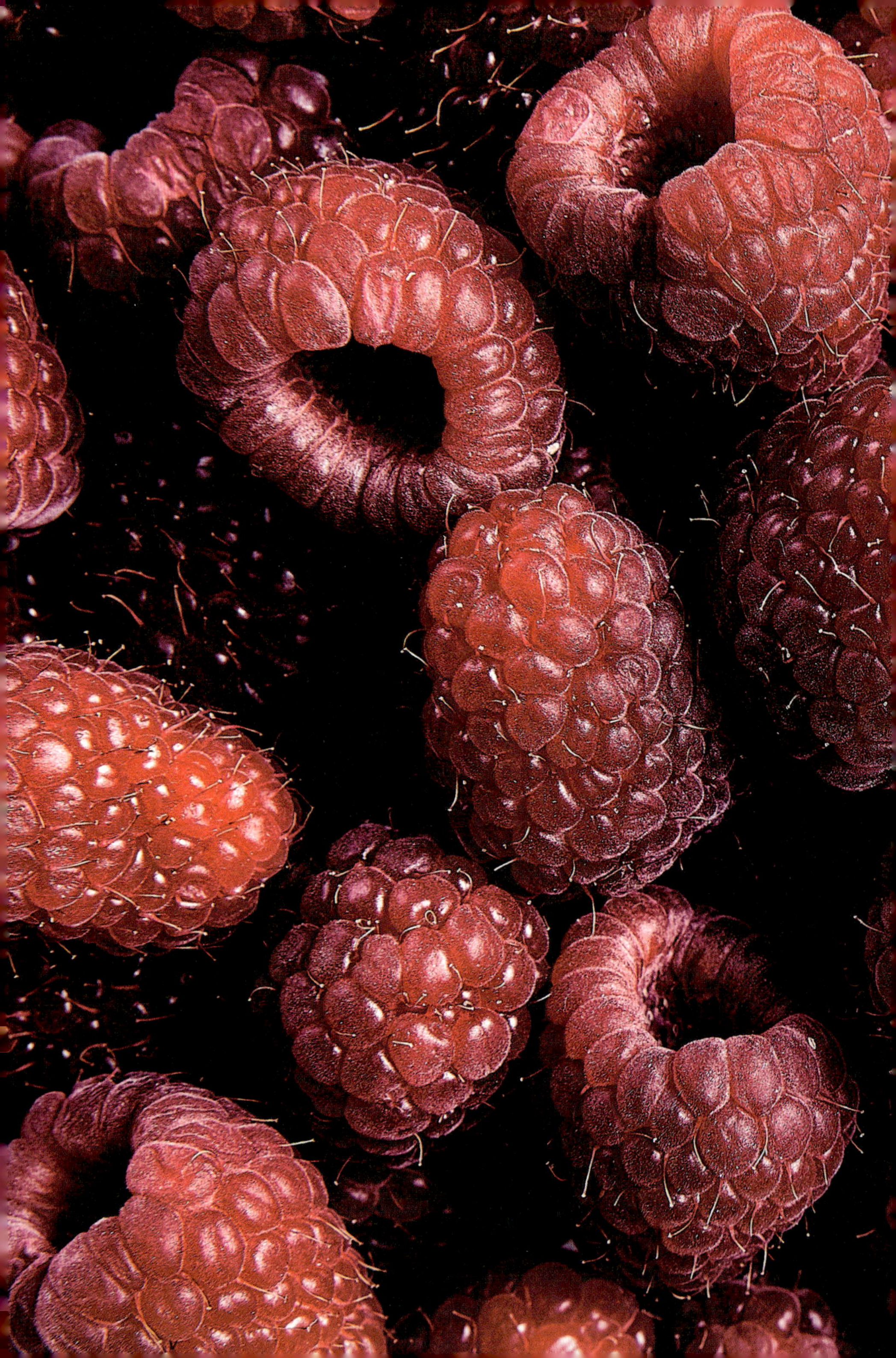

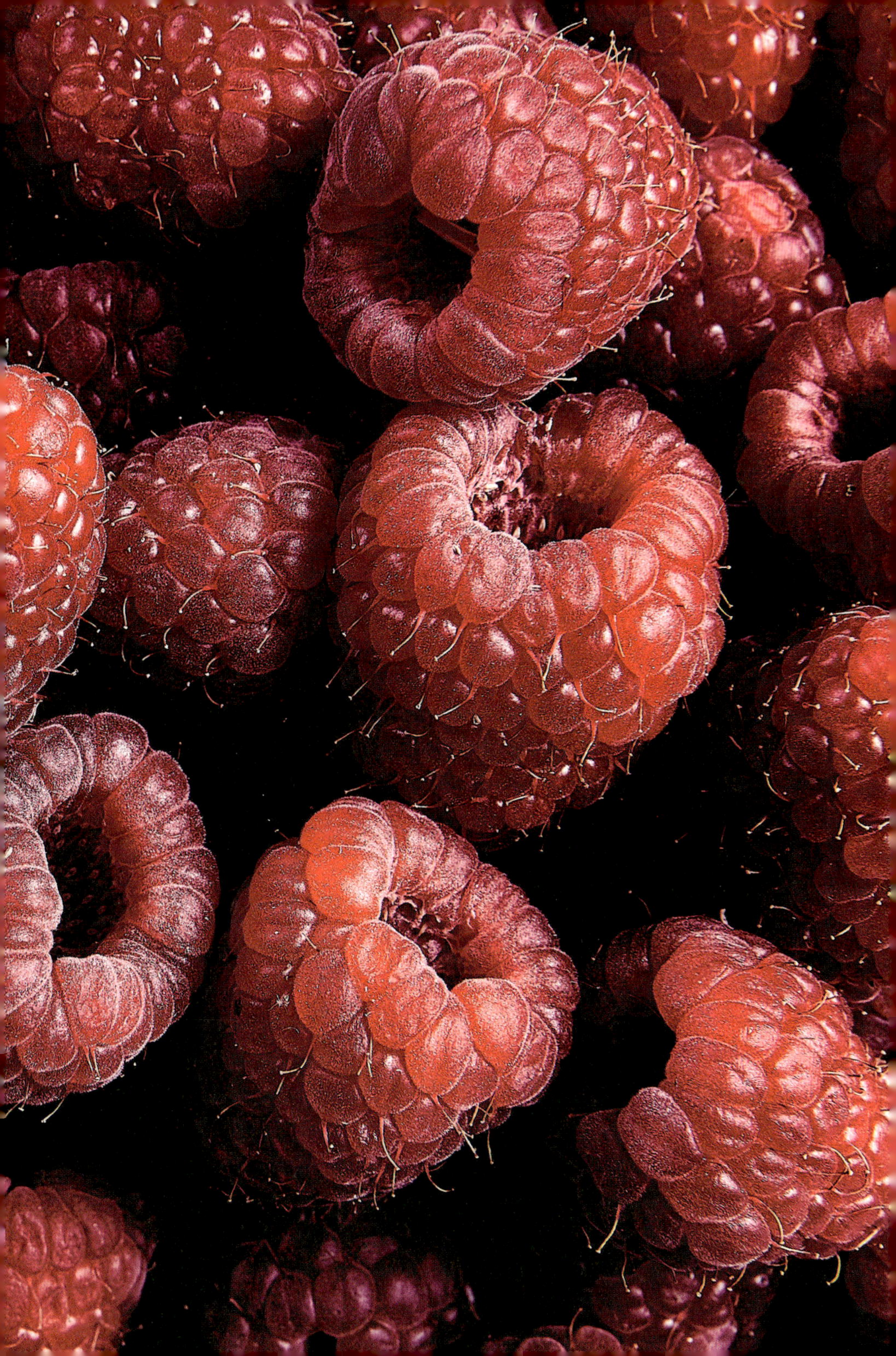

ANALYSING PHOTOS

03

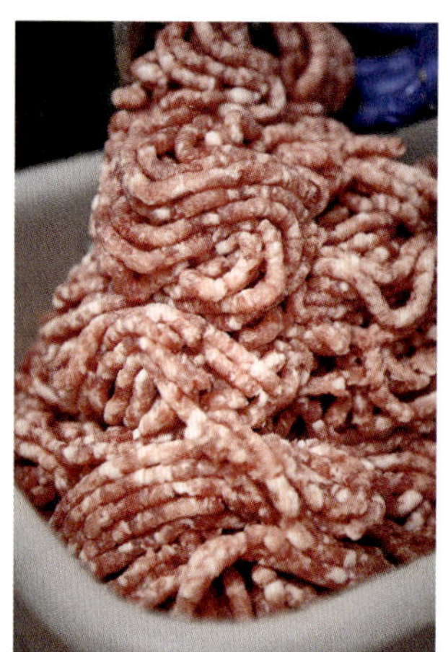

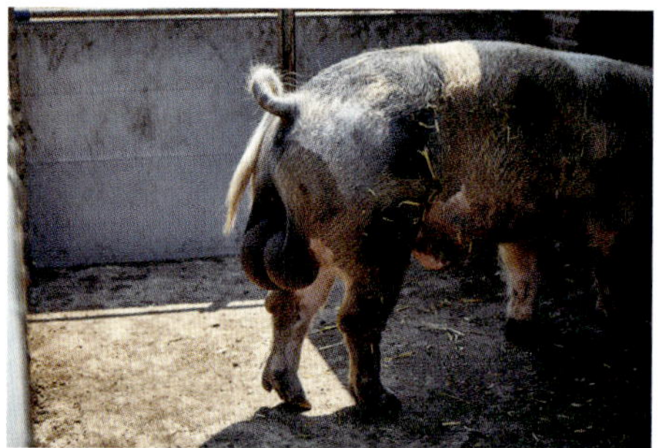

PHOTO SERIES

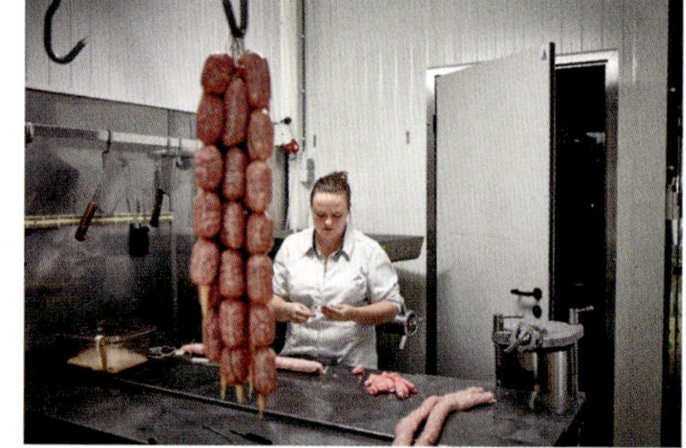

A photo series could also go under the heading of storytelling. Storytelling is just that: telling a story. Showing how a dish is prepared, what the ingredients are. But an empty plate after lunch can also be part of the story.

Certainly it should not be too complicated. Do you have chickens in your yard? Make a portrait of the mother hen, a photo of the eggs in the nest, an assistant breaking an egg above the pan and the omelette with herbs.

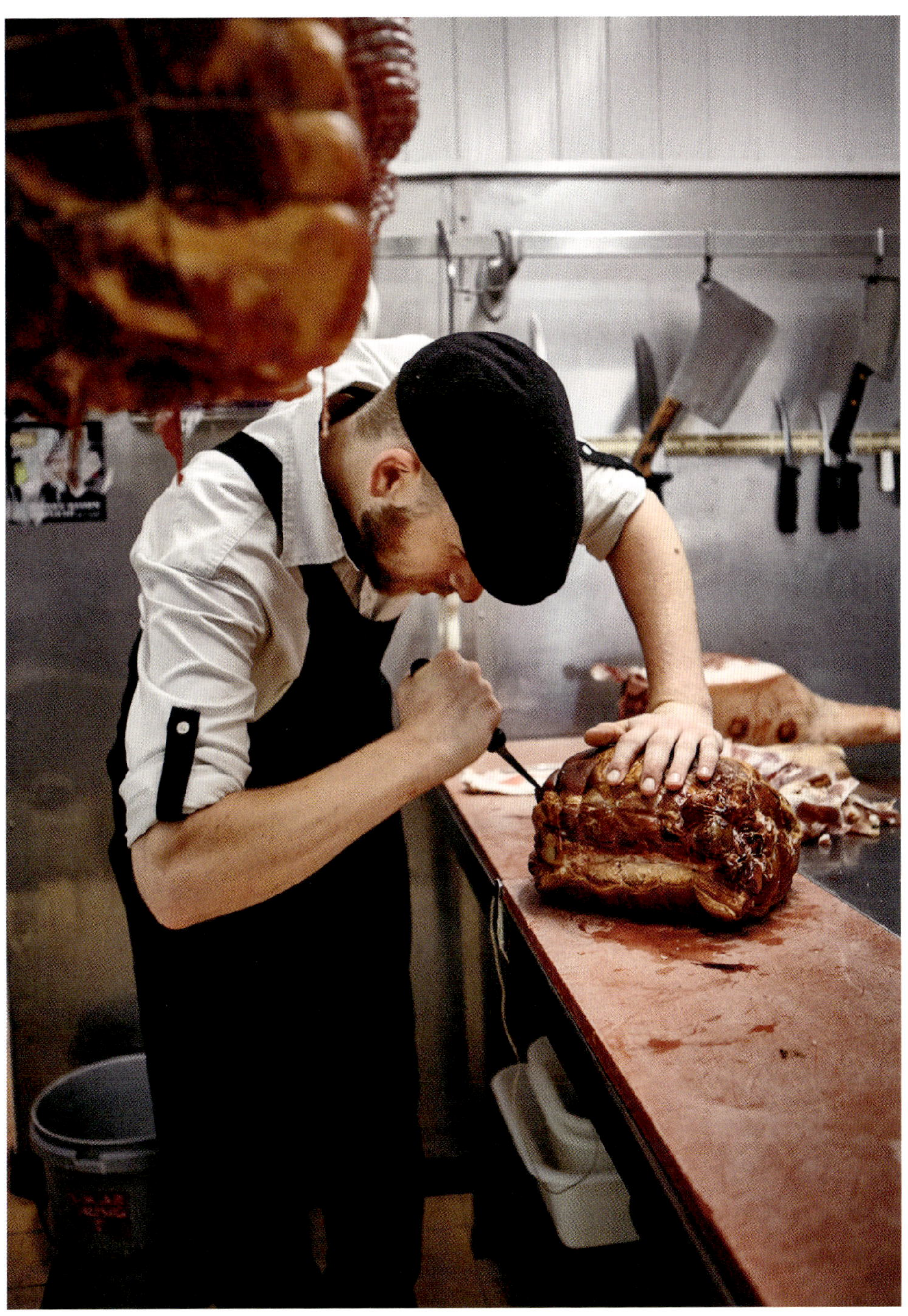

SIDENOTE:

This is a series I made during the grape harvest in a Tuscan village. Kristian and his wife bought a wine estate a few years ago and have been producing organic wines here ever since in very small quantities. I followed them for a day in September and was able to shoot the harvest and the pressing of the grapes. Images I had wanted to make for a long time and now, on vacation, I finally got the opportunity. After picking we were invited to lunch, because la mama had prepared a real Italian lunch for the pickers. For that you don't have to ask me twice. I joined a loud gang of purebred Italians, trying to explain in my best Italian why I had spent all morning peeping through the bushes with my camera. Full to the brim with top wine from a plastic cup, pasta al ragù that was so tasty that it still brings tears to my eyes and an unexpected main course - roast beef with white beans - we rolled down the mountain back to our holiday home.

This is the kind of vacation that makes me really happy. These are moments you don't forget. Photos like these are taken from the heart. If you're able to convey in images how you felt that day, then your series has been successful.

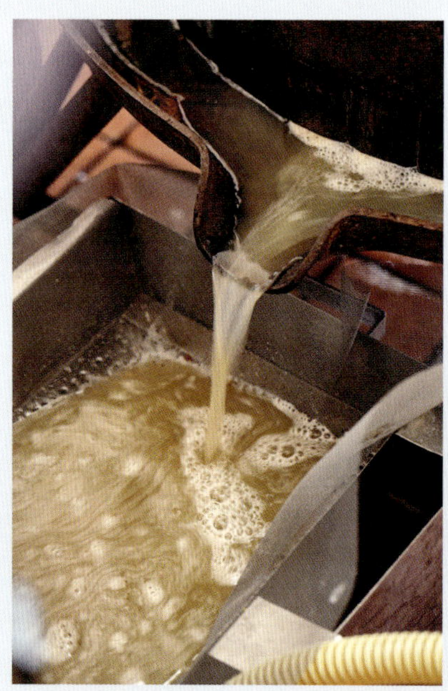

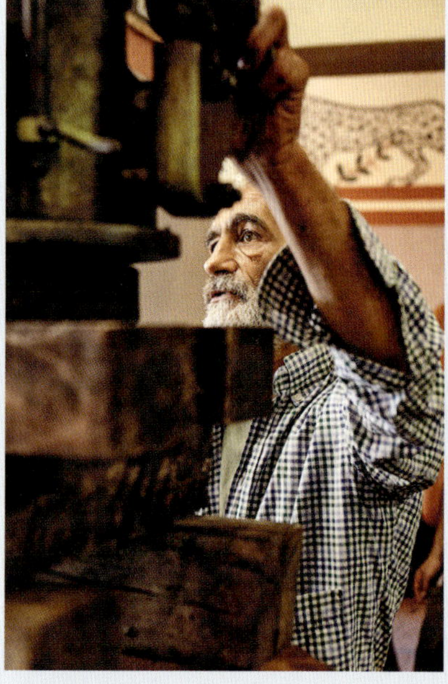

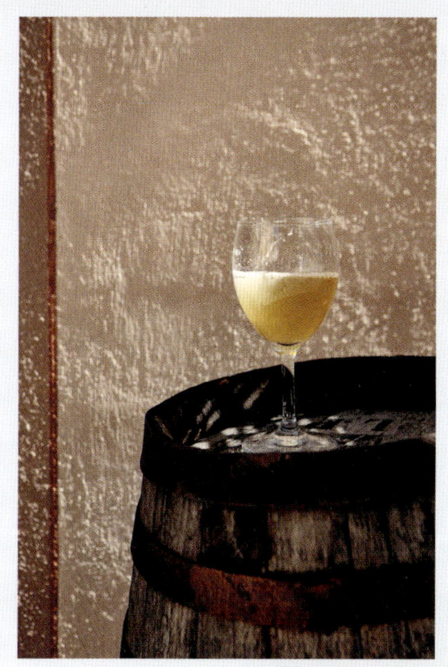

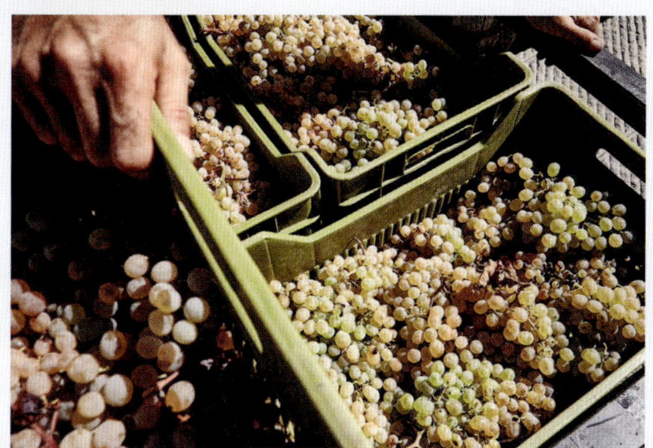

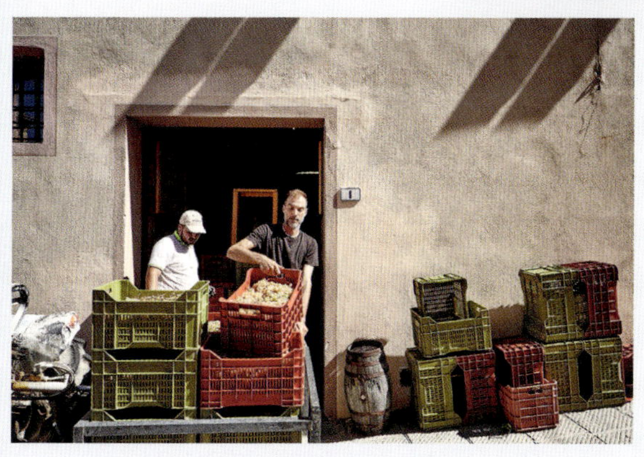

MAKING A SELECTION

You've taken a series of shots and have ended up with fifty photos. How do you then make a choice? Chances are, of those fifty shots, there will be only one that you really like. And that's not bad at all.

KILL YOUR DARLINGS: A SMALL SELECTION OF THREE GOOD PHOTOS OFTEN MAKES A BETTER IMPRESSION THAN A MEDIOCRE SERIES OF TEN.

Take a look at all the photos in the series together. Do they match well? Are there images that show more or less the same thing? Then keep the better of the two in your selection.

With Adobe Photoshop Lightroom Classic, selecting is very easy. There are several ways to rate your photos.

/ Stars: You can give each photo 1 to 5 stars.
/ Colours: you can apply stars and colours together on one photo.
/ Flag: There's a 'choose' and 'reject' flag.

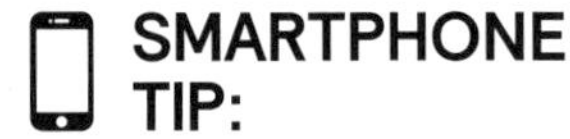

SMARTPHONE TIP:

Install Lightroom Mobile (see below) and make selections from your smartphone photos.

SIDENOTE:

I have a hard time choosing. So bad that, when we go to a restaurant, my friend sends me the menu a day in advance.
With photos it's the same. I've developed my own selection method that works for me. It goes like this: in a first selection round, everything that's compositionally or emotionally good is given a star. During a second round, only the one-stars are visible, from which I make a selection which become two-stars. Those that remain I then leave for a few days, hoping that they will engage in natural selection among themselves. Unfortunately, it doesn't work that way with photos, apparently. The next time round, I take a fresh look to make an even smaller selection.
At that stage, I often let family or friends choose. Sometimes you yourself are so close that someone else can offer an enlightening view.

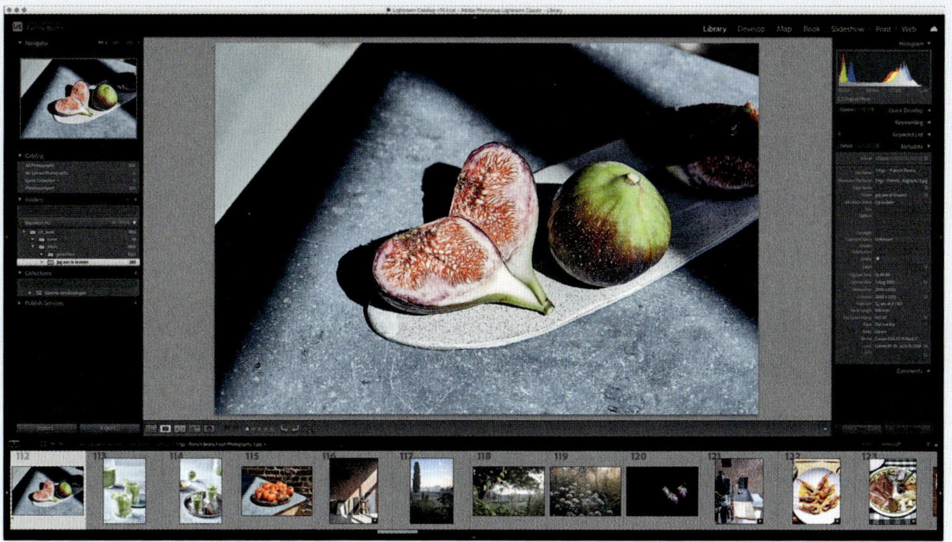

EDITING YOUR PHOTOS

If you set the camera to record in RAW - the largest possible format - the photos will require some editing to bring out the colours. On some smartphones, you cannot photograph in RAW but in high-resolution jpg.

I will briefly mention a few apps for desktop and smartphone, both free and those you will need to pay money. There are also numerous other apps that come and go, but which all do more or less the same. The best thing is to choose one you feel comfortable with.

CANVA

Not so much a photo editing app, but a very versatile tool for placing text on photos. You can choose your own fonts, save colour palettes and even add your logo and other branding elements to your photos.

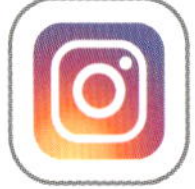

INSTAGRAM

From way back when the app still offered filters with which to quickly add some punch to your photo. If you take your photos with the app itself, you can also edit them with, among other things, contrast, sharpness, colour and shadows.

LIGHTROOM MOBILE

You can use this app on your smartphone, tablet and desktop. Lightroom Mobile is a free light version of Lightroom Classic and is cloud-based. This means that your photos are stored in the cloud.
If you have a large archive, you have to pay for it. The Classic version is not cloud-based. The Lightroom app is free to download for iPhone and Android without an Adobe subscription.

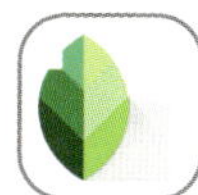

SNAPSEED

A free, easy-to-use and versatile app to make quick edits and also save. Perhaps the most widely used at date of writing.

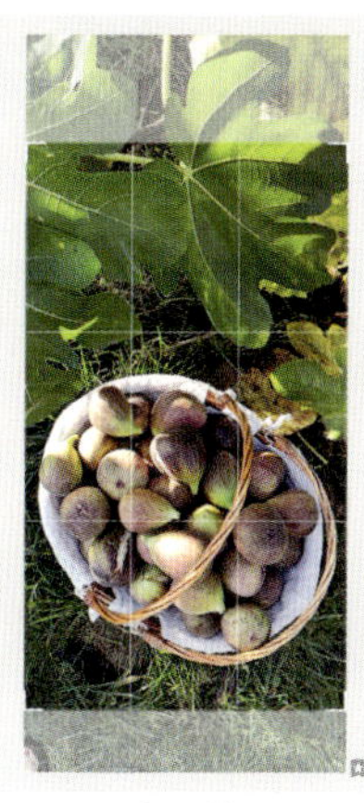

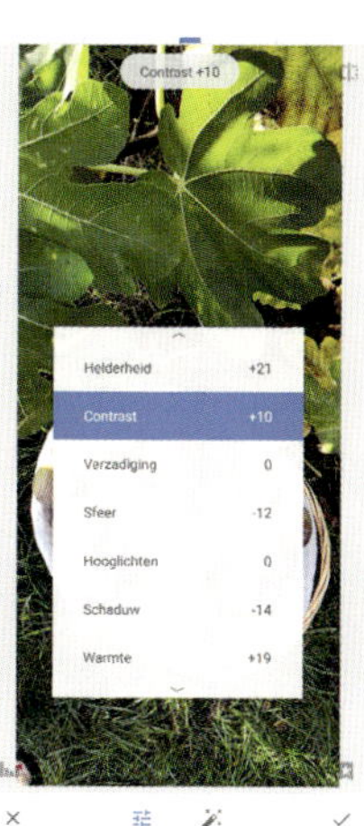

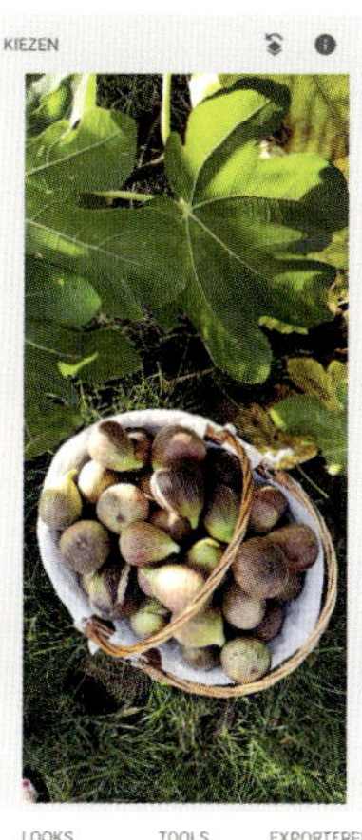

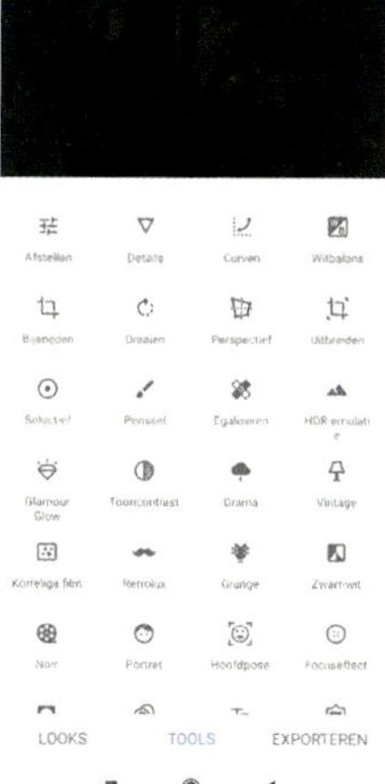

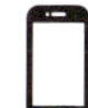

SMARTPHONE TIP:

Check your smartphone settings to change the format in which you record. You can choose between RAW and jpg. In 'Pro' mode you usually shoot in RAW. With jpg it's best to choose the highest possible resolution.

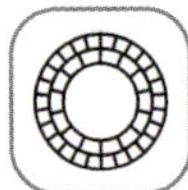

VSCO

Adjust the exposure, the colour temperature, the lens distortion, crop the photo ... Prefer pre-programmed settings? A VSCO filter that works very well for food is F2. It gives a warm tone to the photo, makes the shadows more powerful and increases saturation.
VSCO is also a social media platform on which you can share your creations. Also free of charge.

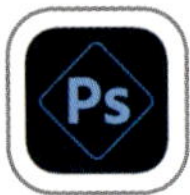

PHOTOSHOP EXPRESS

Like Lightroom Mobile, Photoshop Express is the light version of the desktop version. With this app you have somewhat more options for retouching, in order to 'photoshop' away disturbing elements.

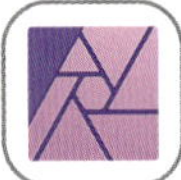

AFFINITY PHOTO

A lesser-known desktop-based software, which is cheaper than Adobe at date of writing. You can do exactly the same things with it and the interface is also similar. Affinity can handle both pixel-based (photos) and vector-based objects (e.g. logos or illustrations).

TIP:

Some small adjustments can upgrade a photo to give your audience an appetite! A bad photo never will be an excellent photo, but you can patch him up.

PHOTOSHOP

Lightroom and Photoshop are both Adobe products. You can buy them together in a subscription. Where with Lightroom you can only make adjustments to one layer, Photoshop allows you to add multiple layers to your photo. This way you can merge multiple photos, but you can also apply certain corrections to only part of the image.

Photoshop lacks a cataloguing system or rating capability. For this you need to use Adobe Bridge. Bridge and Lightroom have similar rating systems and permit similar photo adjustments. Bridge also allows you to convert a RAW photo and then edit it in Photoshop.

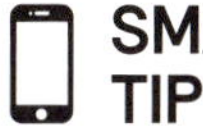

SMARTPHONE TIP:

If you're taking a photo to post on Instagram, don't shoot from Instagram itself, but go to your phone's camera app. Here you can select the maximum resolution and also use manual settings.

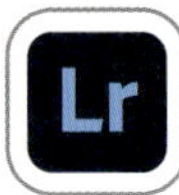

LIGHTROOM

Lightroom is a powerful tool. In addition to the adjustments you can make to your photos, Lightroom comes with a catalogue function. With this tool you can store photos, allocate stars and colour codes, save location information and add a whole lot of other 'metadata' that makes it easier to find your photos, even when they're on your website. The metadata can be used for Google search engines.

If you shoot in RAW format, there will be a number of automatic corrections when you load your photos into Lightroom. The program recognizes the lens and the camera automatically corrects lens distortion and blur that's inherent to the lens.

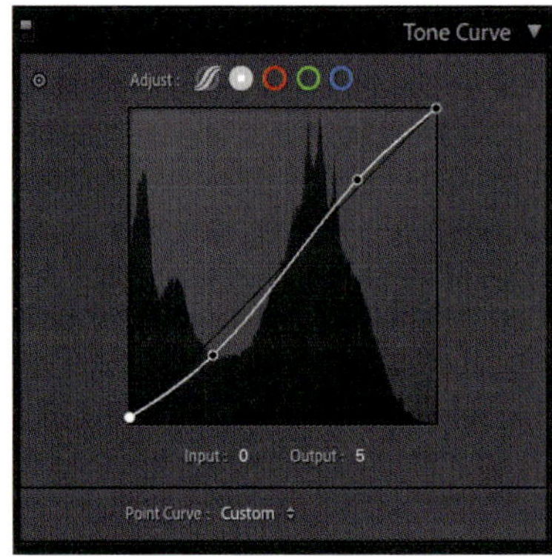

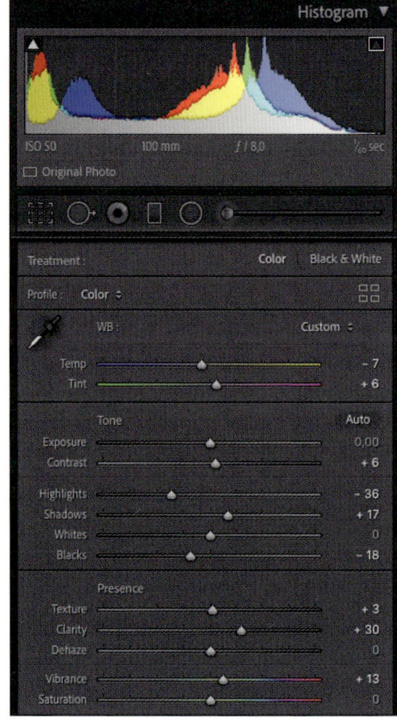

TIP:

The Adobe Photoshop Lightroom YouTube channel offers very clear video tutorials on both Classic and Mobile, for beginners and advanced users.

WHAT ADJUSTMENTS DO I NEED TO MAKE?

The following adjustments can be made to a large extent with each of the apps and software programs above. Names can differ, but functions such as white balance, contrast, lens correction, crop and the like can be found everywhere. I discuss them here using the Lightroom user interface.

White balance

This slider adjusts the colour temperature. If your photo's too yellow, slide the Temperature slider to the left (blue); if it's too green, slide the Tint slider to the right. You can leave the white balance unchanged "as shot", or let Lightroom determine an automatic white balance. If you have an area in neutral grey, white or black in the photo, you can select the pipette and click on one of these colour areas. The white balance will automatically change to give the correct colour rendering to the grey, white or black.

If you shot in daylight with all artificial light sources turned off, your white balance should normally be pretty much correct.

Exposure

With this you can brighten an underexposed photo by sliding the slider to the right.

Contrast

In food photos we move the contrast slider slightly to the right. Not too much, otherwise the lightest parts in your photo (the highlights) will be overexposed and your shadows will be too dark.

Highlights - Whites

The highlights are the most lit points in the photo. In a photo that has a lot of white elements throughout, certain areas may be overexposed. By moving highlights to the left you get more detail back into the highlights again.

Shadows - Blacks

With shadows and blacks you can brighten up parts of your photo that are too dark on one side, making the food appear black, by sliding the shadows or blacks slider to the right.

The sliders for highlights, whites, shadows and blacks have the advantage of affecting only these specific parts of the photo, without having to select them manually. Feel free to experiment with this to see what works best for you.

Texture

This means that the texture is emphasized in a photo, an already well-textured photo.

Clarity

Clarity is comparable to contrast. The difference is that the highlights and shadows are not affected by pushing the clarity slider up. Clarity actually gives more contrast, even without affecting the saturation.

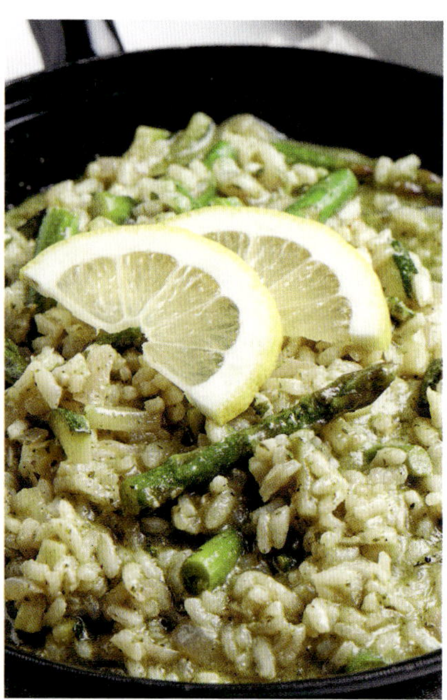

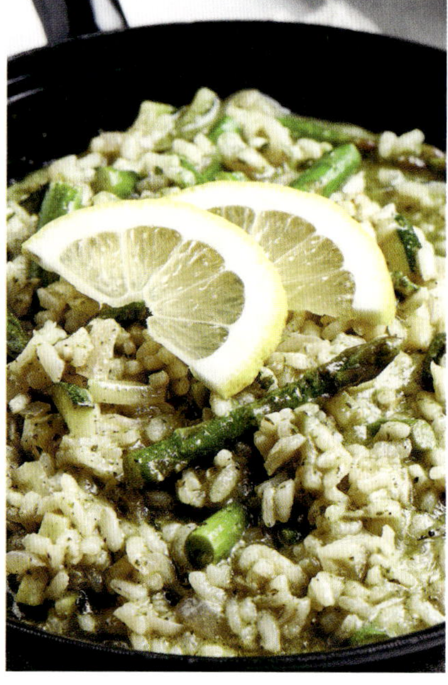

Vibrance
The difference between Vibrance and Saturation lies in the way the colours are boosted. Saturation increases all colours equally, while Vibrance increases the intensity only of dull colours. This prevents intense colours from losing their detail.

Colour grading
One of the latest additions to Lightroom. There are three 'wheels': highlights, midtones and shadows. Each of these wheels defaults to neutral, but you can add colour and increase its intensity. In this way you can put more blue in the shadows and yellow in the highlights to enhance the feeling of a warm sunny day.

Detail
You can't make a blurry photo sharp, but you can make a sharp photo even sharper where it's already in focus. Place the zoom square on the focus point and drag the Amount of detail to the right. In the zoom window you can follow exactly what this slider does. Keep Radius, Detail and Masking low.

Lens Corrections
If it's not already done automatically, check the chromatic aberration and profile adjustments boxes. When Lightroom recognizes the lens being used, it appears in the panel. You can also select your lens manually.

Transform
For me this is one of the best features. Does it infuriate you when the horizon is just that little bit at a tilt? As if the sea is going to drain away. Transform is there to fix that. This function analyses the photo and puts all lines perfectly 'straight' horizontally or vertically.

Effects
Here you can add a vignette. This creates darker corners of the image, pushing the focus more to the centre of the photo. Don't overdo it! When you think: okay, that's right, just slide the vignette ring just that little bit back to normal.

EXPORTING

Satisfied with the post-editing of your photos? Select the photos you want to export for print or web and return to the Library module. Click on 'Export'. In this window you can choose the location where you want to save the photos, give them names and choose the extension. In most cases this will be jpg. Files like .psd and .tiff take up more file space, while .jpg compresses the information in the photo into the smaller file. It is, as it were, ingrained there.

In this window you can limit the file size to, for example, 1000 kB. You choose the resolution here: 300 or 72 dots per inch (dpi). You can also sharpen the images automatically for print or web. You won't be able to see the difference in sharpness with the naked eye, but it's all about a certain crispness.

TIP:

To see if the adjustment you've just made has had the desired effect, you can turn a button on the left on and off for each part of the control panel.

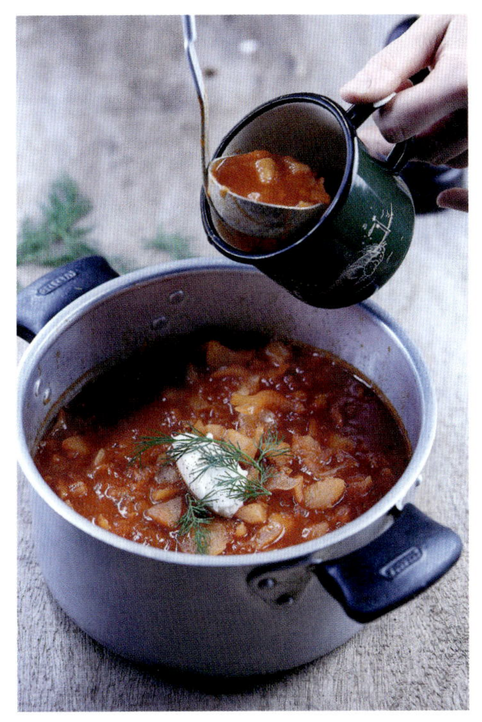

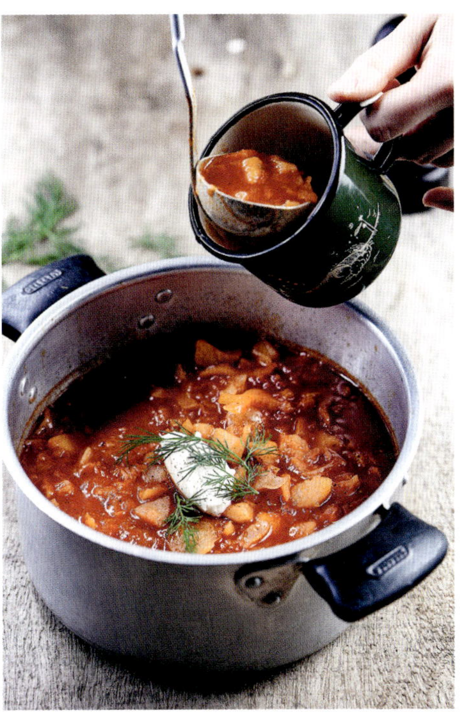

SENSE AND NONSENSE OF FILTERS AND PRESETS

Filters became popular with the rise of Instagram. Swipe to the right for a filter and your photo suddenly looks much 'better'.

VSCO and other editing apps also include filters that you can adjust in intensity to give your photos a custom look. Only you can ask yourself how 'proprietary' that look still is when everyone is using the same filters ...

Enter 'presets'. Presets, frequently designed for Lightroom, are a series of edits that are saved as a filter and can be pasted over your photo with one click. International food bloggers such as First We Eat provide a range of free or paid presets.

The problem with presets and filters is that they always apply the same values to every image, without taking into account the lighting conditions in which a photo was taken. For example, a photo taken in direct sunlight can be over-exposed, while a photo taken in the forest can benefit from that one preset.

COLOUR FILTERS CAN WORK FOR A PHOTO TAKEN IN SOFT DAYLIGHT, BUT HAVE A STRANGE EFFECT ON A PHOTO SHOT IN DIRECT SUNLIGHT.

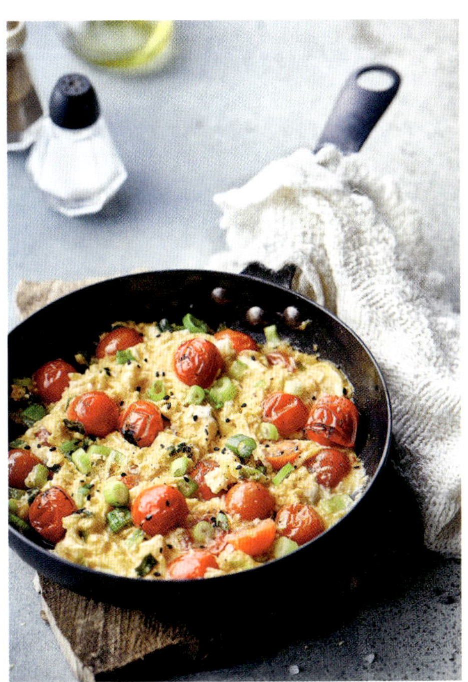

The preset works pretty well for the scrambled eggs, but not at all for the dough balls rising in the sunlight.

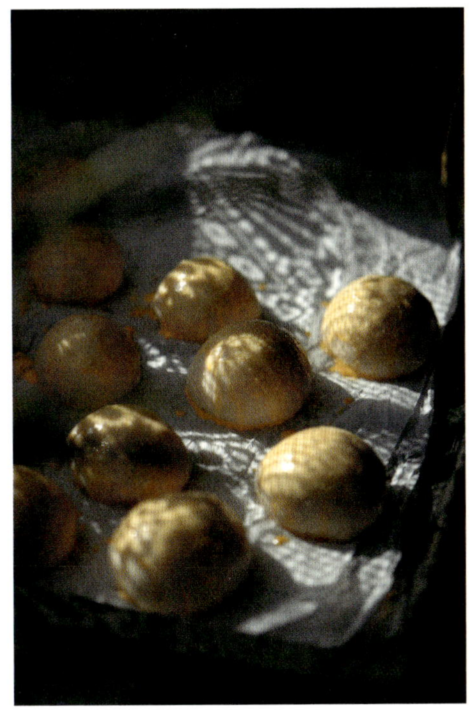

PRINTING PHOTOS

There are many channels for obtaining individual prints quickly. There's even a postal app for having them printed onto a postcard and sent directly to your addressee. The quality of these prints isn't always the best, but for a 10 x 15 cm card it's perfectly adequate.

In general, you usually need a resolution of 300 dpi for print (printed matter), as against 72 dpi for online use. Otherwise, website files would become much too large, making them slower to load.

You cannot enlarge a 72 dpi photo to 300 dpi. The photo will be out of focus and pixelated. But you can reduce photos from 300 dpi to 72 dpi without loss of quality.

Always look carefully at the delivery specifications of the printer where you print the photos. Sometimes they require a resolution of 200 dpi. That may depend on the medium onto which you want to print. Once you've edited photos, you can save them for either print or web.

For photo books I like to choose a quality paper. A book costs a little more, but also lasts longer.

TIP:

View your photos on a large screen before printing. Zoom in on all parts of the image to check that the sharpness is correct and you've not missed any details. Prints, especially in large format, are less forgiving than small online displays.

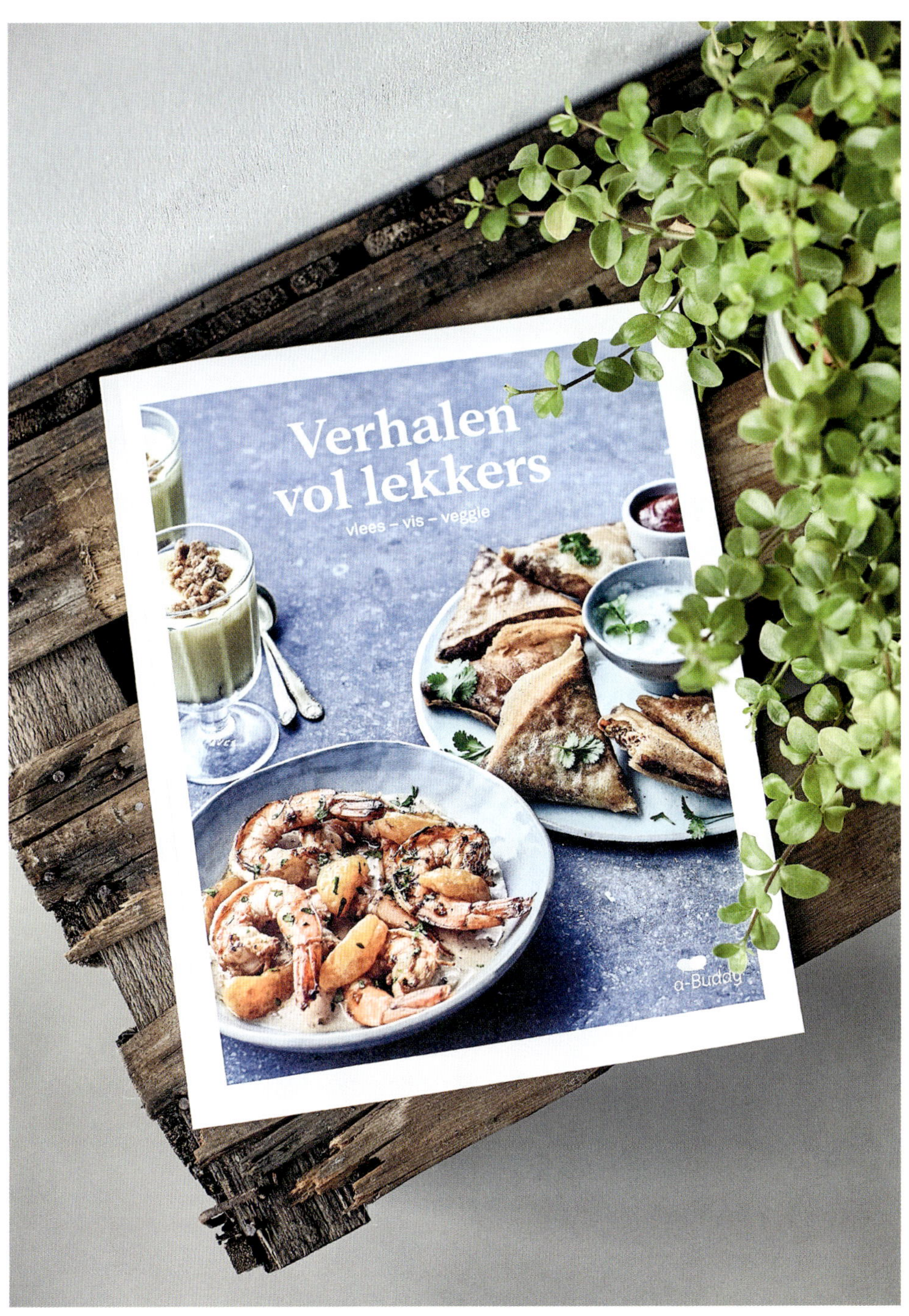
Verhalen
vol lekkers
vlees – vis – veggie
a-Buddy

SHARING PHOTOS

Our photos are viewed more online. And it's also faster. Send your photos into the wide world with a few clicks. Social media have a very wide reach. Use your own website to showcase your photos. You can quickly and easily build your own website with platforms such as Behance, Wix, Weebly, Photoshelter or WordPress. If you have an Adobe subscription for Lightroom and Photoshop, you can build your website with Adobe Portfolio. You can integrate it into Behance, making it easy to add new projects.

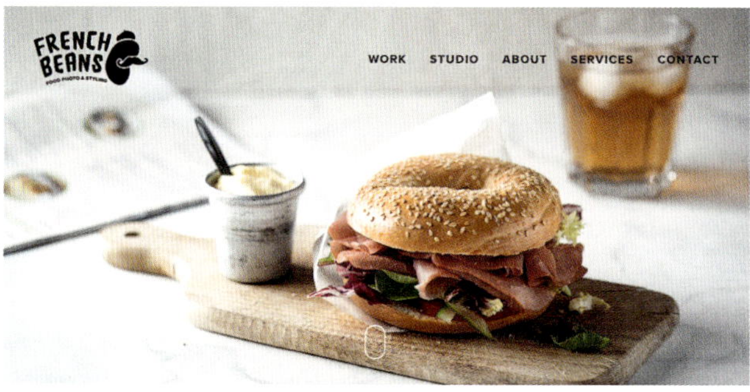

FOOD PHOTOGRAPHY STUDIO

French Beans stands for **expertise in food photography**. We want to capture the natural beauty, beautiful colors and intricate textures of food. We listen to our clients to make sure the essence and vision they want to share is passed on through our images.

In our studio we **cook, style and photograph food** and beverage with great care and precision. With a small **team of professionals**, we create quality images for food and beverage clients in advertising, packaging, editorial, video and social media.

Find out what we can do for you or have a look at the **studio**.

> VIEW OUR WORK

TIP:

Every photo you take is your intellectual property. Even if you take photos for someone else or for a company, the intellectual rights to the photo always remain yours. Unless you also sell those rights, but that's inadvisable.

STORING PHOTOS

Photos you take with your smartphone are stored on your device or on an external memory card. If you shoot in the highest possible resolution, you'll find that this memory fills up quickly.

Synchronize, for example with Google Photos. This way you always have an online backup of your photos. There's also a powerful search system behind it. This enables you to find photos by keywords, such as 'dish', 'vegetable' or 'selfie'. The downside of this system is that you hand over a piece of your privacy to Google.

If you photograph with a system or SLR camera, those files are even larger. It's best to keep these photos on a computer and back them up to a cloud system or an external hard drive.

However, hard drives, internal or external, can fail. Restoring such a drive can be very costly and there's no guarantee that you'll be able to recover all the photos. Therefore, always make a backup with a cloud system or multiple disks that are synchronized with each other (RAID).

TIME TO GET STARTED!

Find a window in your house where you have enough space to place a small table and your tripod, but also room to walk around the table. Best not be too far from your kitchen, so you don't have to go all over the house, up and down stairs, to bring your dish to the set. Best also to keep your props near at hand.

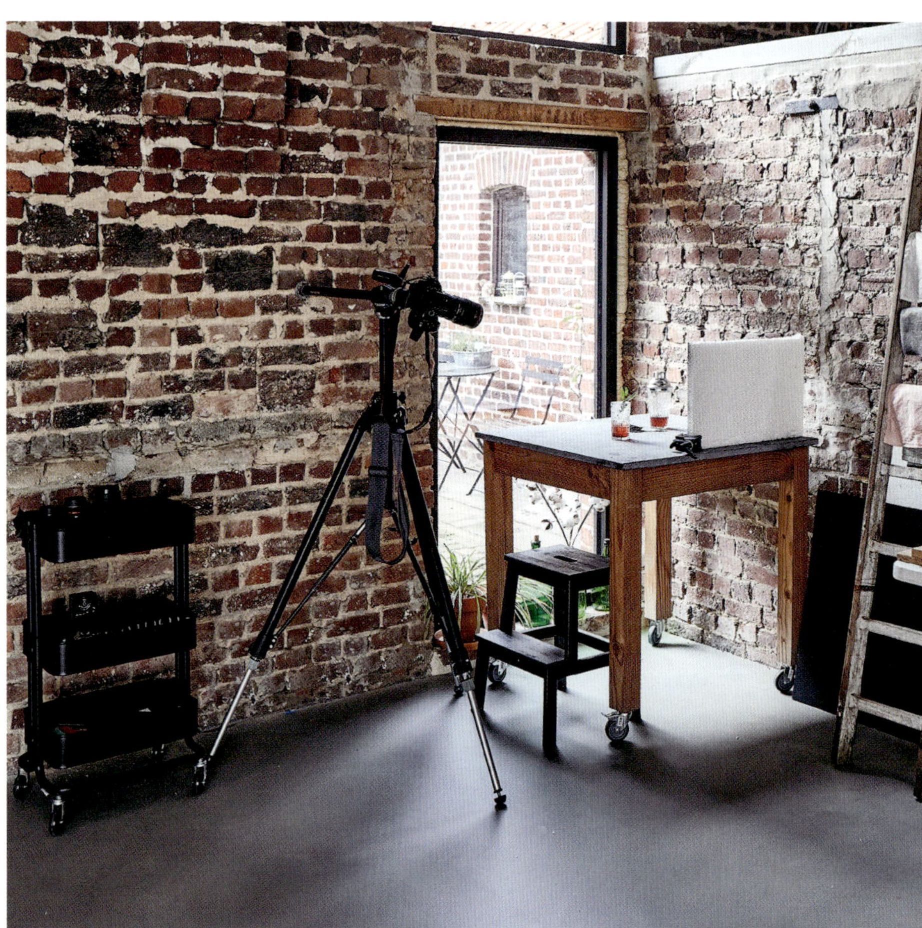

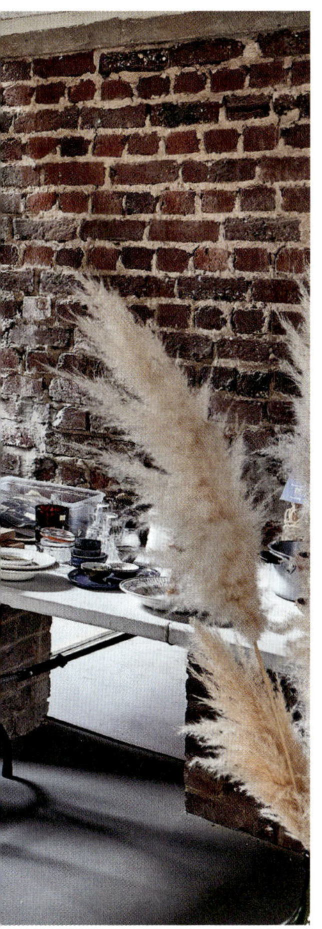

SIDENOTE:

I started with food photography in a small apartment, a 'studio' in the other sense of the term. There was hardly any room to cook, let alone take pictures. We then moved to something bigger. In no time I had taken over the available space with plates, glasses, props, surfaces… The studio was the kitchen, my set was the kitchen table. When my tripod was open, no one could get in or out. We then moved again. The friends who helped us with the move still can't believe where I kept all that crockery. While waiting for the renovation of my photo studio, I was still taking pictures in my living room. My clients were working on the sofa with the coffee table as a desk. Not very smart-looking, but we managed.

01.
TRIPOD

A tripod ensures that your photos are not blurred. But it also makes shooting much easier, because your camera is always in the same place. Suddenly you have both hands free to adjust the composition or your dish.

When buying a tripod, make sure it can support the weight of your camera. There are some very light tripods on the market that can support a lot of weight, even when you use a tree or horizontal arm to take top shots. In this case your camera is hanging above the food, and you don't want it to end up lens-first in the dish you're shooting.

Also check the tripod's minimum and maximum extension. The higher and lower these are, the more options you have to set your camera very low without having to raise the table. If your camera can be mounted on a horizontal arm at about 2 metres, you don't have to work on the floor. And that's better for your back, of course.

02.
STEPLADDER

The higher the camera, the higher you have to be in order to look through the camera and focus! So don't make life too difficult for yourself with a tripod that's too high. A stepladder with three steps will certainly get you high enough.

A tilt screen (also known as flip screen) camera saves you a lot of running up and down steps. Tilt the flip screen towards you to see immediately what you're doing. On some cameras, such as the Canon EOS R6, you can focus via the touchscreen. No more need to climb your ladder for that either.

03.
REFLECTOR PANEL

White reflects light, black absorbs light. A white and a black piece of cardboard, polystyrene foam, paper... are cheap alternatives to the reflector panels you can buy in the photo shop (see Manipulating light p. 78).

04.
TABLE

A small and easily movable table is very useful for 'chasing' the light. You can easily place it closer or further to the window on your own. Place a different surface on it and you've a new table!

05.
EXTRA TABLE

Believe me, you'll need the extra table. As soon as you start making a composition or dressing a plate, within 2 minutes the whole room will be packed with food, plates, bowls, dirty knives, boards, etc.

06.
CAMERA AND LENSES

With your camera mounted on the tripod, your extra lenses are best kept nearby, but away from food (greasy fingers and photo equipment don't mix).

07.
CLAMPS

To use a surface as a vertical background you need something to hold it. Unless you have a very patient assistant on hand who won't budge for a whole day, it's best to buy some heavy-duty clamps to attach that backdrop to a chair or to hold the reflector panel in position. You can also use paper tape to tape a vinyl background to the wall.

08.
LAPTOP

A laptop, desktop computer or tablet are useful for viewing your photos in large format. With programs such as Lightroom or Capture One you can view, edit and export the photos all together to jpg.

09.
STYLING TOOLS

Have the basic tools you need at hand. These are all listed on p. 127 under Toolkit.

10.
PROPS

Don't bring all your props (see p. 148) to your set, just what you think you need. Quickly put away what you don't use, to avoid running out of space while photographing!

11.
FOOD!

The most important thing: the purpose of the exercise! Your prepared dish or ingredients.

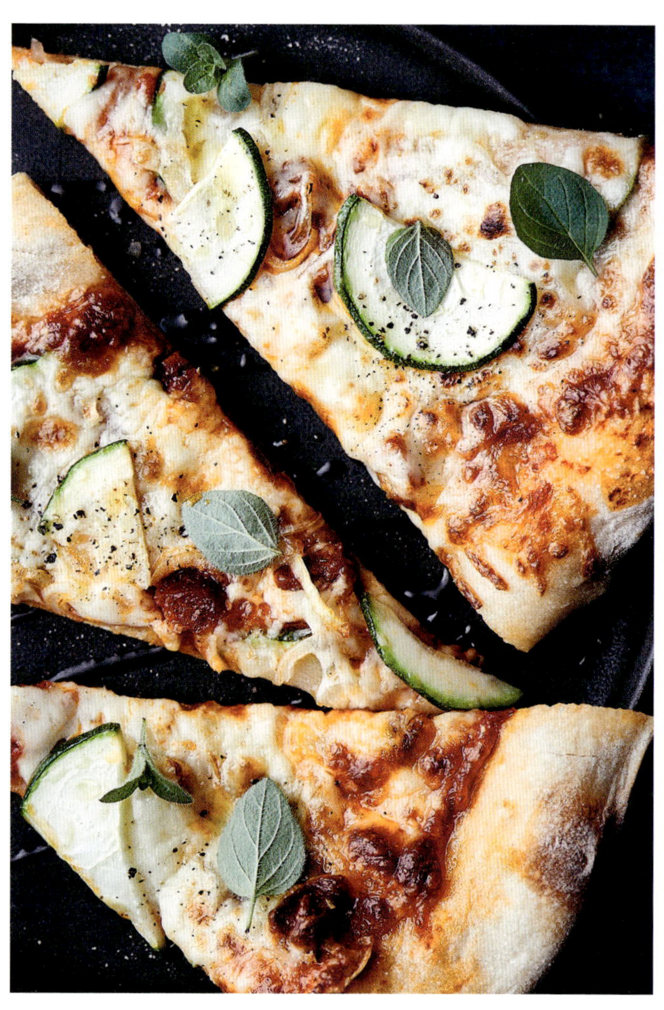

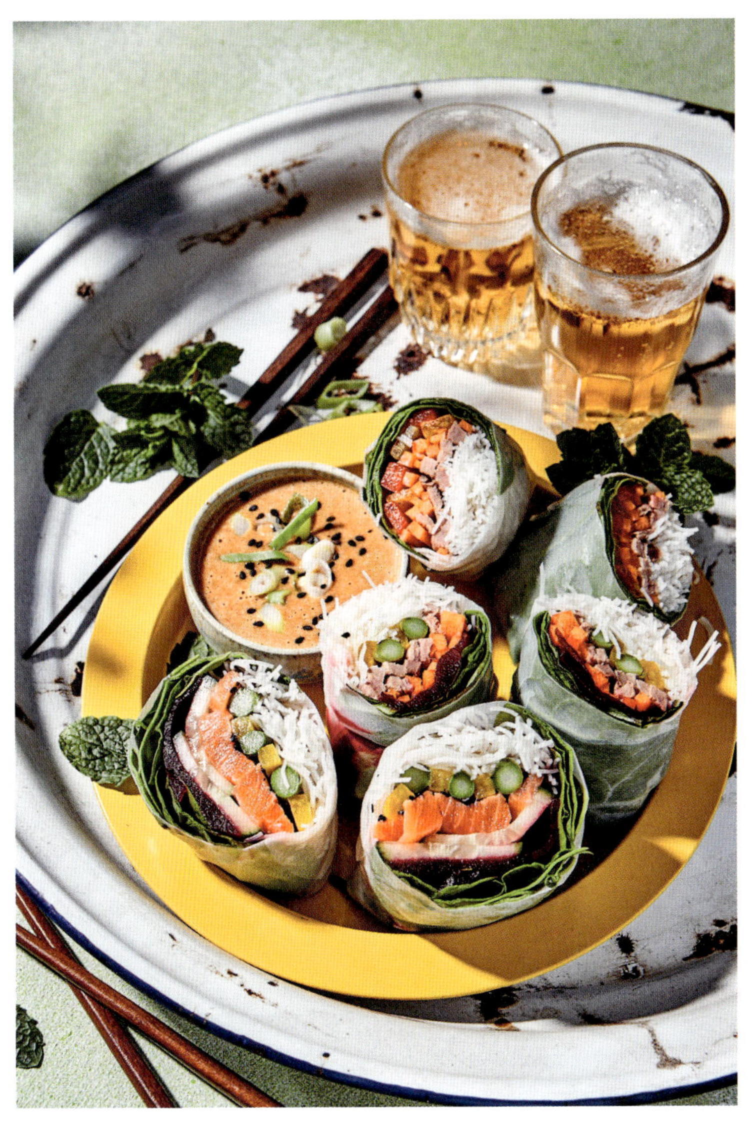

FOOD STYLING

04

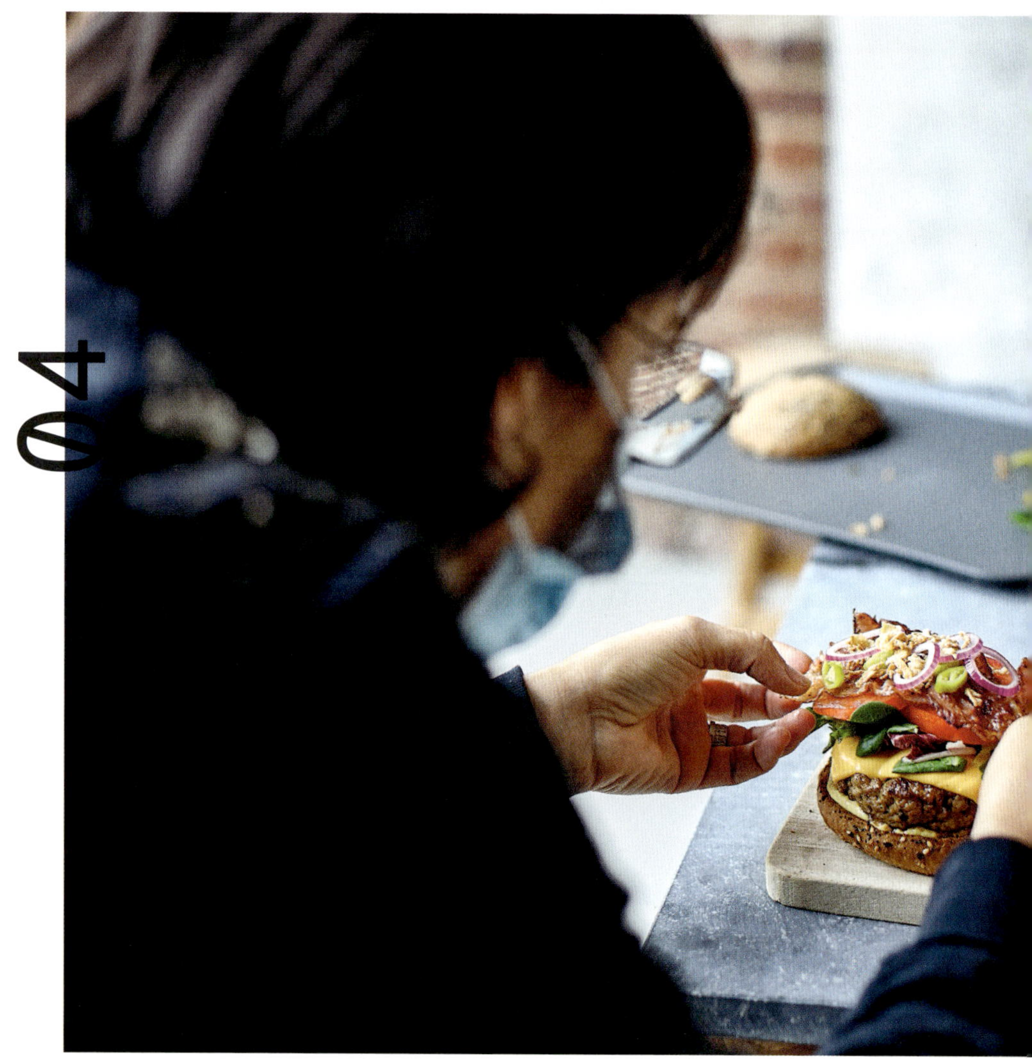

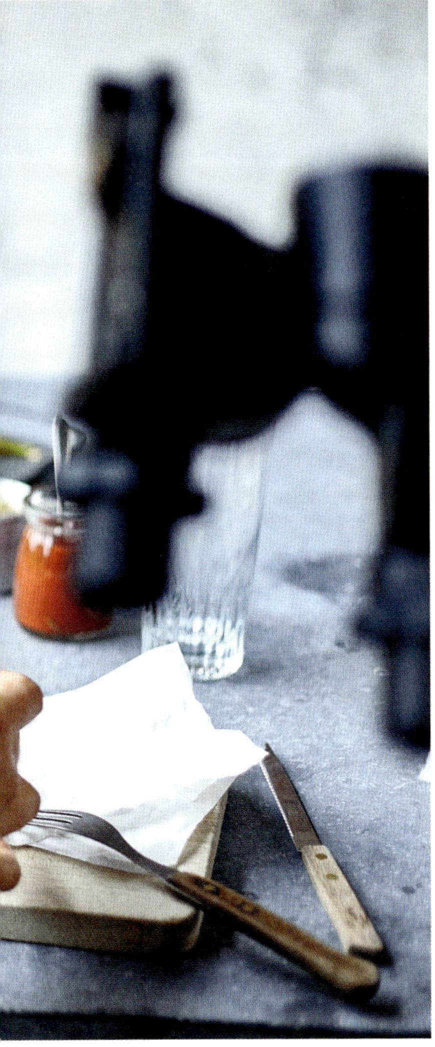

WHAT IS FOOD STYLING?

Food styling is the preparation and dressing of foodstuffs in such a way that the food looks tasty to the viewer.

You've probably already seen on the internet how a chicken is smeared with shoe polish or a stack of pancakes is doused with motor oil. Mind-boggling images. Let me immediately clear up some misunderstandings.

Photos you see in cookbooks and magazines are normally prepared just as you would eat them. No tricks up the sleeve, but oodles of patience, practice, knowledge and a good eye for composition and details.

The type of food styling that speaks to the imagination is sometimes used for advertising purposes. When a dish or ingredient has to be in front of the camera for a really long time, you don't want to be making a new "dame blanche" every 2 minutes, because the ice cream has already melted before it's on set. Okay, that's an extreme example, but with a close-up it can sometimes happen that tricks are used. But still! We often use real, normal ice.

Food styling is not a subject you go to school to learn. At least not in Belgium. As food photography becomes increasingly popular, many workshops or training courses have come onto the market, but you cannot obtain an official diploma.

By the way, did you know that there's a law in America that states that photos and videos of food should not be 'deceptive'? Suppose that a certain brand of milk is being advertised. In this case the food stylist is obliged to use the milk of that brand, for example, if milk is poured into a bowl of cornflakes in the commercial. Even if the milk from another brand looks whiter or thicker.

I can't speak for others, but I like to make sure that my 'work' remains edible. If nothing else, it prevents waste.

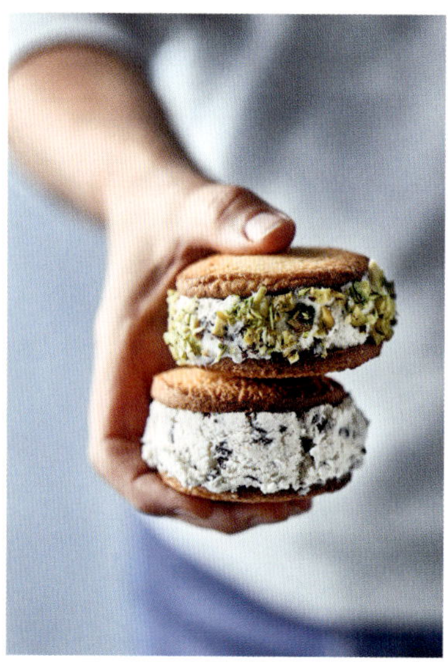

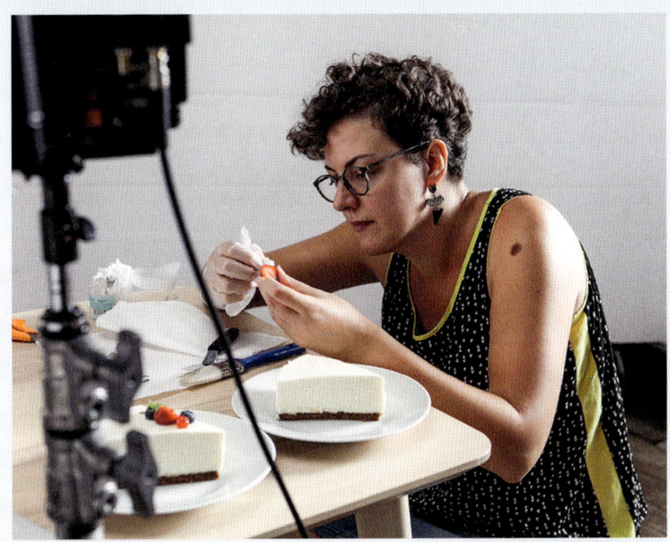

SIDENOTE:

My way to food styling

If you ask me how I ended up in styling, I was more or less thrown into it. I started out as a food photographer and was allowed to assist on a set for a yogurt commercial. It was a world that opened up for me. The endless patience you have to muster for that split-second image fascinated me.

My first assignment as a food stylist was to make cheesecakes. We needed to have a lot in reserve, because the cake would be eaten. On a hot summer morning, I drove to the set with ten cheesecakes in my car and enough spare ingredients to make another five on set, should the need arise. I was very nervous but also very well prepared. Even though my alarm didn't go off at 5 in the morning as planned ...

Leading up to the shoot, I had read about food styling and watched movies until my eyes hurt. Because my lack of experience or training made me insecure.

In order to have some basic knowledge, I took lessons at cookery school, because I'm of the principle that you should be able to present knowledge and/or experience if you're going to offer something you're going to be paid for. I've been able to gain lots of experience in a short time and have frequently gained the confidence of customers. For that I'm very grateful.

THE BASIS OF FOOD STYLING

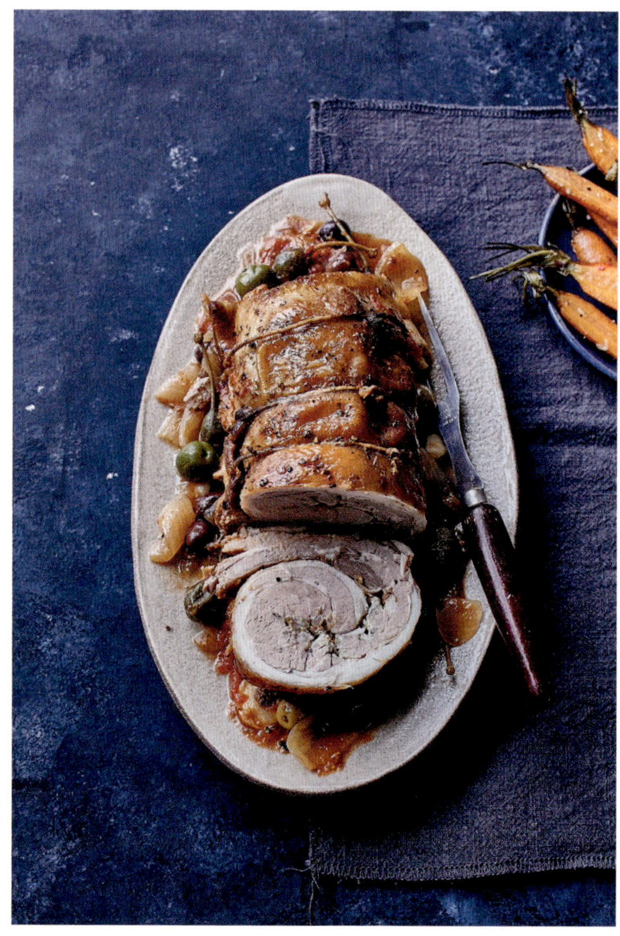

Just before shooting some vegetable oil was brushed on the outside of the roast.

TOOLKIT

In addition to your regular kitchen utensils, there are some handy tools that make styling a lot easier.

Oil

Use a little olive oil and a brush to shine the parts of the dish that are already cooked with fat. Apply the oil only at the very last moment, just before you push the button to take the picture.

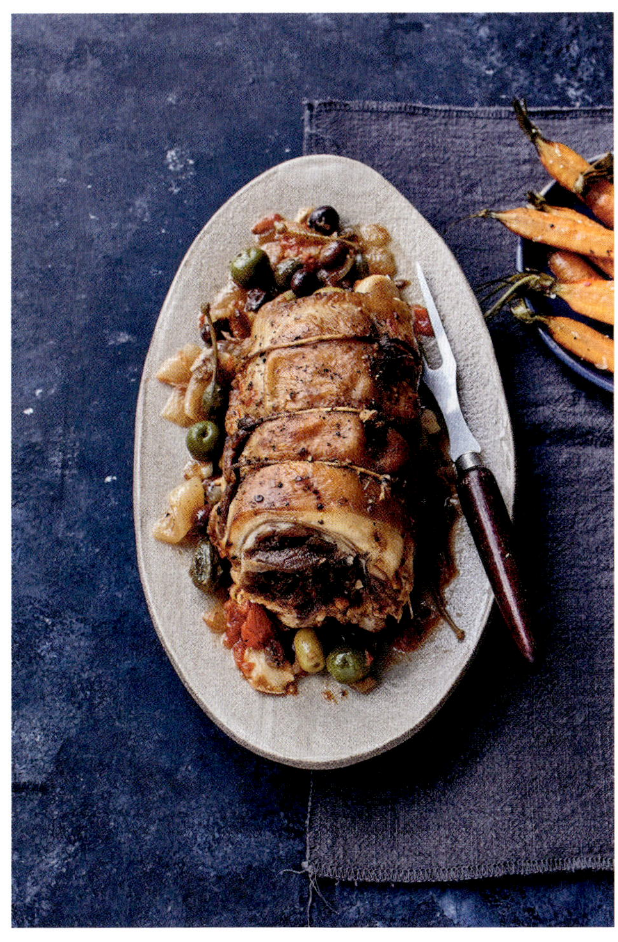

The natural fat from the roast disappears the longer it is on the set, making it appear dried out.

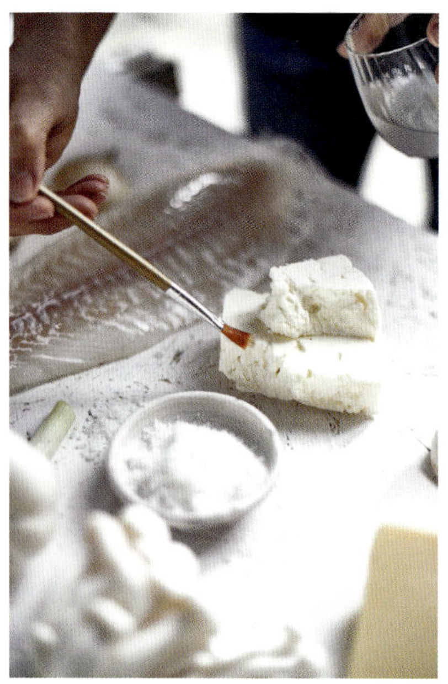

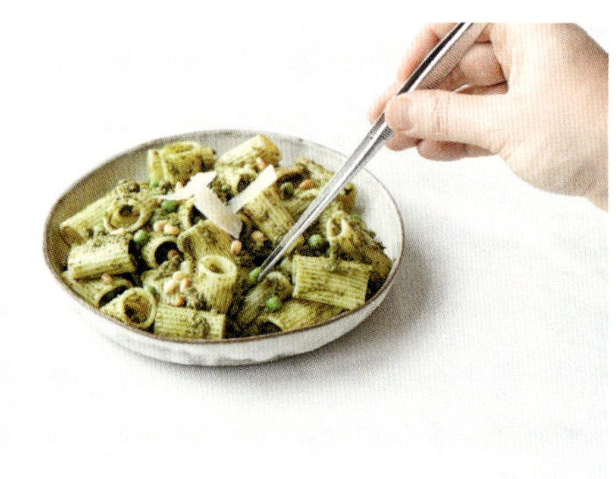

Water

No fat has been used in the preparation of lettuce, raw vegetables, rice, etc. Make them shine by applying water with a brush or spraying with a plant spray. Unless, that is, they're mixed with a vinaigrette, then you can use oil or the remains of the vinaigrette.

Tweezers

Peas, fresh herbs, seeds... have a mind of their own. Move small elements in your dish with tweezers, so as to have them exactly where you want them.

Spoon
Sometimes it's better to use a regular spoon to place sauce, mayonnaise, purée or anything else on a plate than to use special tools. It comes across more natural.

Brush
In addition to applying water or oil, a brush is also useful for wiping away small details. I have several brushes in different sizes. So have a brush that gets the job done for every situation.

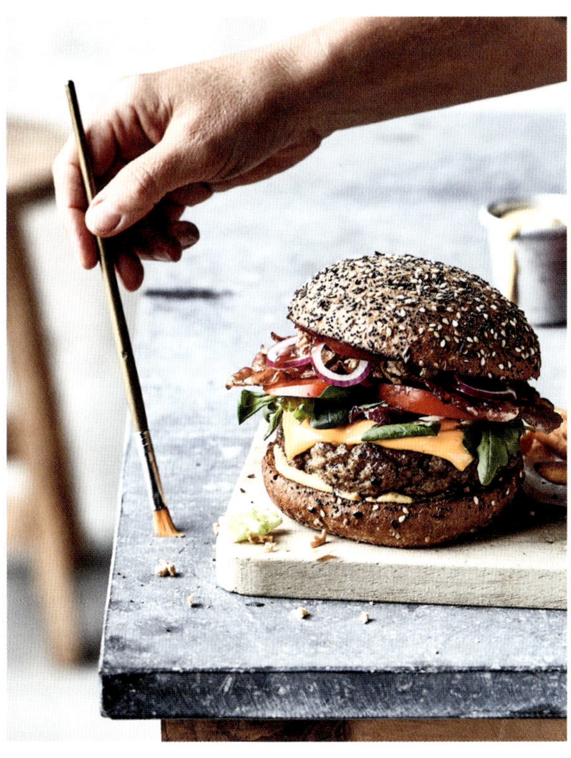

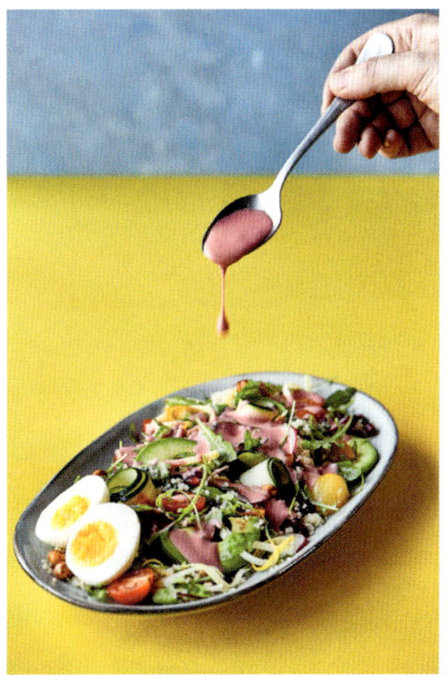

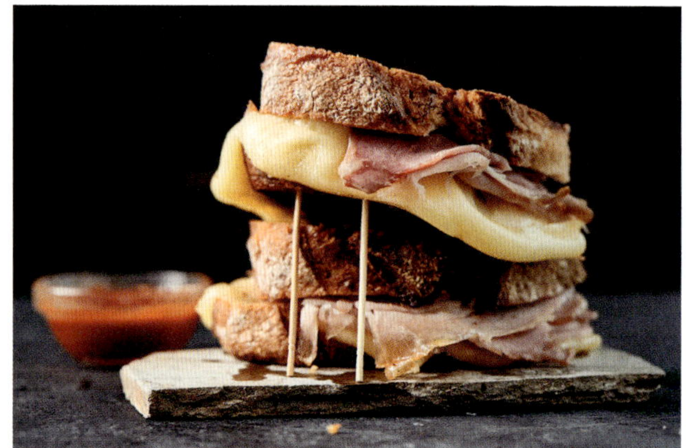

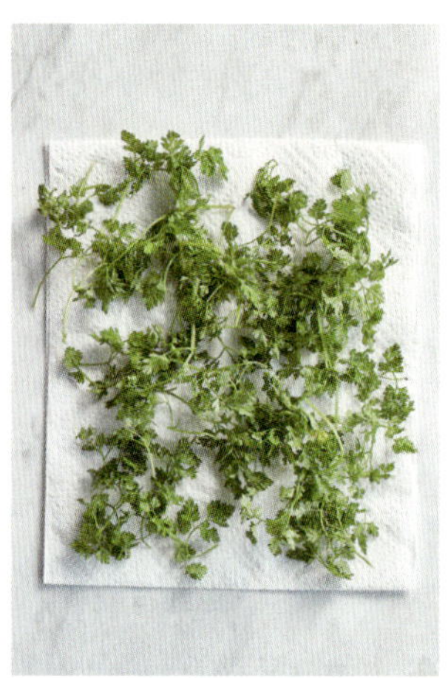

Toothpicks
If an ingredient refuses to stay where you want it, you can use a toothpick - or a broken piece of one - to do whatever you want! Always check that the toothpick isn't visible in the photo and, above all: make sure that all toothpicks are removed before eating the dish!

Kitchen paper
Keep it close to the set at all times, to wipe your hands, to dab a stain, to apply fresh herbs ... A kitchen roll is a real all-rounder.

TIP:

Keep your tools in a small box or in a kitchen drawer. This way you have them quickly at hand when you want to take a photo.

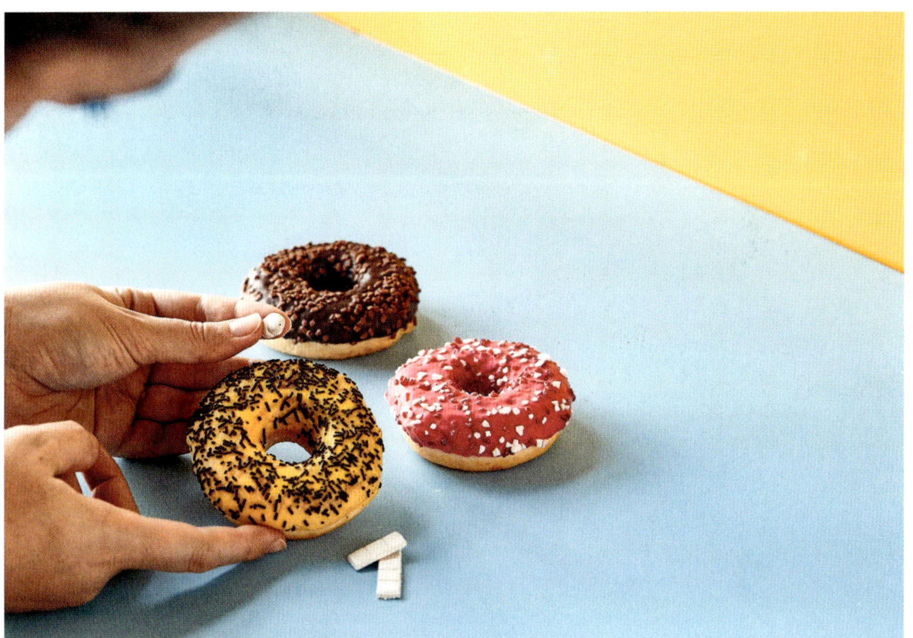

Poster buddies

"What's that chewing gum doing in your tool kit?" I sometimes hear. These are poster buddies, the most versatile tool for having to hand. You can mould them into any shape and use for supporting not too heavy ingredients. An alternative product: Blu Tack.

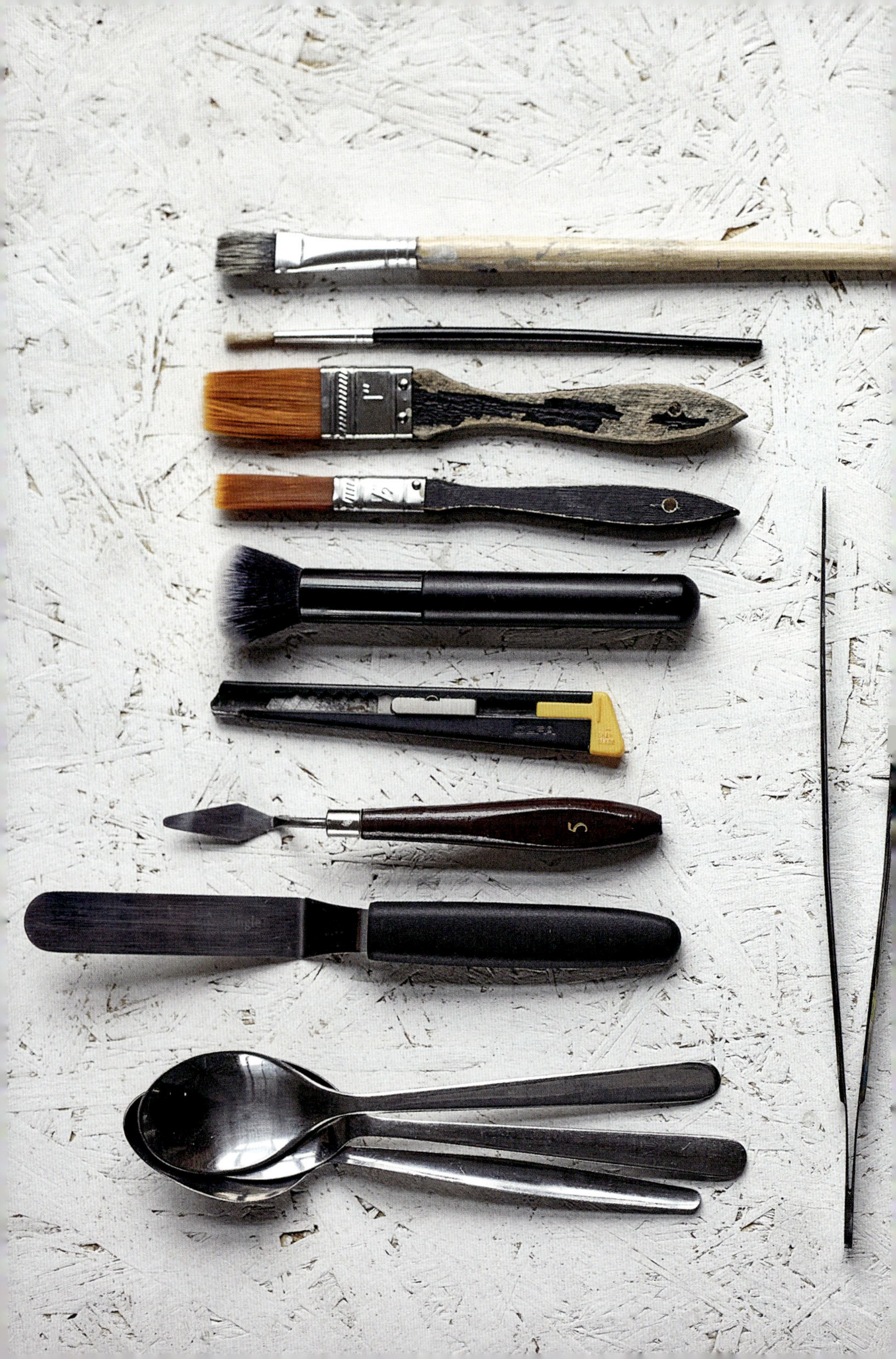

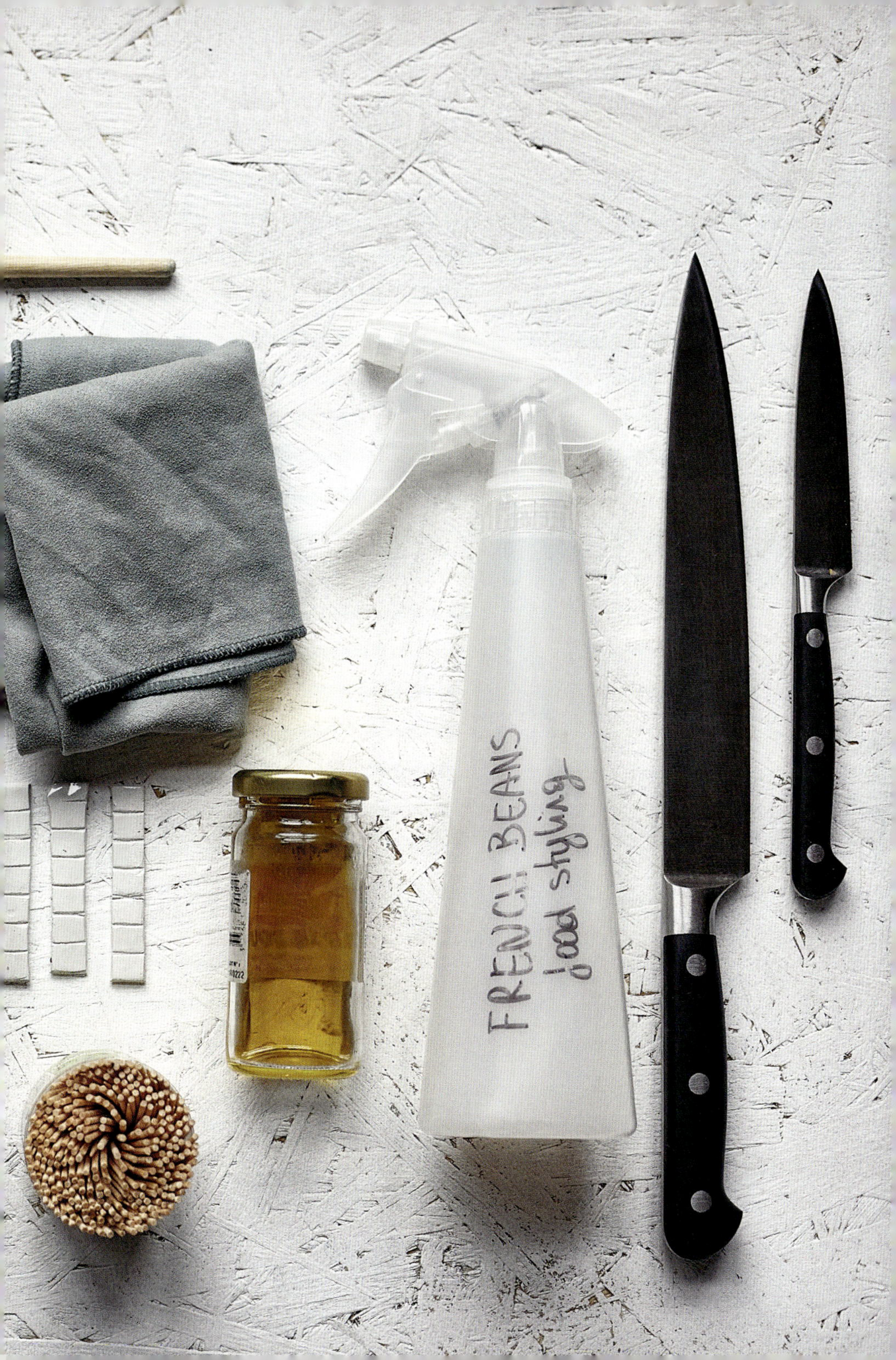
FRENCH BEANS
food styling

PREPARING DISHES

Know what to expect. Make sure you've an idea of what your dish will look like. If you've prepared the dish before, you'll know better what to look out for. Dishes you make for the first time will always turn out a bit of a surprise. But that can of course also be fun!

No matter how attractive the composition, with the most beautiful light and the right props, if the dish isn't tasty, then the story isn't correct. Use recipes that are proven to be delicious. A photo of a dry-looking salad won't make your mouth water.

Is the rice overcooked or are the pancakes burnt? Hungry mouths will forgive you, but the camera won't. Something that's well prepared also looks good on a photo. In addition, there are some cooking techniques that make certain ingredients look better. I list a few below:

Grilling

A grilled steak, BBQ brochettes, courgette slices in a grill pan and so on look like they're asking to be eaten with their beautiful straight grill marks. Make sure the pan is hot before you start grilling anything. Don't lift your meat or vegetables too often to see if the stripes are already nice, or you won't get sharp marks.

TIP:

Always buy the finest and freshest looking ingredients. While shopping, check carefully that there are no spots or irregularities on your ingredient. A good start is half the battle!

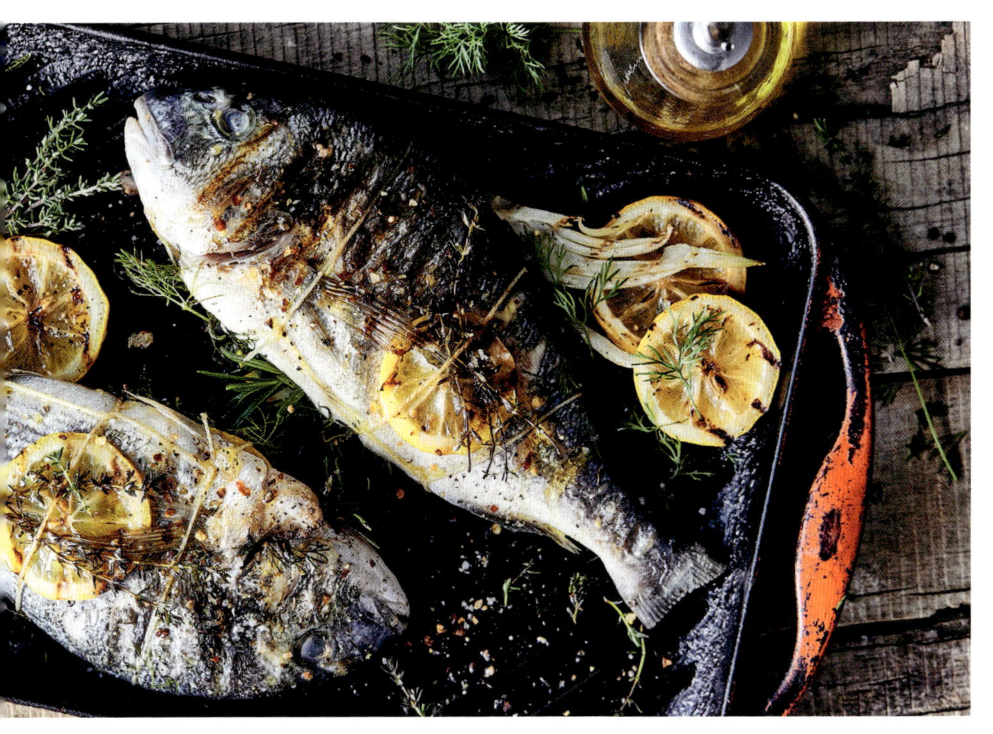

Steaming
Fish and vegetables, such as broccoli, cauliflower, etc., retain their shape and colour when steamed. You can steam fish and then place it in the grill pan to give it colour.

Blanching
In general, vegetables look better when blanched briefly instead of completely 'cooked'. Bring plenty of salted water to the boil, add the vegetables and reduce the heat. The cooking time depends on the vegetable, it's difficult to put a time on it. You can test it: if, for example, you still hear 'crack' when you break an asparagus in two, it's good. If it bends in half, it's overcooked. Carefully remove the vegetables from the water and scald in ice water.

Sauce
It's better to keep sauces separate and to dress them just before taking the photo. Tomato sauce for scampi diabolique, for example, gives colour to the scampi. It's best not to put the scampi and sauce together until your set is ready.

Ice water
Fill a bowl with water and ice cubes. Put your lettuce and fresh herbs in it. This way they stay fresh longer. Don't take them out until just before you start shooting. You can also wrap them in a damp paper towel and keep them in the fridge.

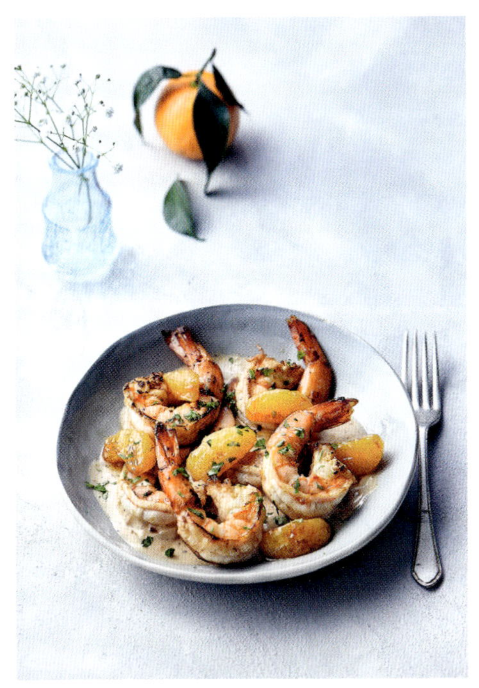

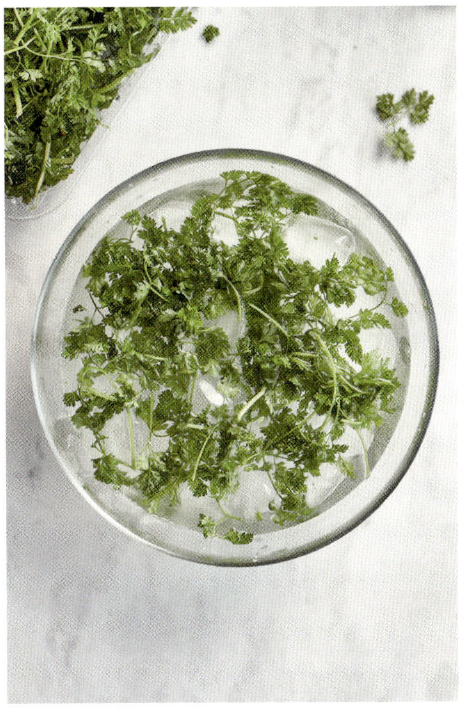

RECIPES

Whether you're an experienced chef or starting hobby chef: a recipe has to work. Don't just assume that a recipe you've tracked down online (or even in a cookbook) has the correct quantities, preparation method or processing sequence. The fact that your result doesn't look like the picture in the book doesn't always relate to your performance or qualities as a food stylist or photographer. Often the recipe has not been tested or has been partly copied from another recipe without proper thought.

MORE IS BETTER

Especially when photographing fresh ingredients, it's better to buy a few extras. Cut fruits or vegetables dry out quickly or don't look like you expected when cut open. Just think of our ever-loved avocado. Better to buy too many in advance than to run to the store during a shoot.

MORE IS BETTER - YOU WILL HEAR ME SAY THIS ABOUT ONLY ONE THING: THE AMOUNT OF FOOD.

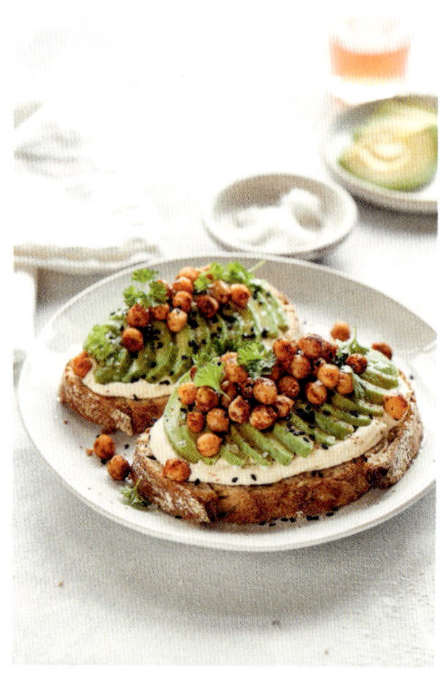

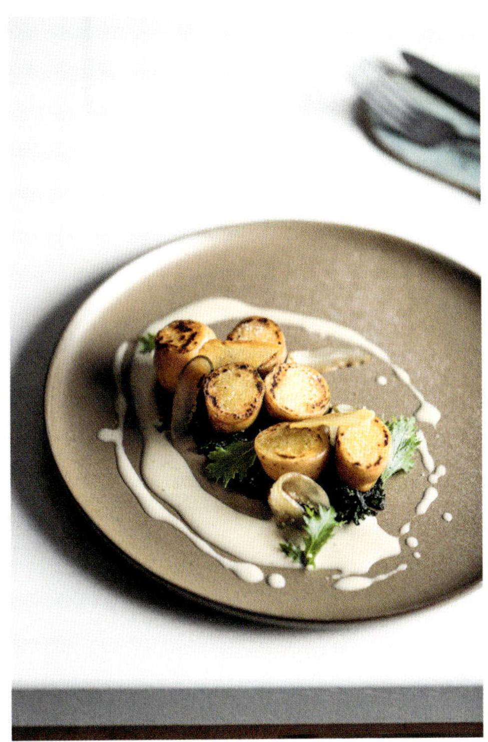

PLATING

Techniques exist to turn your plate into a true work of art. I'll mention a few:

/ Add depth by placing meat on a bed of vegetables.
/ Spoon a little sauce under your meat (substitutes) or fish instead of over it.
/ You can also place sauce next to the plate in a separate jug or little bowl.
/ Something green as a finish will make your dish look fresher.
/ Wipe off any disturbing stains of spilled sauce or gravy.
/ Don't overfill the plate, rather choose a larger plate.
/ Play with shapes and height, for example a tuft of pasta with a slice of tomato leaning against it.
/ Not everything has to start from the centre of your plate. Start in an upper half and zigzag down.

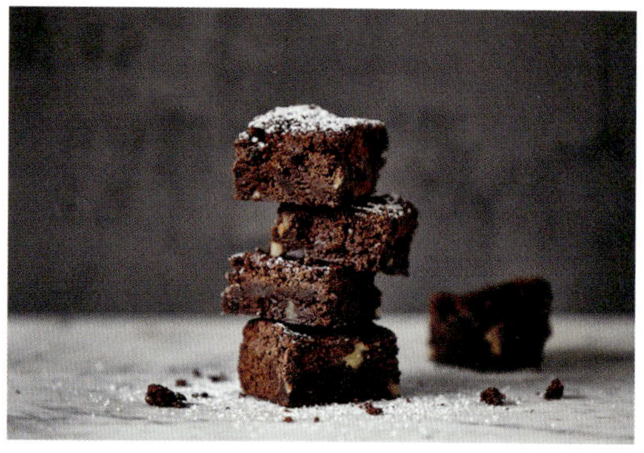

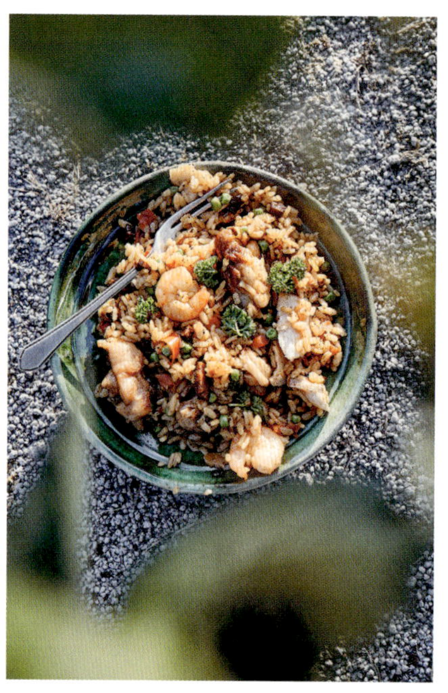

COLOUR

Fresh herbs add colour and structure to dishes. But the days of pressing a crown of parsley into the middle of a dish are past and gone. Be a little more casual. And don't use garnishes too lavishly. The focus must remain on the dish itself.

TEXTURE

Dishes with little texture, such as pudding, soup, sauce, stews, etc., can be textured with ground pepper or coarse sea salt. Oriental dishes, for example, go well with sesame seeds. Desserts can be helped along with icing sugar, grated coconut, grated lemon peel or cocoa powder.

A dish with little texture can be given more depth by the way you dress it. Take a paella. In itself, it's a mush. Use tweezers or pliers to pull a few pieces upwards, a piece of chorizo, some peas, chicken ... This way you can better see what has been mixed in and it's no longer a flat mush.

THREE ISN'T A CROWD

Odd numbers work very well in compositions, including on the plate itself. For me a repeat of three works best. One is often too little, five is too much. The group does not have to consist of three identical pieces, but can also consist of, for example, a whole strawberry and two halves.

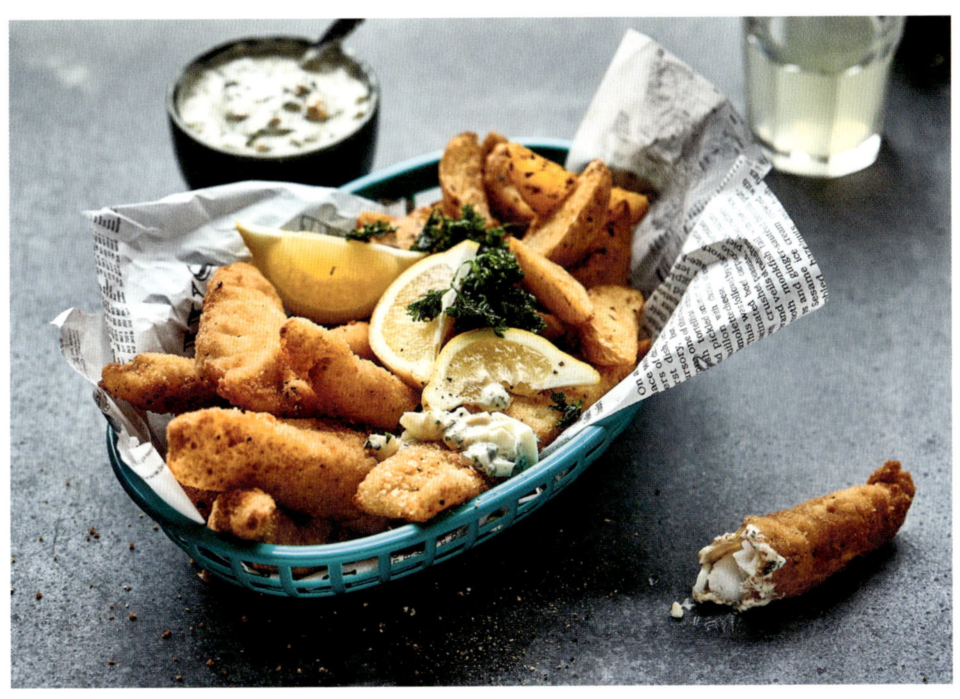

A SERVING OR A DISH?

When it comes to macaroni and cheese, a whole dish equals one serving to me. Sorry, silly joke!

There are many oven dishes that look nice as such. Or cakes that are beautifully decorated. It would be a shame to photograph only a portion of them. That's why I first photograph the whole and then take a picture of a portion, possibly with the dish in the background.

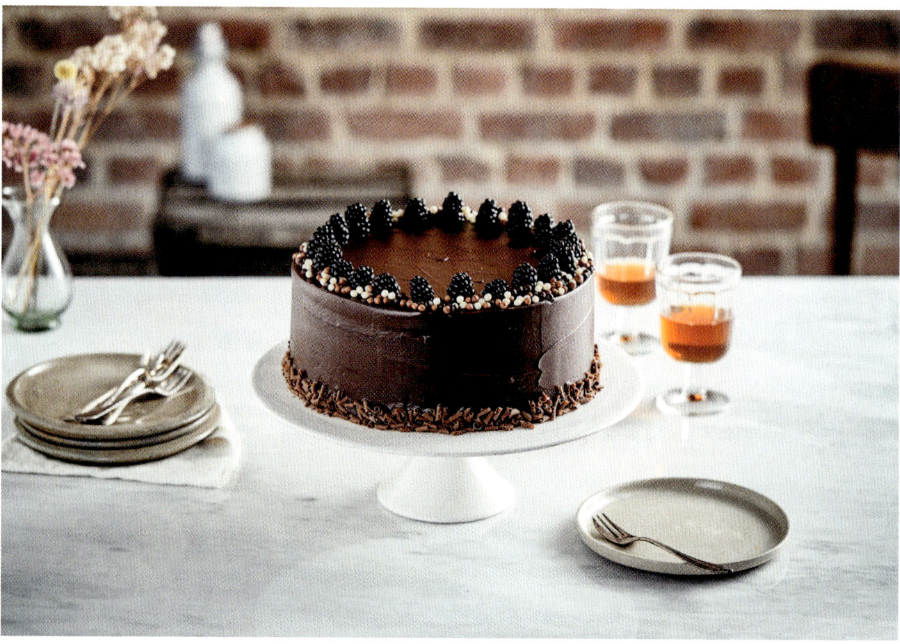

THERE ARE ONLY THREE RULES FOR FOOD PHOTOGRAPHY: FORGET ALL THE RULES, DARE TO MAKE MISTAKES, PRACTICE, PRACTICE, PRACTICE ...

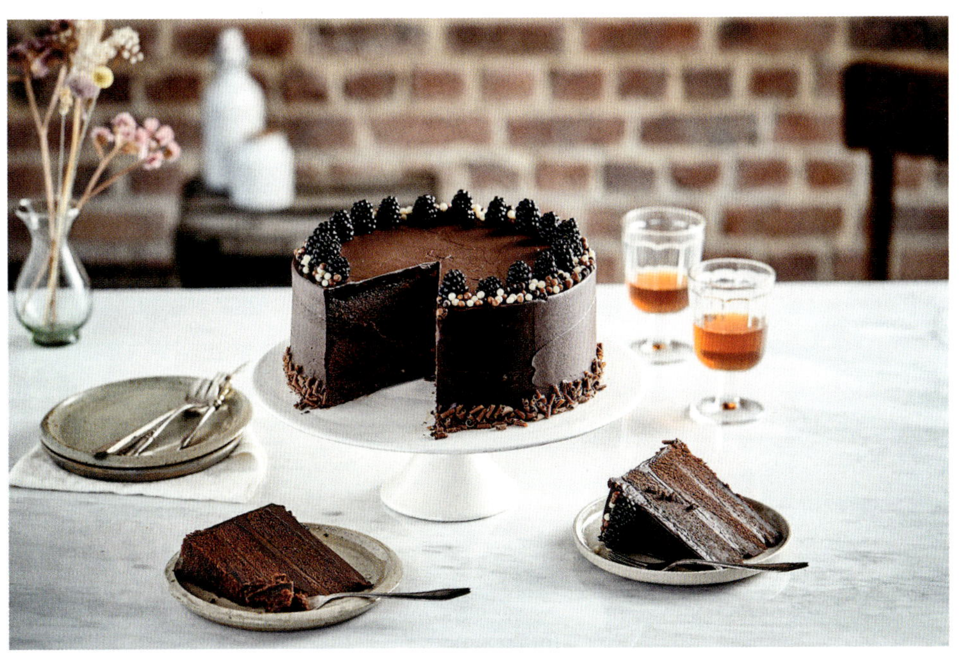

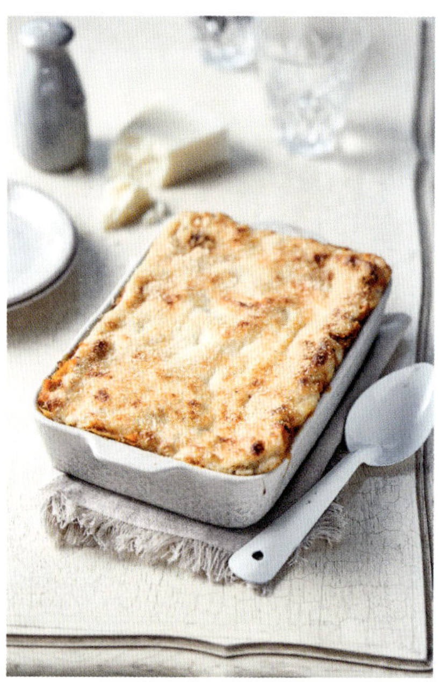

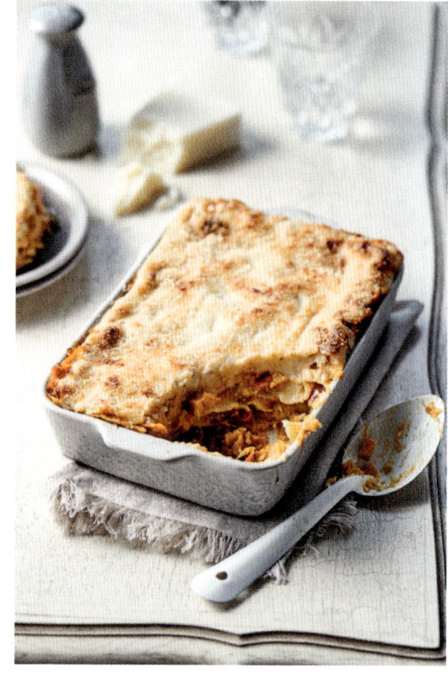

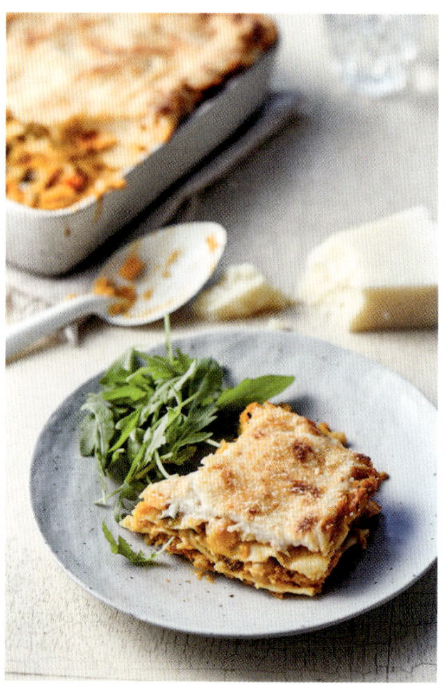

TIP:

Fresh, green herbs give every dish a fresh touch. A little greenery and your stew suddenly takes on colour, texture and freshness.

Oven dishes, especially layered ones, show their best side when you display what is in them. Take a portion, or scoop some out, and arrange it nicely on a plate as well. In this way you'll have the option afterwards to choose the best photo from three different set-ups:

/ the dish
/ the dish with a scoop removed
/ the portion separately

OVERSTYLING

There's such a thing as over-styling. Too much is too much. Something looks natural when it's natural. Yes, styling means lending reality a helping hand to make it beautiful to the eye of the camera. But something raw will never look cooked. Something cold can hardly look warm.

A greasy hamburger, for example, is permitted to look really greasy. A lettuce leaf can be crooked. The sauce is allowed to run out. A clean burger just looks less tasty!

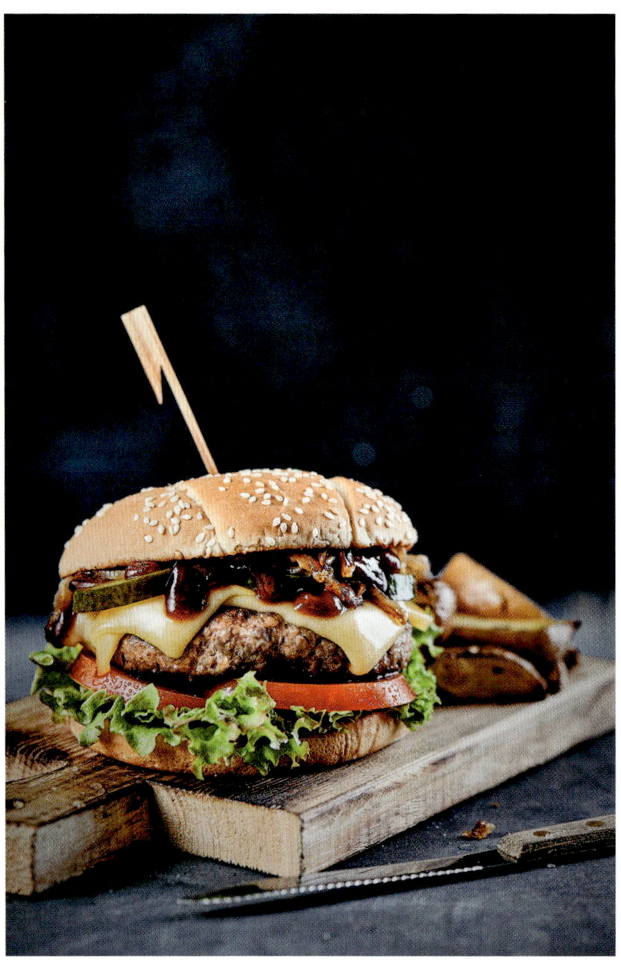

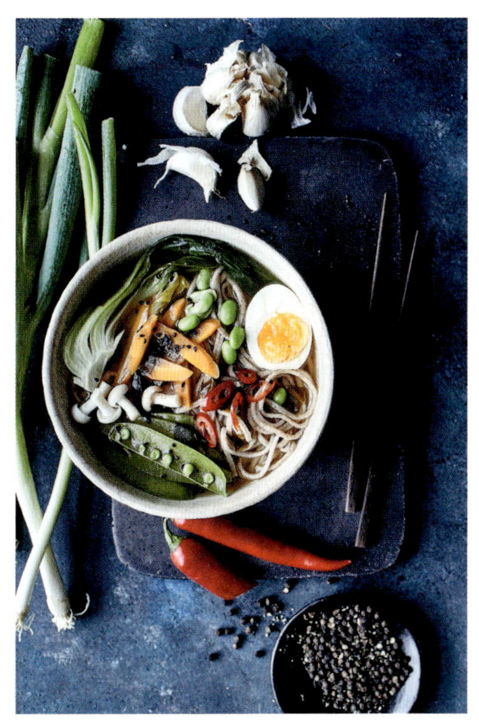

TIP:

Is the picture correct? Only use garnishes that enhance the dish. What you've left out of the dish can be beautiful, but in the dish creates confusion rather than convey the message.

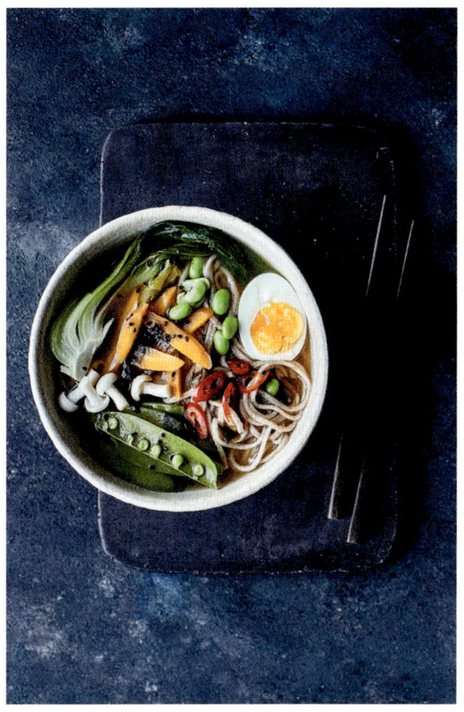

PROPS

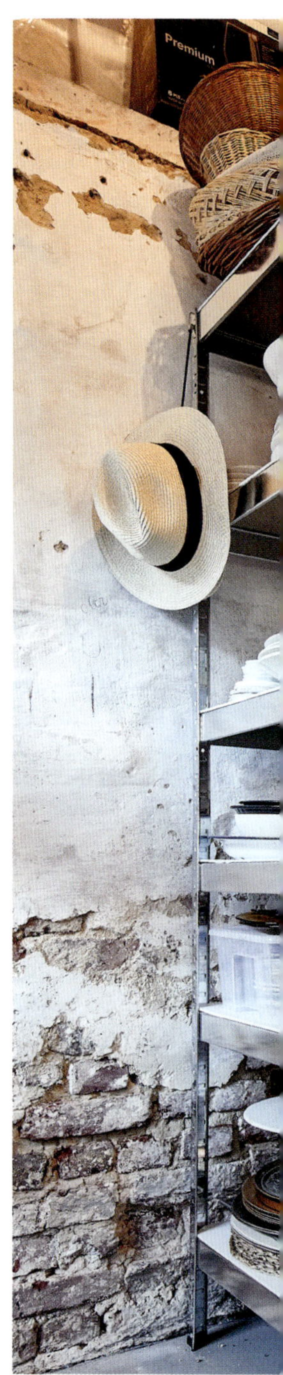

You may be familiar with props from the theatre and film world, where they refer to objects that appear in the picture and are necessary for telling the story. You can also see them as playing the same role in food photography.

BACKGROUND

For me, a background and a backdrop are two ways of saying the same thing. A background placed against the wall is a backdrop. To make it easier I'll talk of backgrounds.

You can find backgrounds everywhere and everything can serve for this purpose: a floor, table, wall, (arm)chair, grass... you name it.

The range of commercially available surfaces or backdrops for food photography has increased enormously in recent years. The advantage is that they're printed on a washable material and can also be rolled up. The disadvantage is that most of them are too small, which limits your options for placing several plates on one photo or for photographing in side view.

Printed stone surfaces are popular, because a real marble top for example costs a lot of money and is also heavy.

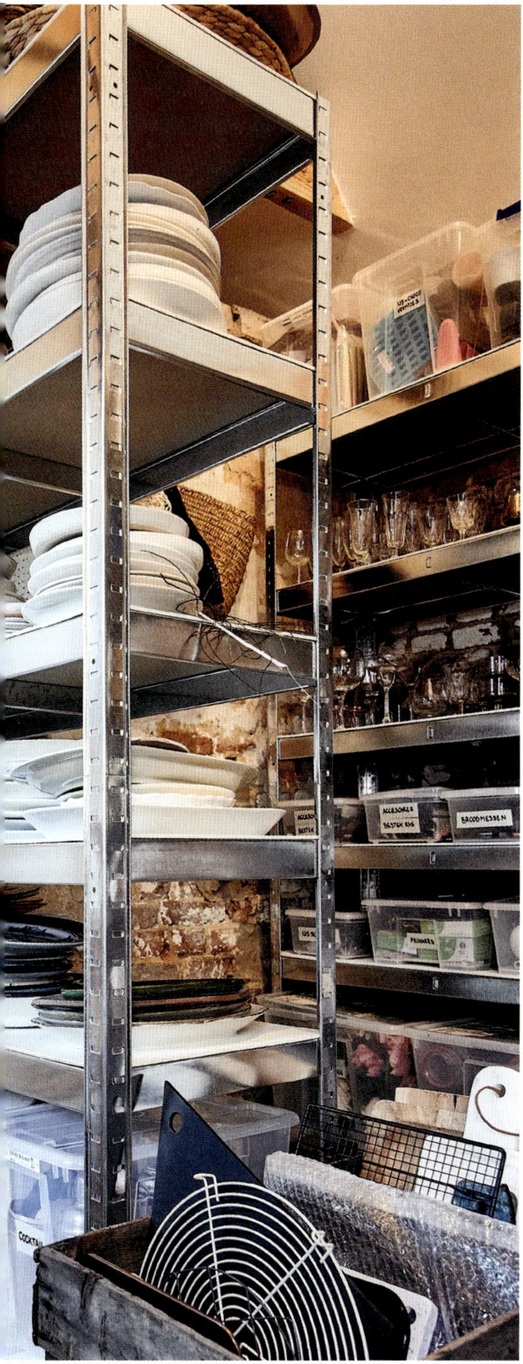

SIDENOTE:

The best things in life are free. That may not apply to everything, but it certainly applies to surfaces! For example, I've already put my car to the test a few times, drummed out my sweetheart and sent my father out on the road to pick up a free piece of marble somewhere in Belgium, a table, a few chairs, a door ... So thank you, Dad and thank you, Leander.

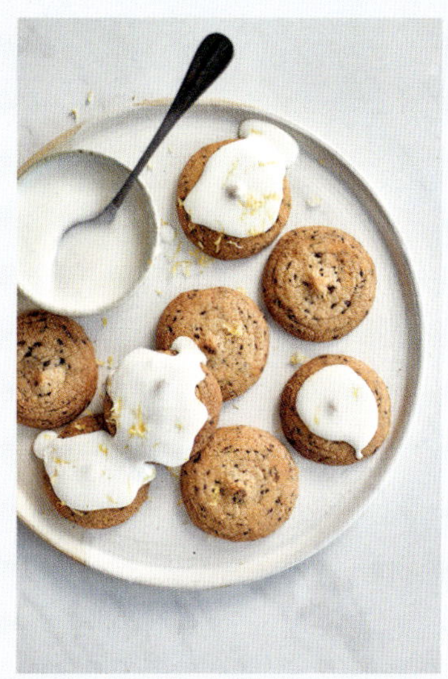

Prints of wooden planks have the disadvantage of losing the texture. With real wooden planks, the light falls into the grooves and veins, which are picked up in the plate's shadow. With a printed surface you lose these details, making the shot often appear less realistic.

PERSONALLY, I LIKE TEXTURED MATERIALS BETTER, SO I SEARCH FOR OR MAKE MY OWN SURFACES. THE ADVANTAGE IS THAT NO ONE ELSE HAS THE SAME BACKGROUND, WHICH MAKES THE PHOTO UNIQUE.

What kind of things can be used as backgrounds?

/ The usual suspects: the kitchen table, patio table and kitchen worktop are obvious choices when things have to be done quickly.

/ Textiles: a tablecloth, bed linen, a towel, linen shirt, leather shorts, carpet, pillowcases, the armchair ...

/ Wood: an old door, (painted) planks, a tree trunk, chair, table, cutting board ...

/ Stone: the floor, bathroom tiles, marble, natural stone, ceramic tiles, the windowsill, driveway, the terrace ...

/ Paper: coloured paper, printed paper, wallpaper, even a drawing or painting! Or take a photo of a nice texture yourself and print it on matte paper. Unfortunately, not washable.

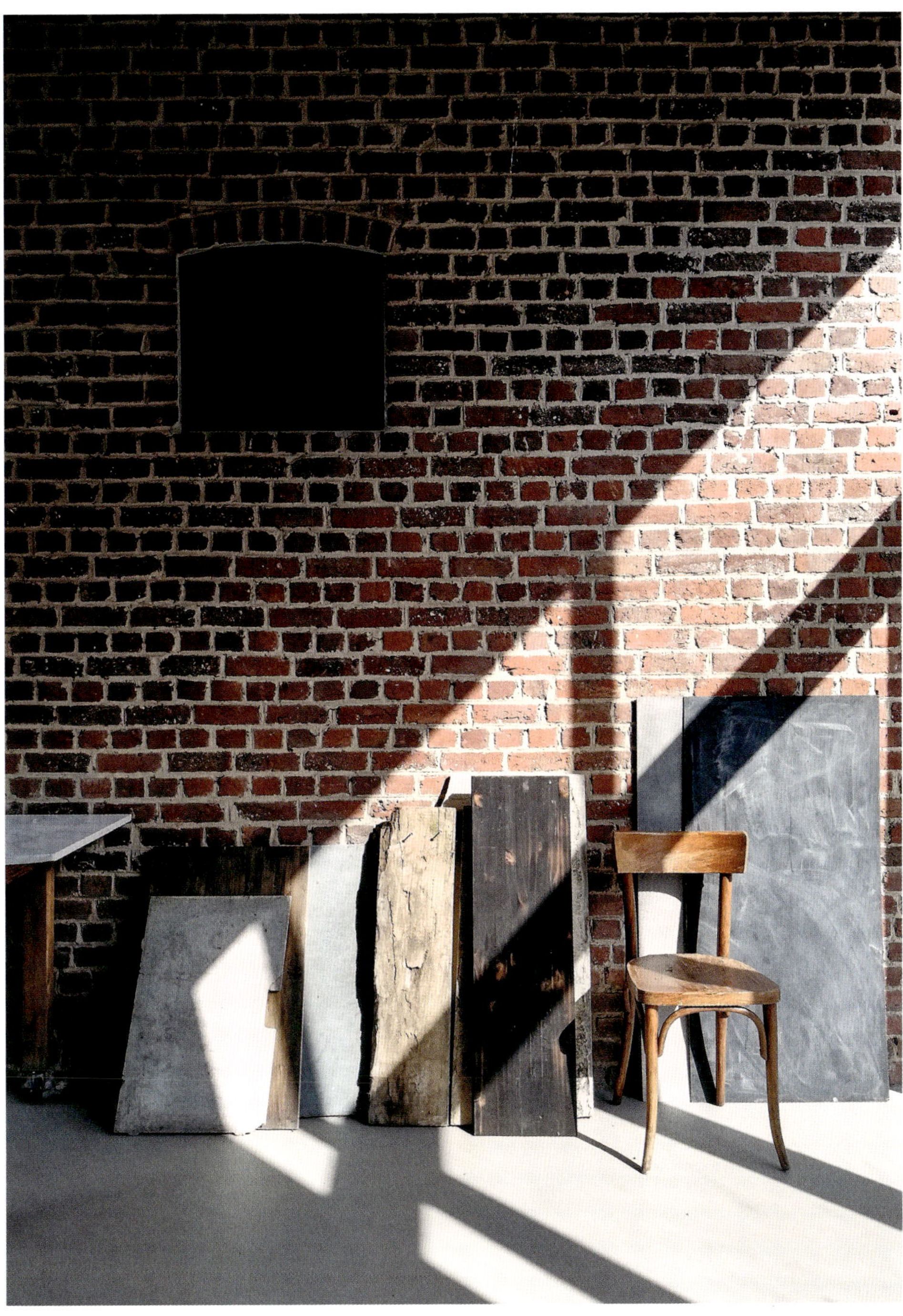

EXERCISE: PRODUCING YOUR OWN BACKGROUNDS

What do you need?

- ☐ Acrylic paint in several colours
- ☐ Texture paste or sand
- ☐ MDF panels, 150 x 75 cm
- ☐ Paint rollers
- ☐ Paintbrushes
- ☐ Filler
- ☐ Filler knife
- ☐ Sponges

TIP:
Some DIY stores sell test pots of wall paint. You can also use this as long as it's matt.

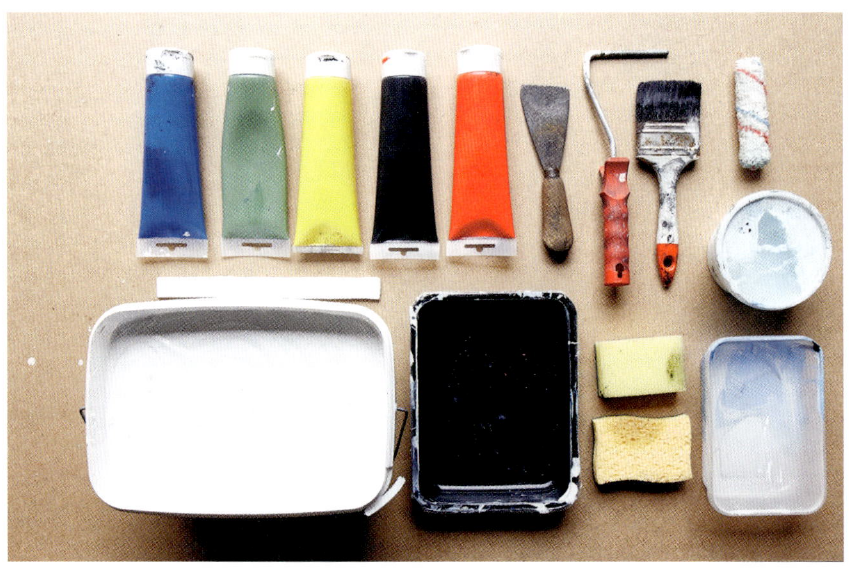

1. Start by applying a layer of primer to your background. White wall or ceiling paint does the job perfectly.
2. With a roller you can easily paint even surfaces, with a brush or a sponge you get more texture and colour shading. I often take the roller in one hand and the brush in the other and alternate: rolling a bit, then brushing and also dabbing with a sponge in between. Let yourself be guided by feeling and try not to think too hard about it. When this layer is ready, leave it to dry for a while before starting the next layer.
3. Use a plastic container that you can mix paint in. With a sponge you can mix the colours in such a way that a bit of each colour can still be seen. Paint that's not perfectly mixed gives you a nice effect.
4. The next layer can be a shade lighter than the previous one. To do this, mix white paint with your base colour and a little water. You can then dab on a second layer with a sponge. The layers certainly don't have to be even.

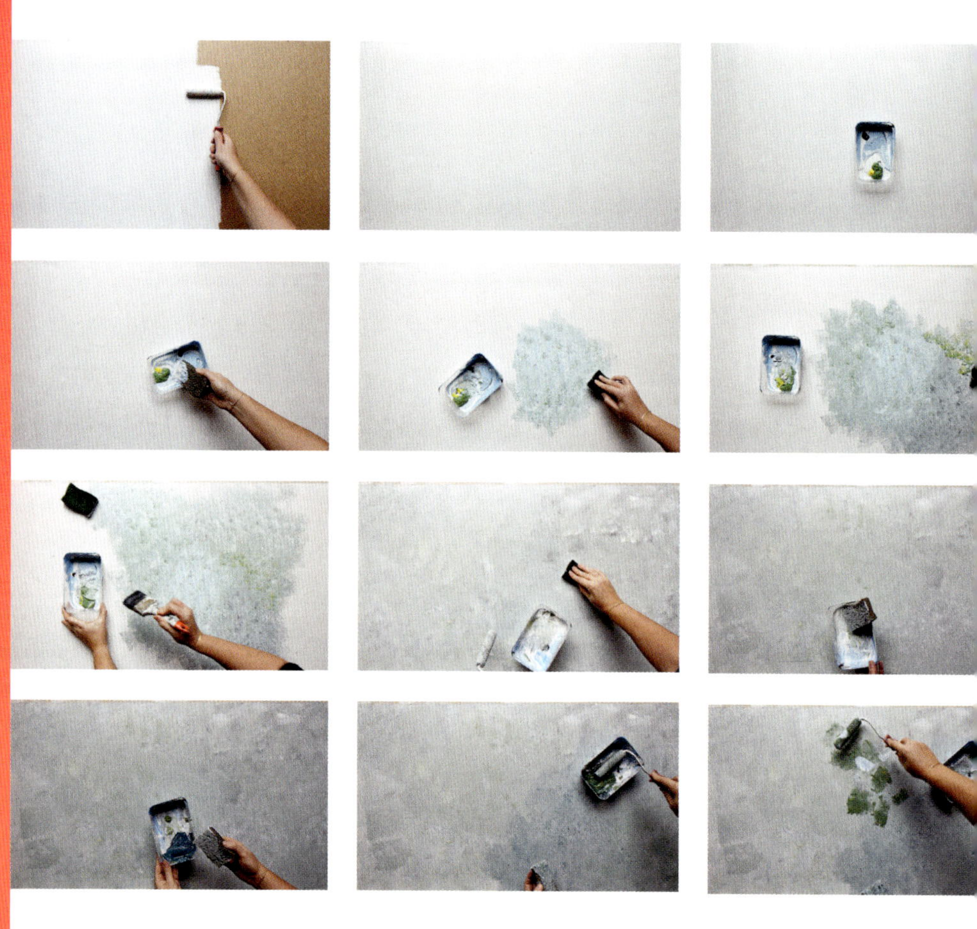

On the left of the photo you can see the effect of painting with the roller. In the middle I dabbed the paint on with a sponge. On the right I painted with a brush. The roller job looked the best in this case, so I went back over some other pieces with the roller using my intuition. On other pieces I found dabbing with the sponge gave a nicer effect.

A beautiful background doesn't always come across that way on the photo. Photograph textures and surfaces that you like. Do they come across well in a photo? This is a good exercise for learning to recognize a surface that works.

Cool colours generally work well in food photography: light blue, grey, black and white. This is because these colours contrast with that of the dish, which is usually in the warm tones. Feel free to experiment with warm background colours, such as pastel yellow, light pink or beige.

In general, complex patterns and bright colours are out of the question, as they take the focus away from the subject. But they can also strengthen the story, just think of a spaghetti bolognese on a red and white checkered tablecloth. A real classic!

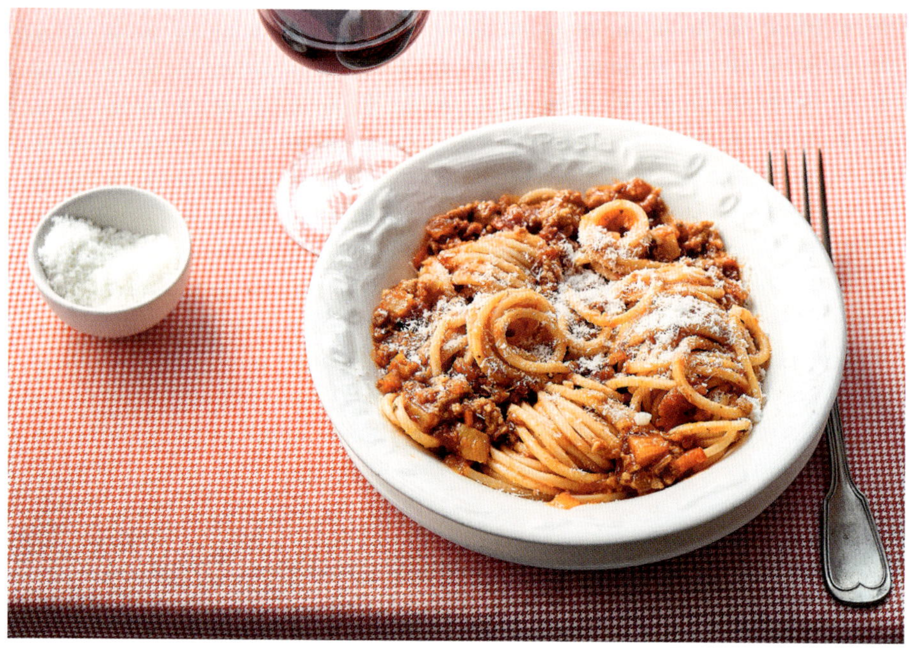

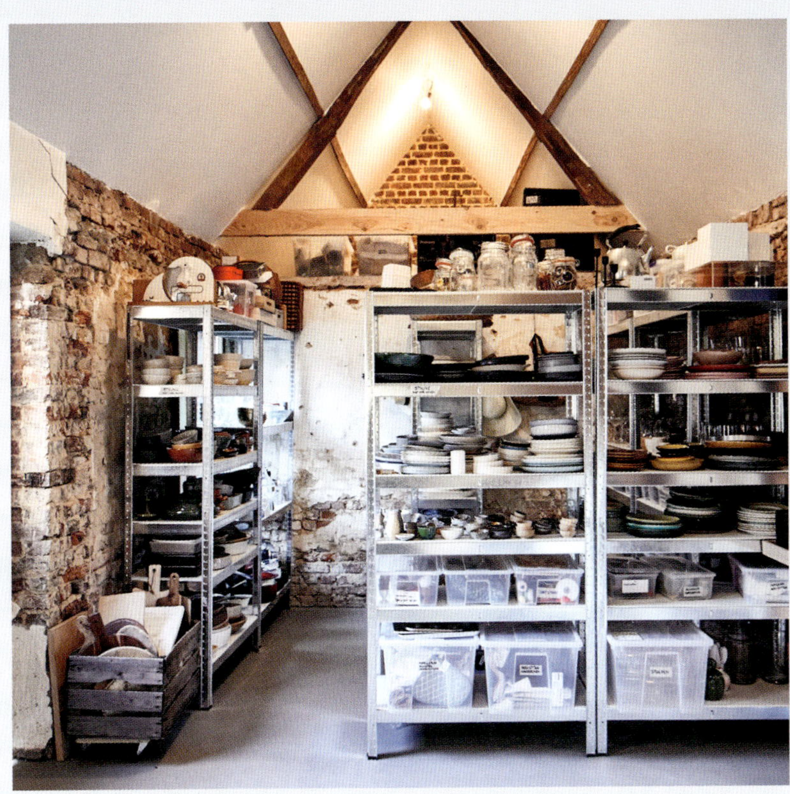

SIDENOTE:

When I started my collection, I had a craze on coffee cups. Today I have a rack full of porcelain and earthenware cups, which I hardly ever use. On the other hand, I seem to be constantly short of plates.

What you need most depends on what food you prepare most. If you like to bake, those coffee cups can still be useful. As cake trays, and little bowls for cookies and dessert dishes.

Props in one particular style or colour palette come in handy if you mainly shoot for yourself, your own blog or social media. This ensures unity and recognisability in the feed. You work towards your own style, something that tells your followers that this is your photo. A mood board can help with this and is often a good starting point for deciding what props you want to bring into your home or not.

PROPS

Keep It Simple Stupid (KISS)

The KISS principle also applies in styling. Too much is too much. Five empty plates stacked on top of each other, with a stack of pancakes on top, that's either a pile of dishes or the picture just doesn't add up. Two or three empty plates in the background with a few forks on top, to show that several people are coming to eat, that does makes sense.

A particular plate can work very well for one dish, but not at all for another. Props with busy patterns quickly attract attention. Which makes them difficult to combine with a complex dish. Even so, there's no law that says busy prints per se should not be used. In certain cases they do an excellent job.

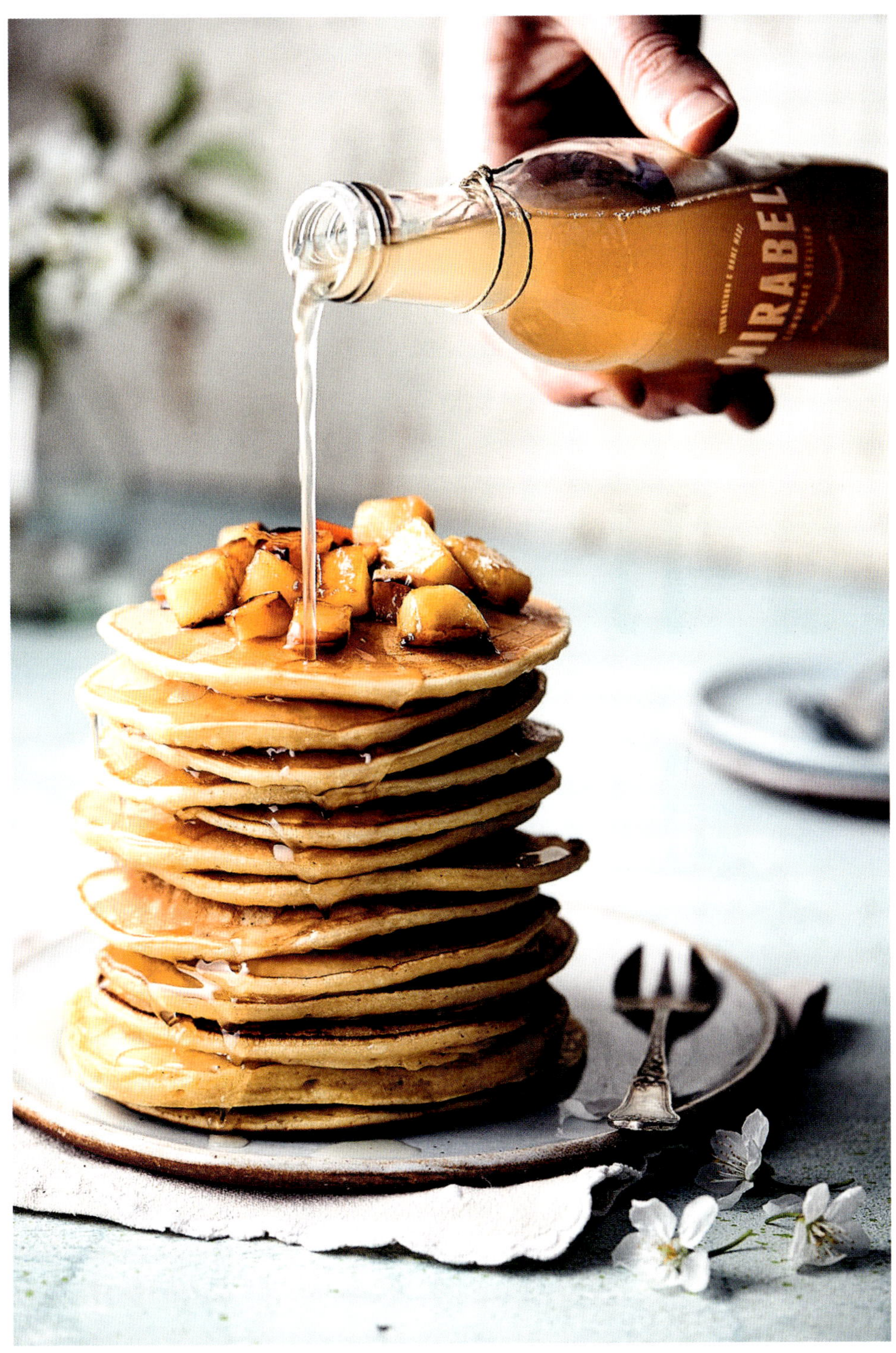
MIRABEL

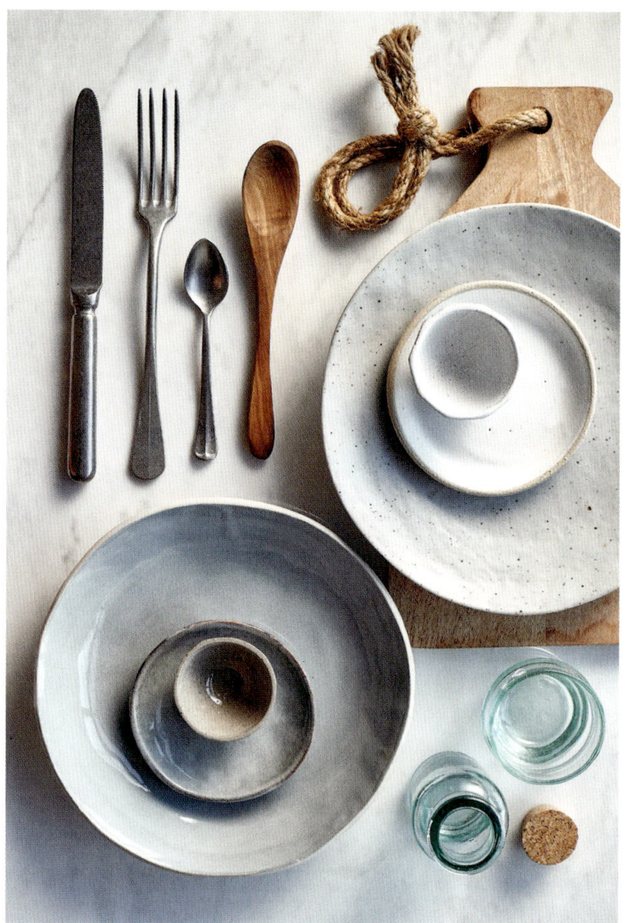

Plates

In most cultures people eat from a plate. Your collection of props will therefore consist largely of plates. Flat, deep, big, small, oval, square (although a square plate can be a real nuisance to style) and so on. Plates come in all shapes, but also in all colours!

Do you have to run out and buy every type of plate straight away? No, of course not. Start with a few simple (white) plates that aren't too shiny and have a certain texture. Handmade ceramics have all these properties and are also completely unique!

Bowls

Small bowls can fill an 'itching void'. They can contain grated cheese, fresh herbs, lemon wedges, et cetera. Anything, as long as it makes sense in the picture.

Larger bowls should not be too deep. A shallow bowl throws fewer dark shadows, which makes lighting easier. In addition to which, you don't have to make super-sized portions in order to fill them.

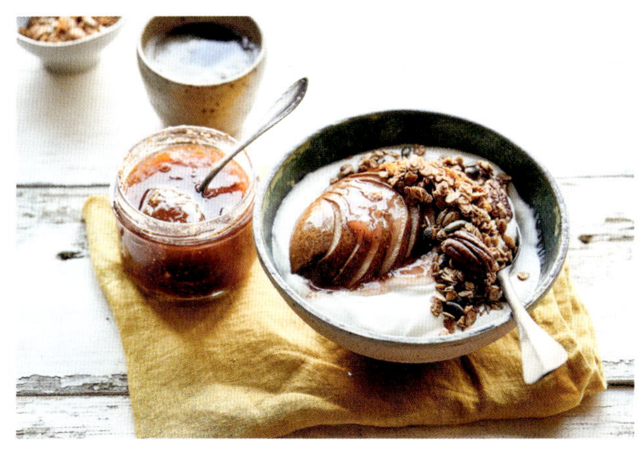

Both bowls have the same top diameter. However, the same amount of yogurt appears much less in the deep bowl than in the shallow bowl.

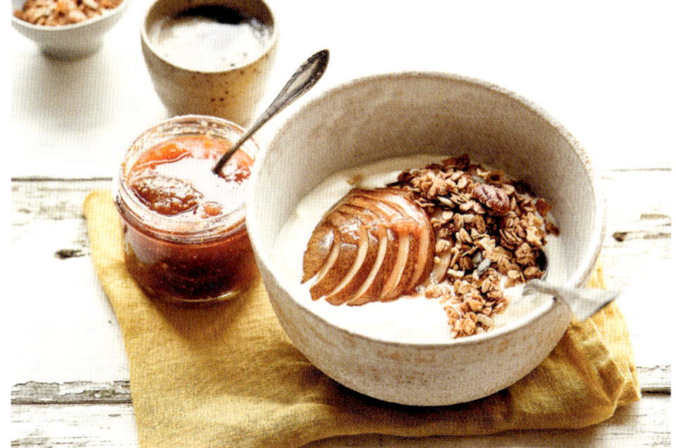

Glasses

A glass of water or a wine glass in the background is a logical prop for a dish. Go for neutral glasses that don't demand too much attention in an image. You don't have to buy a full set of the same glasses. If you mainly photograph cocktails, your collection will consist of glasses of all shapes and sizes.

Boards

I have a bit of an obsession with wooden boards. Large, round cheese boards, small cutting boards with and without handles, boards on a support ... in different types of wood and preferably slightly used. For bread and cheese of course, but by placing a board under a plate you create additional layering.

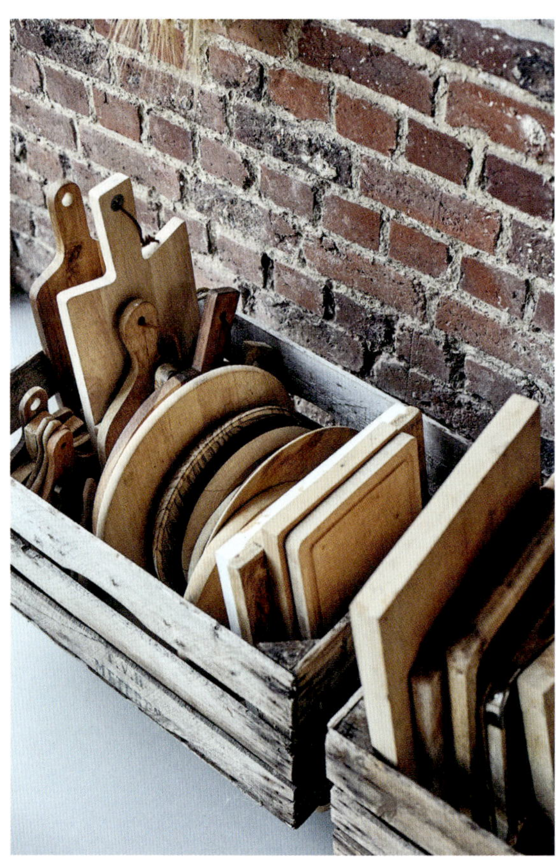

Cutlery
Knives, forks and spoons are the basis. In an otherwise too empty picture, they can be the solution without demanding too much attention. Providing they're are well placed in the composition, of course! Start with some attractive pieces that aren't too shiny. The harder the shine, the more reflections you will see. This can disturb the image, especially with spoons.

Pots and pans
Sometimes you want to present a dish in a cooking pot. Why? Pots are ugly and unwieldy, aren't they? Indeed, the large, stainless steel cooking pots that most people use on a daily basis are just that. But there are also smaller cooking pots and pans in enamel or cast iron, in different colours that you can match with your setting.

Oven dishes and baking tins have the same difficulty: they're often large and bulky. Go looking for stone oven dishes with a slightly rougher surface. A glass Pyrex dish can also be useful, for example with a layered dish. Old baking tins that have lost some of their shine are exactly what you need for the picture.

TIP:

When you go hunting, buy two to four pieces of the same, no more. Your storage space fills up faster than you think and you rarely need more than four plates. I only have one of most plates in my stock. The same goes for glasses and cutlery.

Vases and decoration
A vase with flowers in the background, a milk jug, salt and pepper shakers, honey pot... These are all kitchen items that you'll find on a real kitchen table. They bring life into the picture and also belong there.

I'm a big believer in less is more. Too many items to fill an image only distracts from what's important.

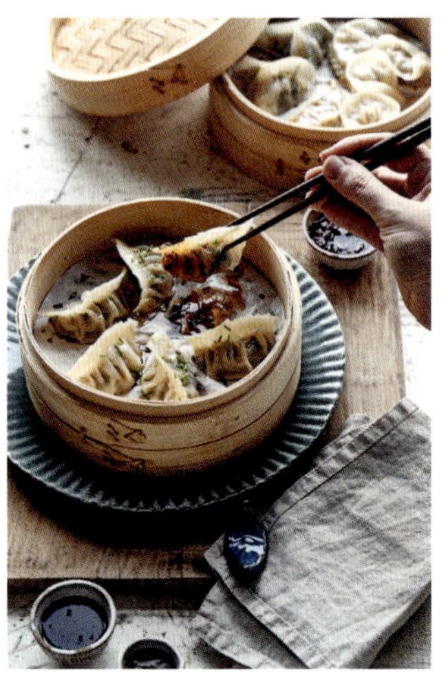

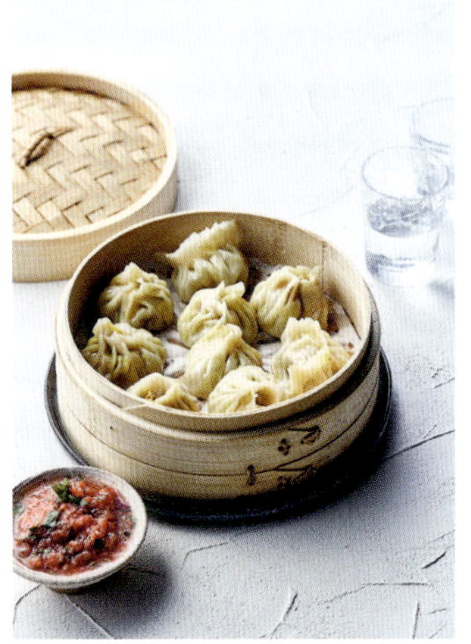

TIP:

Do you feel stuck, that your composition is blocked? Then remove props one by one. Does the picture still work without that last prop? You'll often find there was too much going on in the composition and that everything balances better with fewer props.

COLOUR

Don't choose your props just because you like them. Think carefully whether they go with your dish. The colour of your dish can often set the tone for the overall colour palette of the photo. You can use these colours to hang your props on.

Complementary colours, such as yellow and blue, combine very well in food photos. A dish with lemons on a dark blue background needs little else. That stands out!

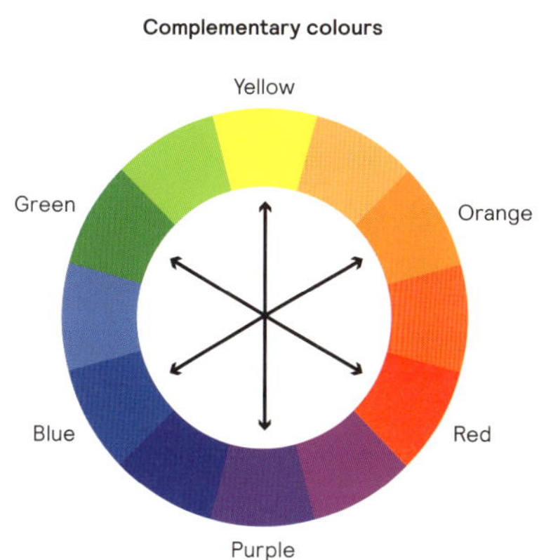

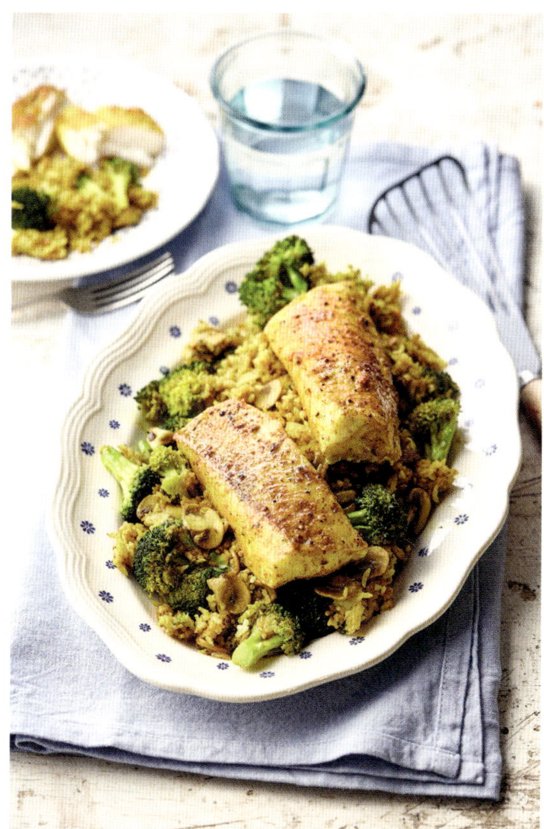

Ton sur ton, or elements from the same colour palette, are an artistic choice. For example, high-key and low-key photos use only white or only black elements respectively with subtle differences in hue to build the image.

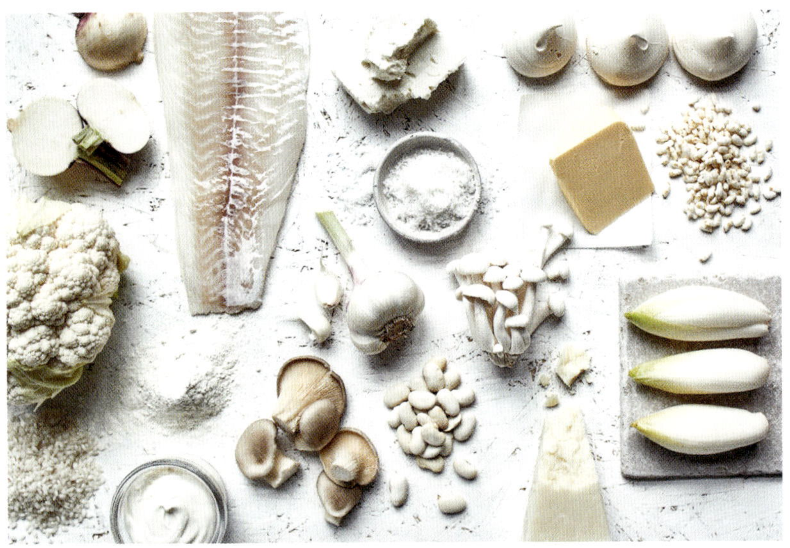

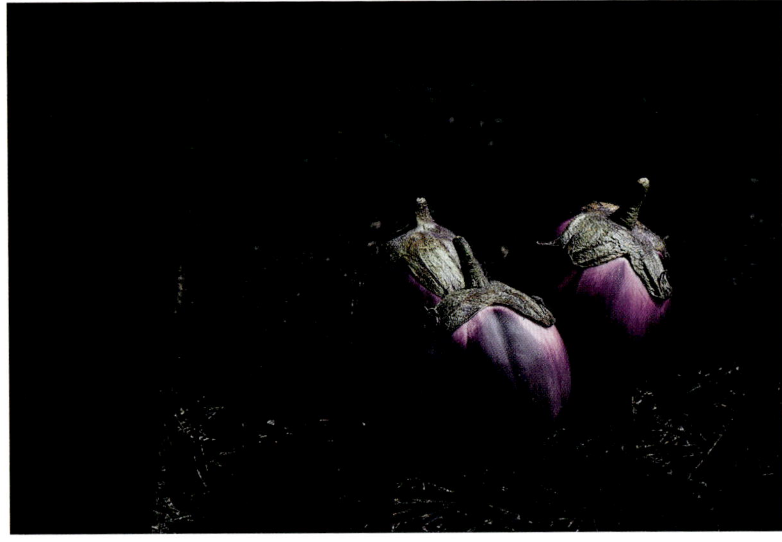

Colours evoke feelings. Blue gives a cool impression, but combined with warm colours such as yellow, red, orange, it can appear warm and attractive. White and light pastel colours evoke a summer feeling, especially in combination with harsh light and tightly defined shadows.

Green tells you that something is fresh. Health and organic products often have a lot of green in their image style. Brown and other dark dishes with little colour gradation benefit from green. Not only are they complementary, but a literal leaf of green freshens up the whole dish and adds some more texture.

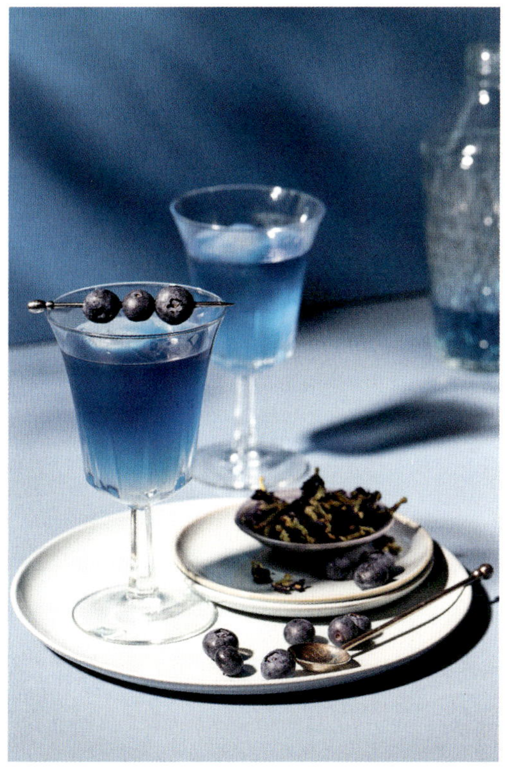

The idea behind these photos was to pick up the colours of the dish in the props and the background: ton sur ton.

TEXTURE

More texture in plates or glasses makes surfaces appear to matter, reducing the harshness of the light's reflection. There's more life in an imperfect hand-turned plate. A subtle drawing or pattern gives rhythm.

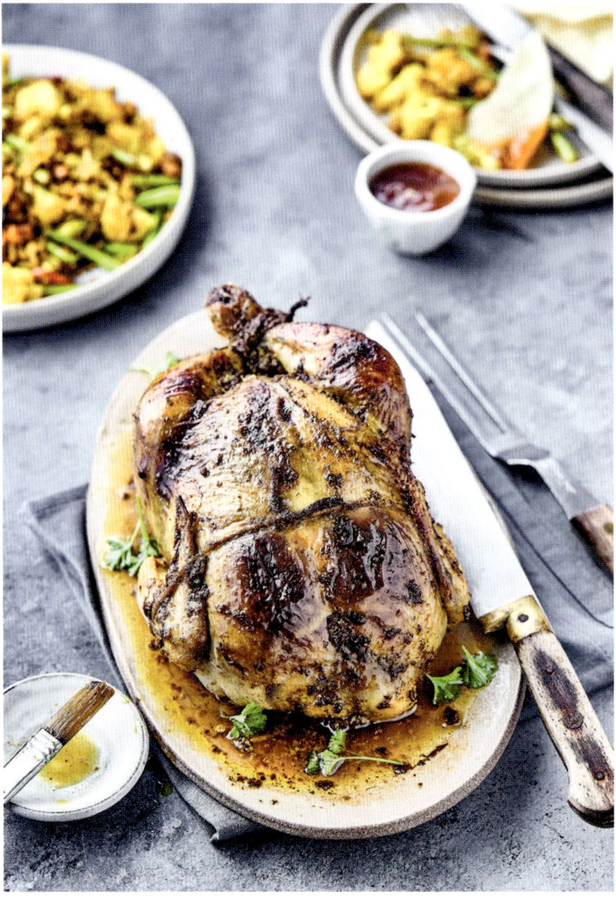

A little detail: all the plates in this photo are handmade by me. Ceramics is a hobby that serves me well as a photographer.

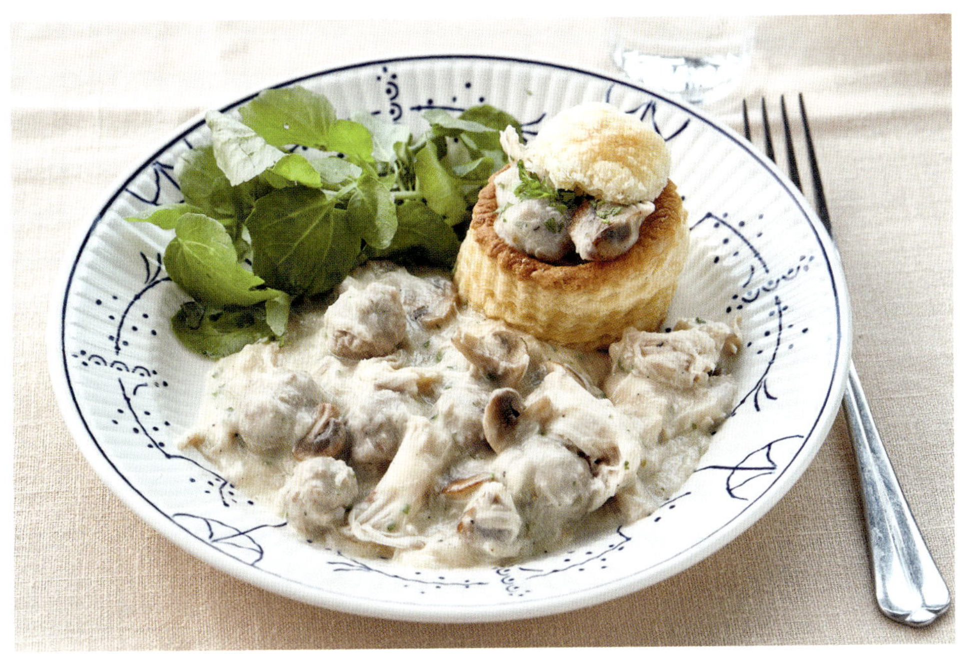

Figurative prints on crockery or textiles usually grab too much attention. But it is also possible to consciously work the print into the photo. Experiment here: artistic freedom prevents uniformity.

LAYERS

Work with layers to create texture and shadows. A tray, board, flat plate, napkin, tile, etc. under the plate or a bowl add depth to your composition.

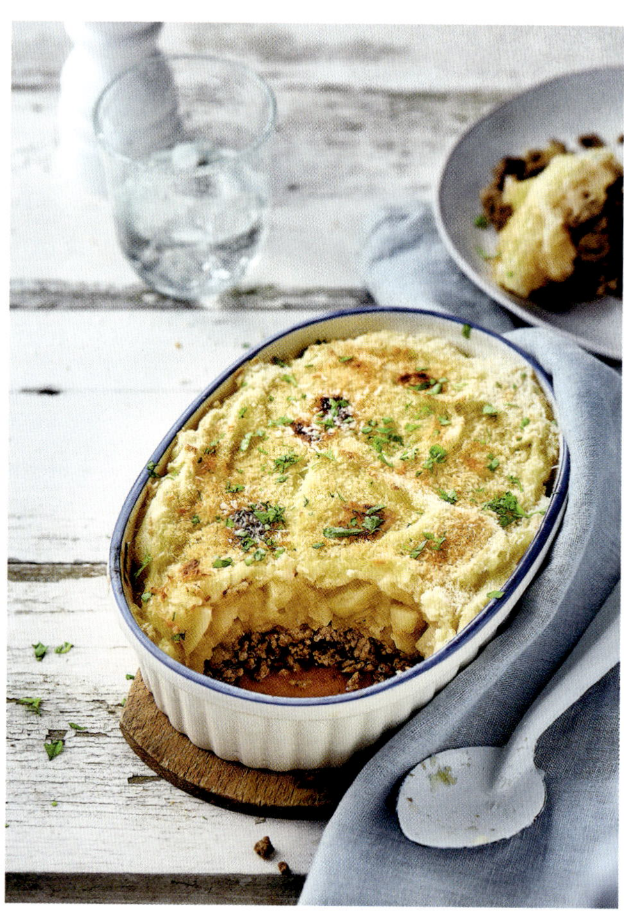

SHAPE

Many props are circular in shape. Plates, cups, glasses, bowls ... Connect them by placing elongated elements that guide the eye through the image.

Oval plates and dishes look very nice on their own and require few or no other props. A fork or a spoon maybe, but nothing more. That works perfectly.

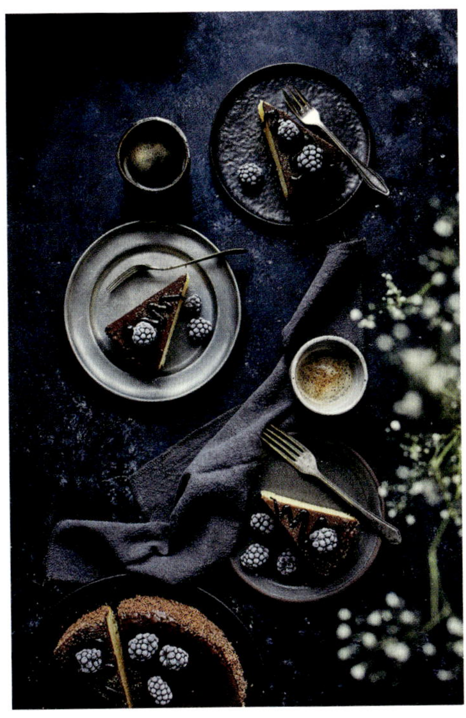

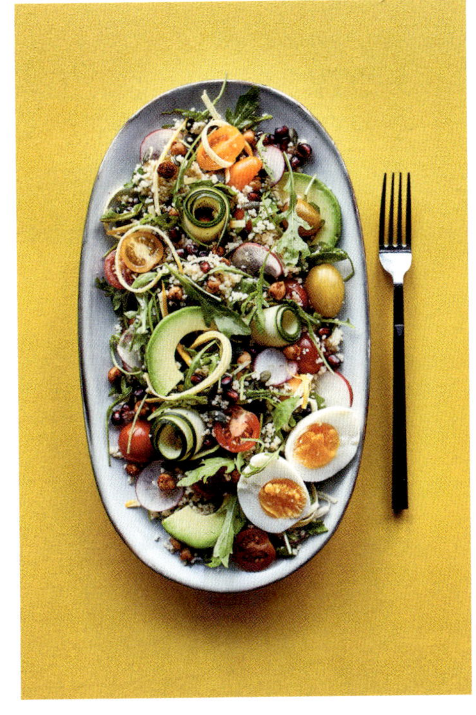

Trends

Square or rectangular plates refer to a certain trend of a few years ago. Long before that, there were grandma's plates with floral prints on the edges. Likewise, the rustic props that are popular today will also go out of style in a few years' time. If you've a sense for trends, you can also use this to your advantage to reflect a particular zeitgeist in a photo. Or maybe flower prints are part of your personal style and provide recognisability.

SIZE

"Your eyes were bigger than your tummy again!" I was often told as a child. There's something to be said for this when it comes to size of tableware for food photos. A small plate fills up faster and gives the impression of being fuller than a large plate. There's more space to display a glass or bowls, while a large plate takes up lots of photo space and looks empty. Without any scale reference, such as a hand, a small glass can appear normal sized and a large wine glass can be huge!

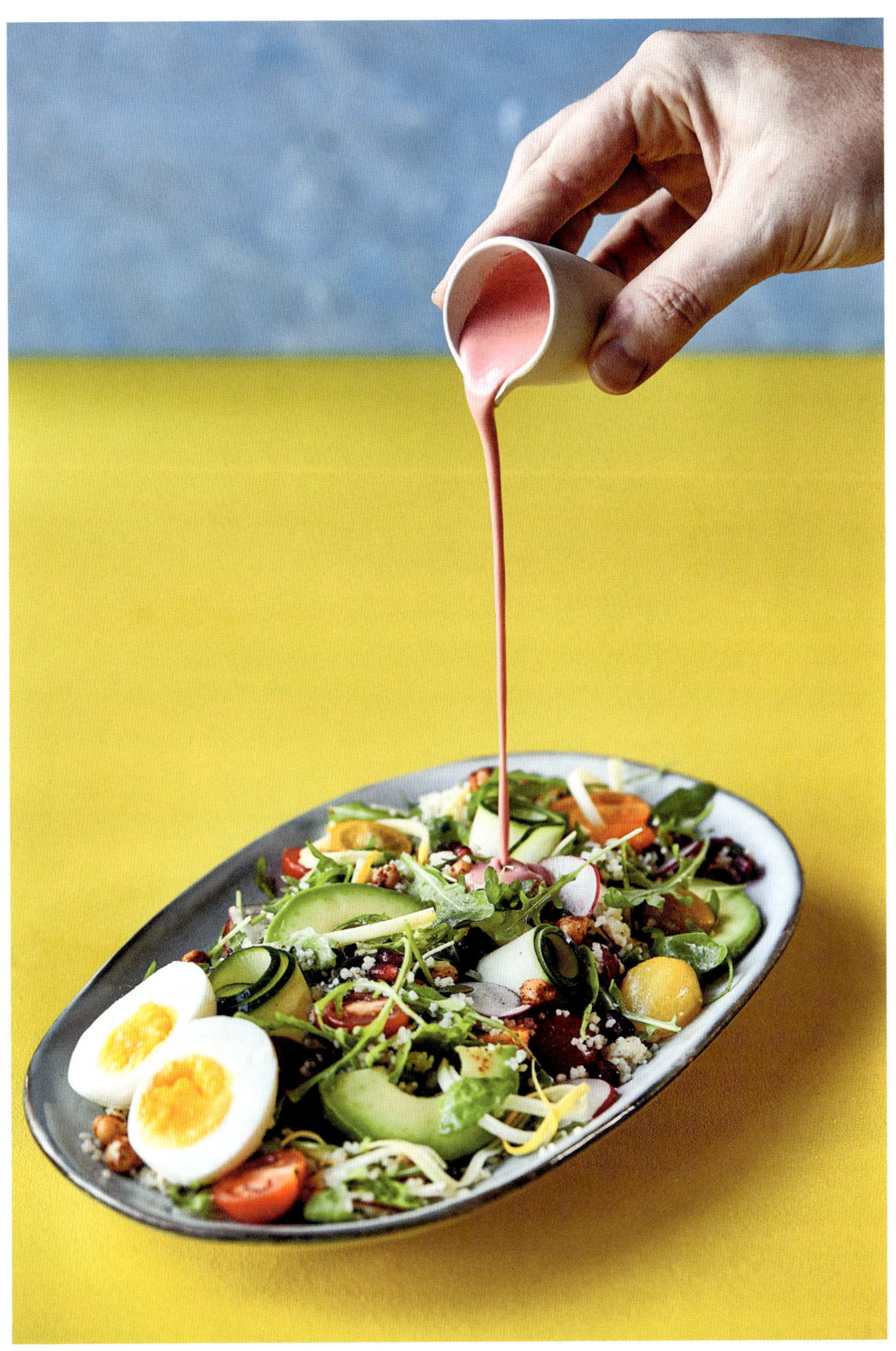

WHERE TO FIND IT

Collecting props has become an occupational disease for me.

You don't always have to go out of the house to find attractive surfaces or props!

The possibilities are actually endless and before you know it, you're going to have to clear a room to store your props. But for those who don't know how to get started, let me give 'the basics':

/ Interior design and cooking stores: it's here you buy new pieces in the latest fashion trends. If you like sleek design dinner services or modern glasses, then these are the places to go looking.

IN THE MOST UNEXPECTED THINGS, IN THE MOST UNUSUAL PLACES, I SEE AN OBJECT THAT CAN LOOK NICE IN THE PHOTO.

/ The bargain shop: if you're looking for a series of props with character, you can certainly find them in bargain shops. Don't just buy what takes your fancy, but also ask yourself: will it look good in the photo?
/ Flea markets: these are my happy places. What is junk to one person is worth gold to another. If I can also buy a cast iron cooking pot for one euro, it's made my day!
/ Ceramists: Buy some handmade pieces from a ceramist and cherish them. Not only are you supporting local craftsmen, you'll also always have a unique plate or cup!
/ From grandmother: Visiting family? Throw a line by subtly stating that you're looking for an old ladle. Chances are your grandmother has several of them hanging around.

/ Online: the internet is large and there's a lot to be found. You can buy on craft platforms like Etsy, via Instagram from local designers ...
/ In your own home: you're richer than you think. Don't limit yourself to your kitchenware. There's an attractive fruit bowl sitting in the living room. The coffee table has a characteristic wood grain, the pillowcases can serve as napkins, the bed linen can double as tablecloths, the concrete floor in the garage is ultra-hip and the stable door is suddenly a new table!

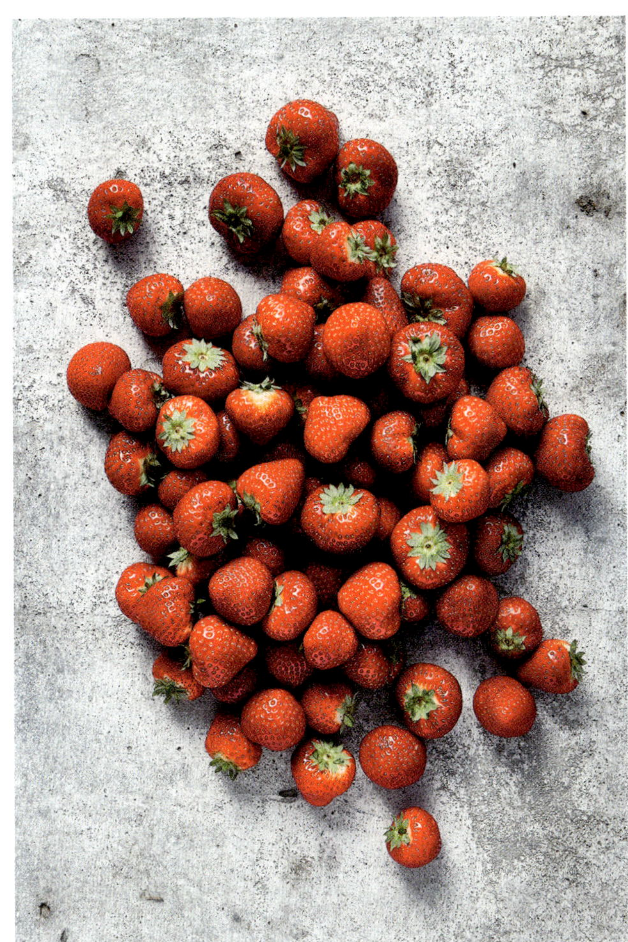

I recovered this background surface during our renovation. It's unique and has a story attached to it.

EXERCISE: TREASURES IN THE ATTIC

You're richer than you think. This assignment consists of looking in your house or apartment, in the garden or on the terrace for something that could pass for:

- ☐ a background surface
- ☐ a plate
- ☐ a board
- ☐ something green (flowers or twigs)
- ☐ a napkin

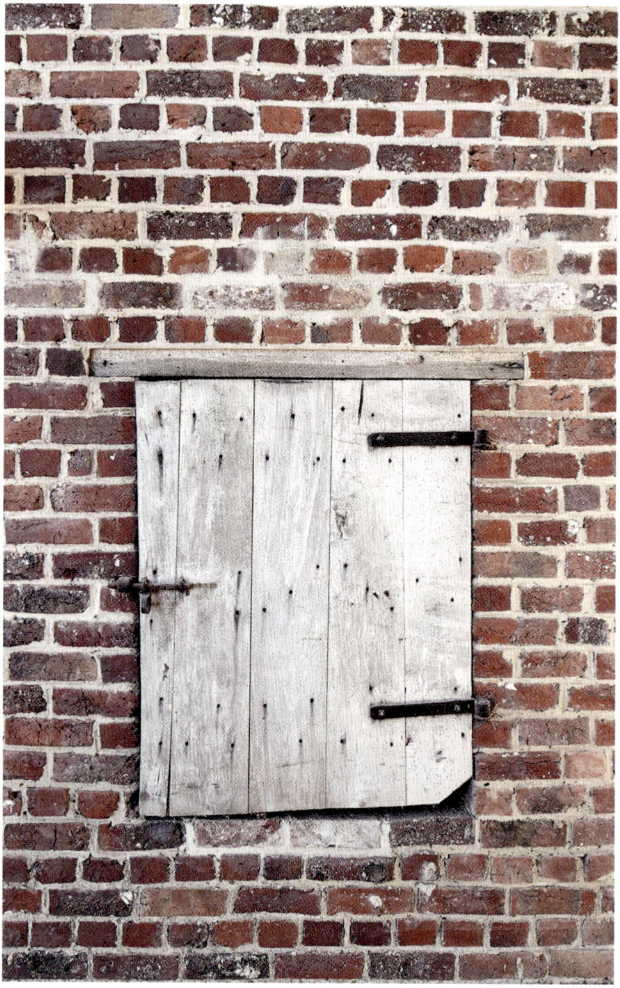

EXERCISE: COPYCAT

Just copying a photo is never okay. But analysing a photo to find out how the photographer built up the image correctly, what light he used, what makes the composition so good, what colours and textures he combines ... You can learn a lot that way. Recreate the photo yourself and try and make it look as close to the original as possible.

Then analyse this photo:

- ☐ Where does the light come from?
- ☐ Which light source was used, how far away from the subject and what diffusers or reflectors were used?
- ☐ From what angle was the photo taken?
- ☐ What lens could this have been and how far away from the setting?
- ☐ Look for a background similar to the one in the photo.
- ☐ What choices did the stylist make for the props? How big and deep are they, what colour and texture are they?
- ☐ How is the dish structured?
- ☐ What makes the composition so strong?

Once you've answered these questions to the best of your ability, you can recreate the photo. Always keep the original.

TIP:

You can then post the result of your exercise in the Facebook group *Foodfotografie & styling*. And you'll get free feedback from myself and group members!

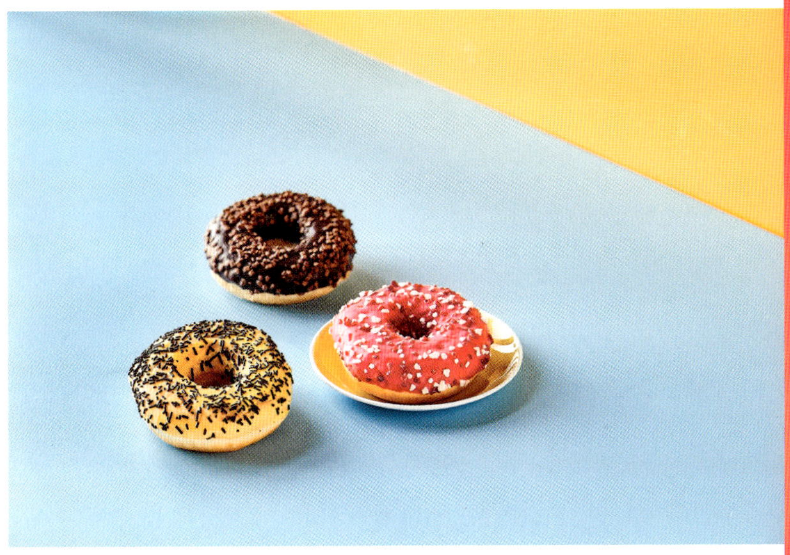

THE PERFECT FOOD PHOTO

Before you start taking pictures, eat something and thank me later. On an empty stomach, I'm an over-hasty food photographer.
You're at the stove on a weekday. When your food's ready, you think: gosh, how delicious! I have to take a picture of that. You grab the first plate from the cupboard and shovel out your food. But it looked different in your head than how it now looks on the plate, didn't it?

01. RESEARCH

Look for sample photos of the dish you want to photograph. If necessary, create a mood board (see p. 20).

02. SEARCHING FOR PROPS

Select the appropriate props based on the dish and your research (see p. 148).

03. GETTING IT ALL IN PLACE

Make sure you have all the ingredients at hand, plus extra. And don't forget the fresh herbs! Already be thinking about what you can prepare for when the time comes to shoot. If you're shooting straightaway, prepare everything separately.

04. PREPARING THE SET

Place your table by the window and your camera on a tripod. Make sure to have your reflector panel and your basic styling kit (see p. 127) at hand on set.

05. COMPOSING THE PICTURE

Before preparing any food, you can place the props and surface in the right composition.

06. USE STAND-IN FOOD

A filled plate looks very different from an empty plate. If you're working with a dish that has only a short set life, you can use a replacement portion that's not styled. This will give you time to see if props may need repositioning.

07.
ADJUSTING THE LIGHT

You may need to move your reflector panel closer now that the plate is filled or put the exposure one stop higher. Often the image appears darker when you've added the food. Or maybe the sun has just disappeared behind a dark cloud.

08.
PREPARING/FINISHING THE FOOD

Put the finishing touches to the preparation, for example stir the sauce, fry the fish or scoop the ice cream. In the meantime, feed hungry housemates with their own portions to allow you to shoot in peace.

09.
DRESSING THE PLATE

Dress the plate. Look through the camera viewfinder at regular intervals and take a photo now and then to see the intermediate result. Finish with the garnishes.

10.
TAKING THE PHOTO (AT DIFFERENT ANGLES)

Taking the final photo is the least hard work! The preparation work is done, all that's left to do is to push the button. Approved? Then take your camera off the tripod and take a few more photos from a different vantage point. As long as the food looks good, you can keep taking photos.

It sounds cumbersome, but steps 1 to 3 can be done perfectly well for several dishes together at the weekend. When you've found a good spot in the house for photographing, you can keep it 'ready for use'.

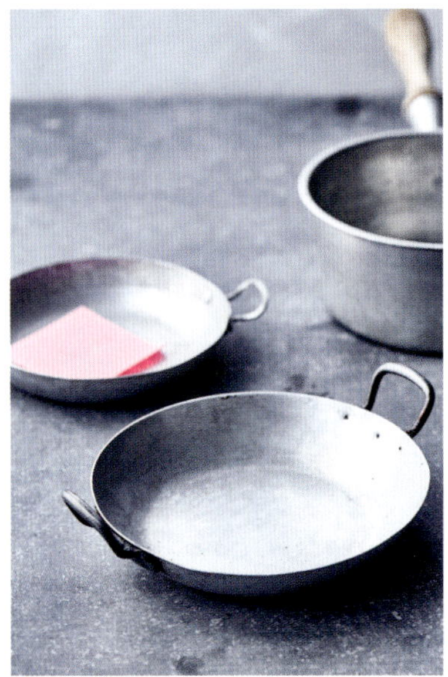

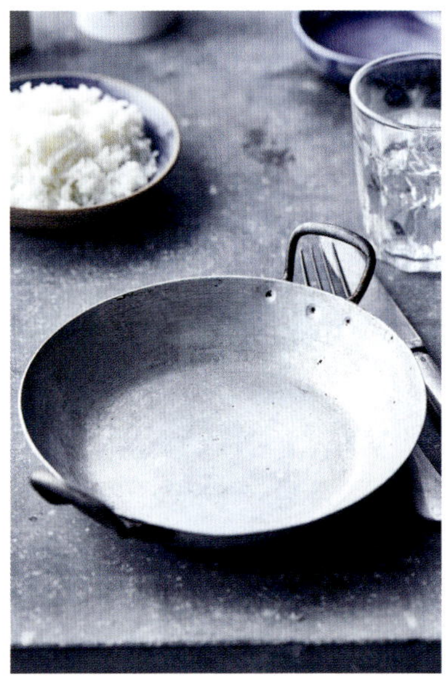

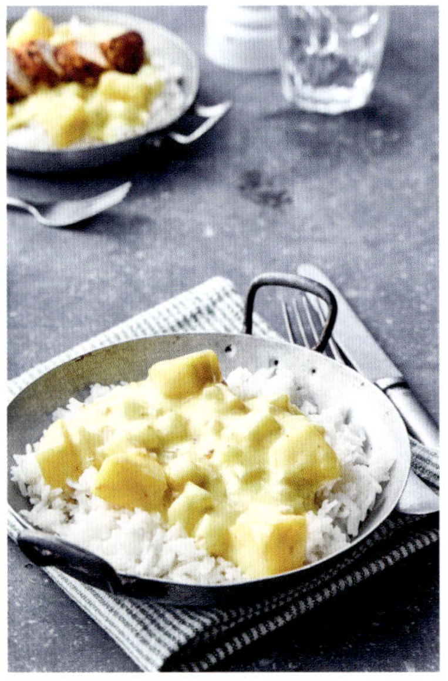

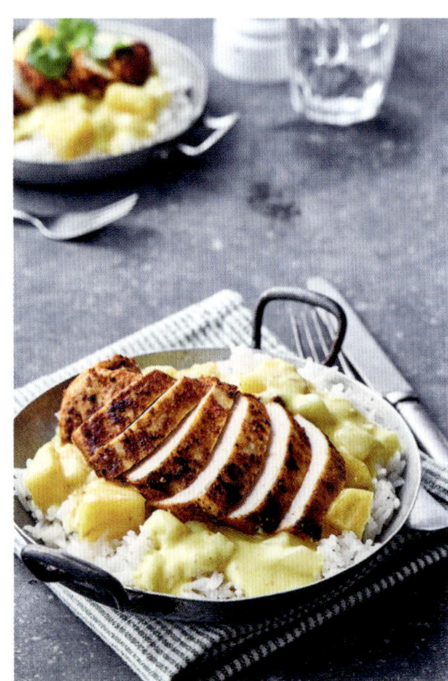

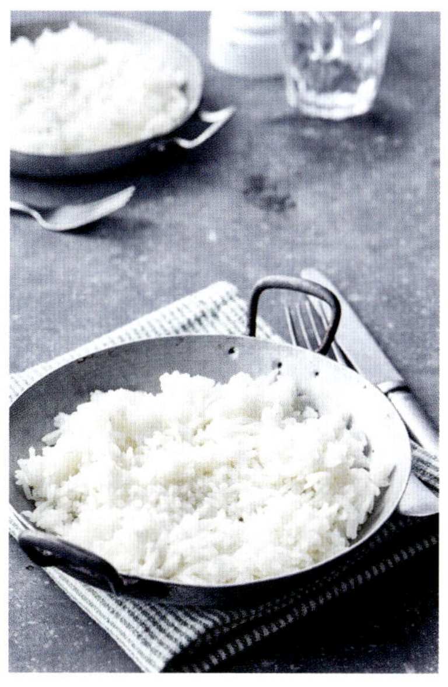

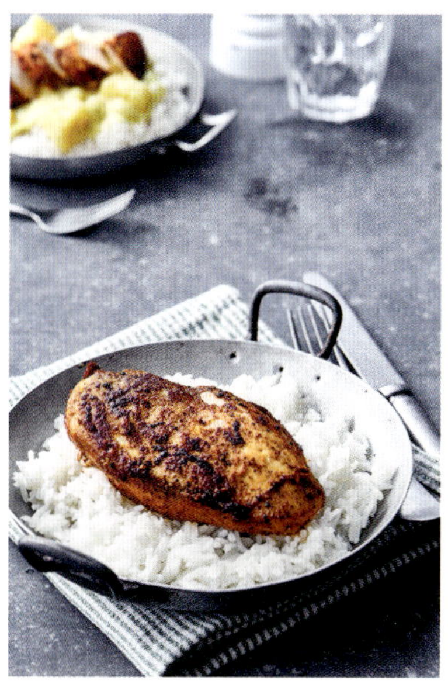

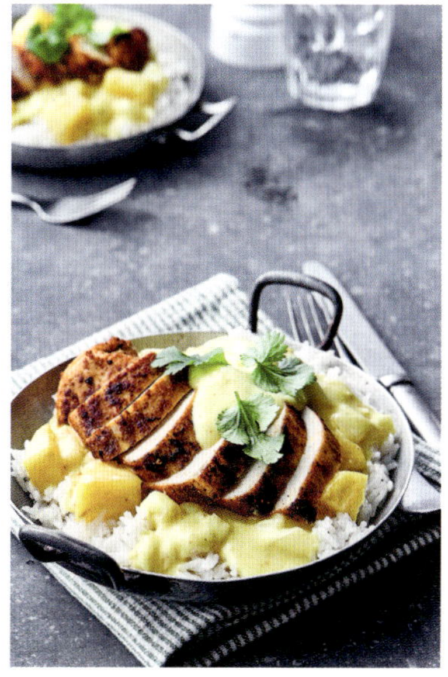

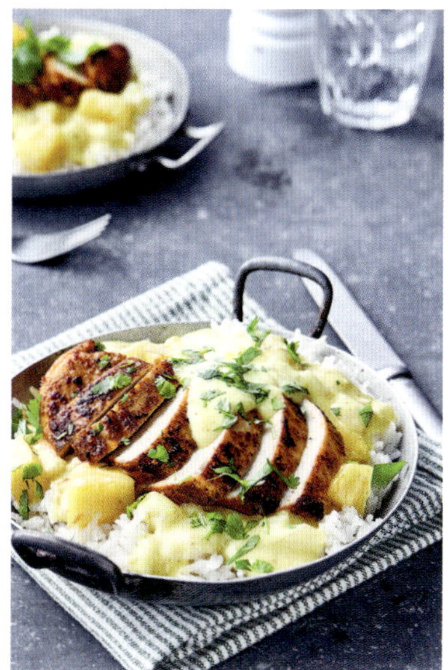

CASES

05

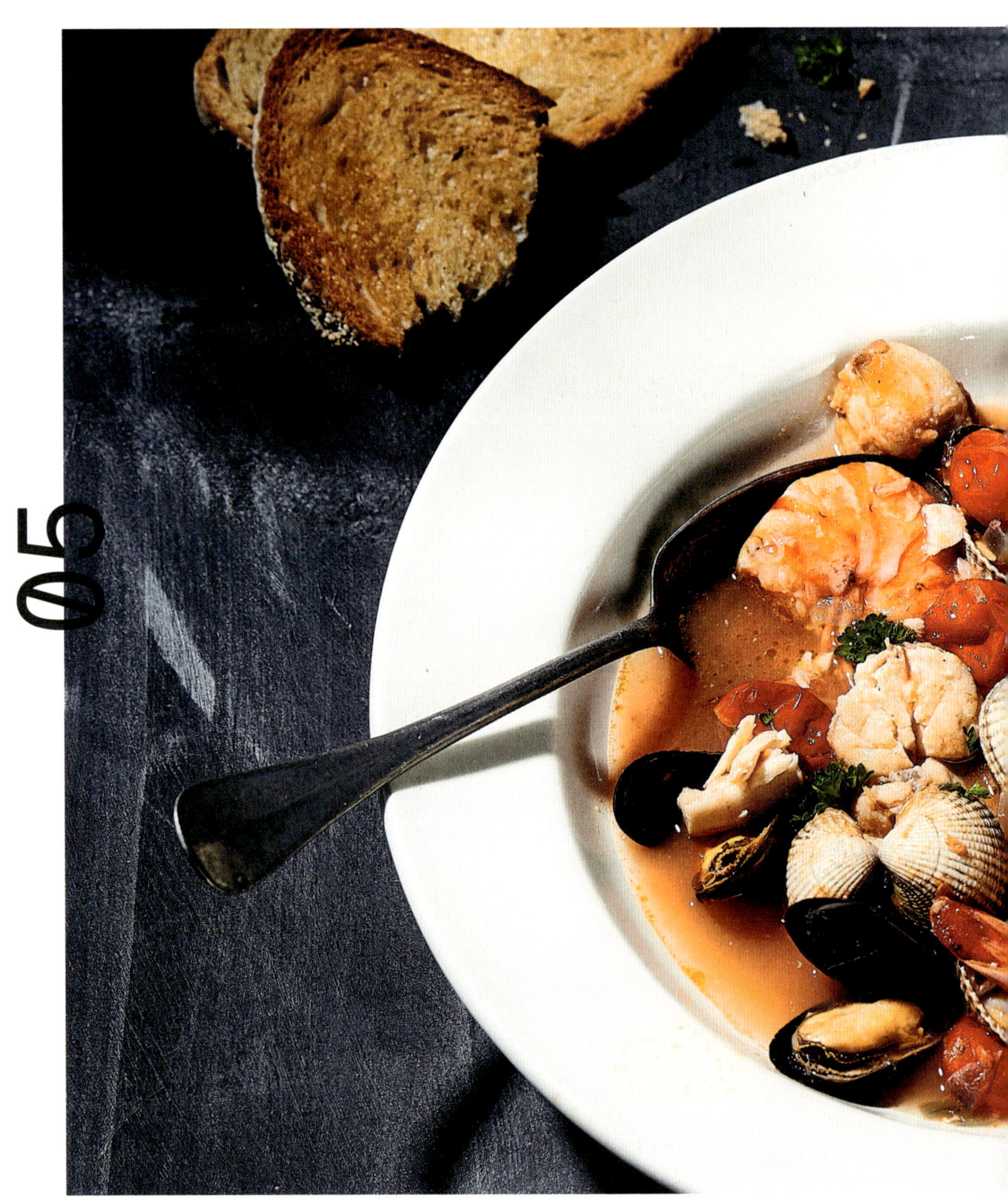

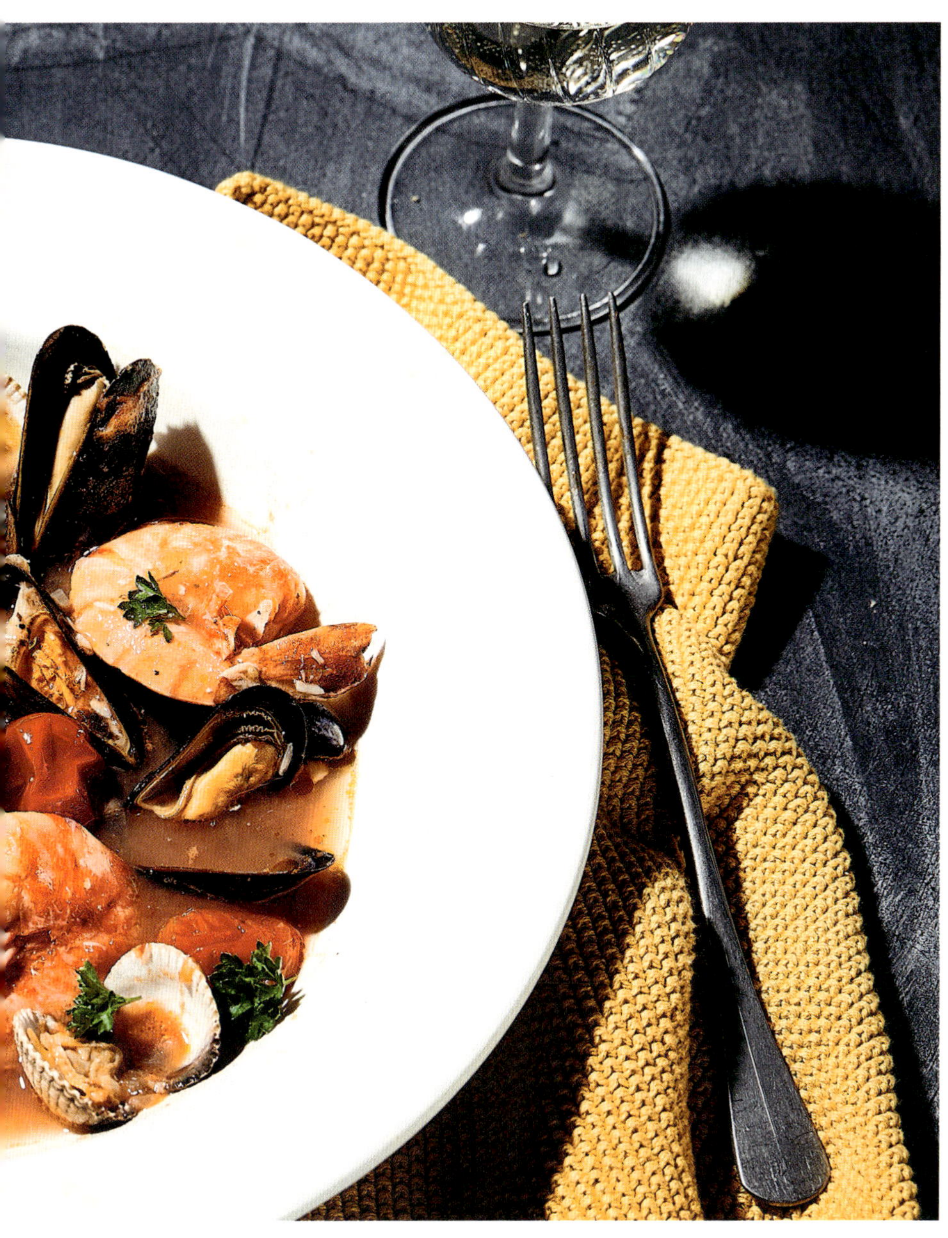

PIZZA

Problem

A pizza is basically a flat disk with flat ingredients that are usually hidden from view by the delicious, thick layer of melted cheese covering. You cannot manipulate it like a salad or a pasta. It is what it is. So you have to use other things to make a wonderful picture of it.

Atmosphere:

The home-made authentic Italian pizza, straight from a wood oven with a wafer-thin base and dark brown crispy bubbles in the crust. You can still hear the hot mozzarella crackling and the scent of oregano storms into your nostrils. You have the knife ready to cut a slice out of the pizza. The spicy oil drips down your hand when you take the first bite and you immediately imagine yourself in an Italian pizzeria.

Solution:

Emphasize the elements that make up the story around the pizza. Photograph someone on a sunny patio holding a slice of pizza.

Don't worry too much about preparing your pizza. With older food styling methods, the dish was often not fully cooked. But the strength of contemporary food photography is that not everything has to be perfect. Here too the principle applies that something that's not completely cooked will never look cooked. Nobody wants to eat raw pizza, right?

When topping the pizza, bear in mind the cheese that's usually sprinkled over the topping. Keep back a few ingredients. After sprinkling the cheese on top, add a few extra slices of mushroom or ham before placing it in the oven.
Cut the pizza into slices and place them in a seemingly disordered fashion one piece a bit more out of the circle than the other. You can also cut a homemade pizza, which does not have to be perfectly round, in zigzags.

In restaurants they often give you rocket on your pizza. You can add some in moderate quantities just before taking pictures, but careful: the heat will quickly collapse the rocket and make it stick flat to the pizza. You can also use fresh oregano leaves as a topping.

If you photograph a pizza from above, bring some movement to the image by already removing a piece, taking a bite from the tip of a slice, a hand holding a piece ... In side view you can emphasize a detail of the pizza, with possibly a second pizza or another dish in the background.

Don't make it too clean. Pizza is comfort food and it's allowed to be greasy!

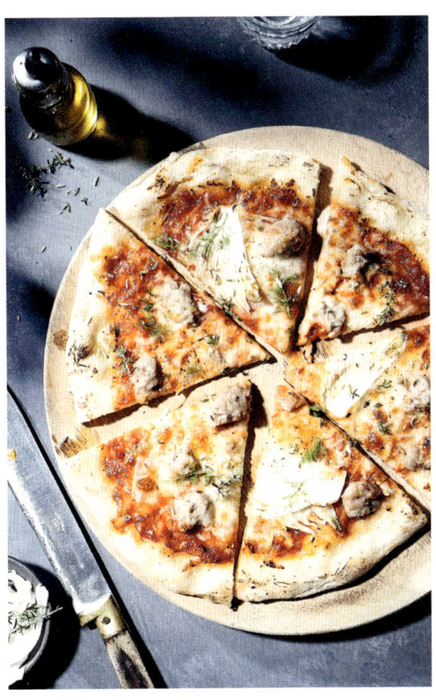

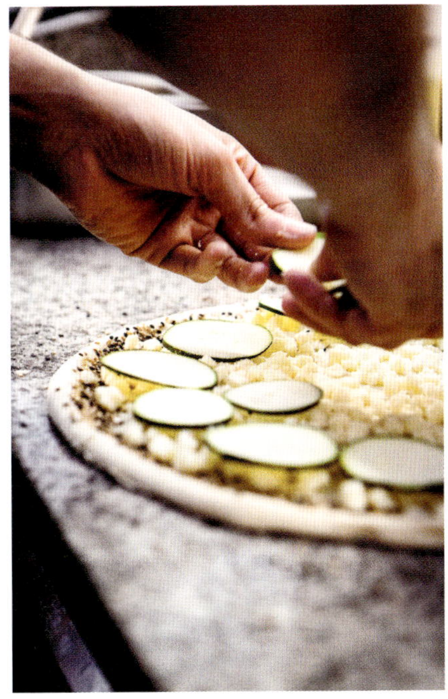

BEEF STEW

Problem:
Grandma's given you a recipe for stew with French fries and you want to photograph it. But a brown mash is and will remain a brown mash. And once stew's gone cold, a gelatine layer forms. Time isn't on your side!

Atmosphere:
Grandma is proud of her recipe. It's been passed down through five generations, including two wars. For her, this is the only real stew. With French fries and home-made mayonnaise. A beer to go with it. Dark beer, of course, because that gives the most flavour.

My grandma served beef stew on blue Boch plates. We ate at a table with a white floral tablecloth. Freshly cut fries on the plate, a good dollop of mayonnaise and Piedboeuf beer from what had started life as a Chocomel glass.

Solution:
Embrace the brown mash. Prepare the beef stew properly. Don't tell grandma, but you might just thicken the sauce a little if it looks like soup on the photo.

The photo has to speak of texture and colour. Make sure you can still make out the meat lumps in the sauce. If necessary, show a broken-open lump. Some fresh thyme and mill pepper add texture and colour. Yellow French fries next to it will have the same effect.

Never photograph cold stew. The sauce will look crumbly from the gelatine coming to the surface. This applies equally to other animal-based sauces such as cream, milk and gelatine.

If you want to photograph stew in the pot, make sure that the amount of stew is in proportion to the size of the pot. More than 2 centimetres of free rim means you'll have to look very deep into the pot on the photo. In this case the picture will show more pot than stew.

There are three methods to make your stew pot appear more full:

/ Make more beef stew. Another trick: the most obvious solution, and yet the most overlooked:
/ Use a smaller pot for the photo: prepare your beef stew in a regular cooking pot and choose a smaller diameter pot for the photo.
/ Place an inverted bowl at the bottom of a pot to get a more filled pot with the same amount of beef stew. The biggest disadvantage of this method is that the liquid - the sauce - sinks. It runs along the bowl to the bottom of the pot, giving you a much less saucy stew. Many viewers won't notice this, but it's for sure that grandma will wonder where all the sauce has gone. My least preferred method therefore.

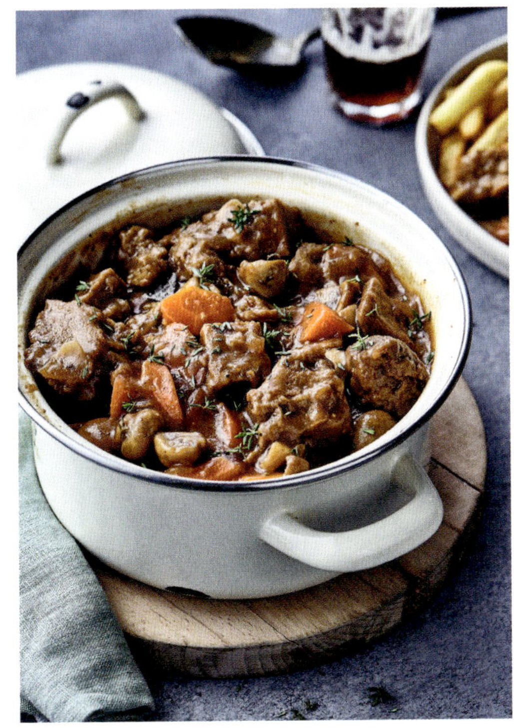

COLD DRINKS

Problem:
Drinks can cause problems in several areas:
/ reflections
/ spots
/ cold drinks get warm

Solution:
Polish the glass thoroughly with hot water and soap. Remove dust with a static cloth. While you're at it, it's best to clean two or three glasses at once. If something goes wrong with the first, you already have a spare without having to do the dishes. Hold the glass with a glove to avoid fingerprints.

Shoot close to a window and place a diffuser screen in front of the window. This way you won't see the window latch or the car in the street reflected in the glass. If you want bright sunlight, you can of course omit the diffuser screen. Turn off all lights in the room and block light entering the room through another window.

Condensation on the glass makes a drink look fresh. If the liquid isn't completely cold or the glass has been on the set for too long, spray water on the glass where the liquid is with a plant sprayer.

But careful: spray water only where there's liquid in the glass. If you've water droplets right the way down the glass, it no longer looks natural.
You can work with fake ice cubes, but know that really good fake ice cubes cost around 20 euros each! Fake ice doesn't float, while real ice does, which hinders credibility.

Glass has the advantage of transmitting light. With backlighting, light passes through the glass and your drink. Where there are ice cubes, even more light comes through and you get beautiful colour shades. Backlighting also leaves small points of light in the condensation droplets. In most cases, you'll need to soften the shadow on the other side of the backlighting (the camera side) with a reflector panel.

GLASS TYPE

We recognize hot drinks better in a porcelain cup. But if the content matters, for example the colour of the tea, you can also opt for a glass cup.

Choose your glass to match the type of drink. A cosmo cocktail is an elegant classic that everyone knows in a wide, funnel-shaped glass on a tall thin base. While a mochito belongs rather in a long drink glass.

Glasses on a base are usually more difficult to photograph, because they pick up reflections from many angles.

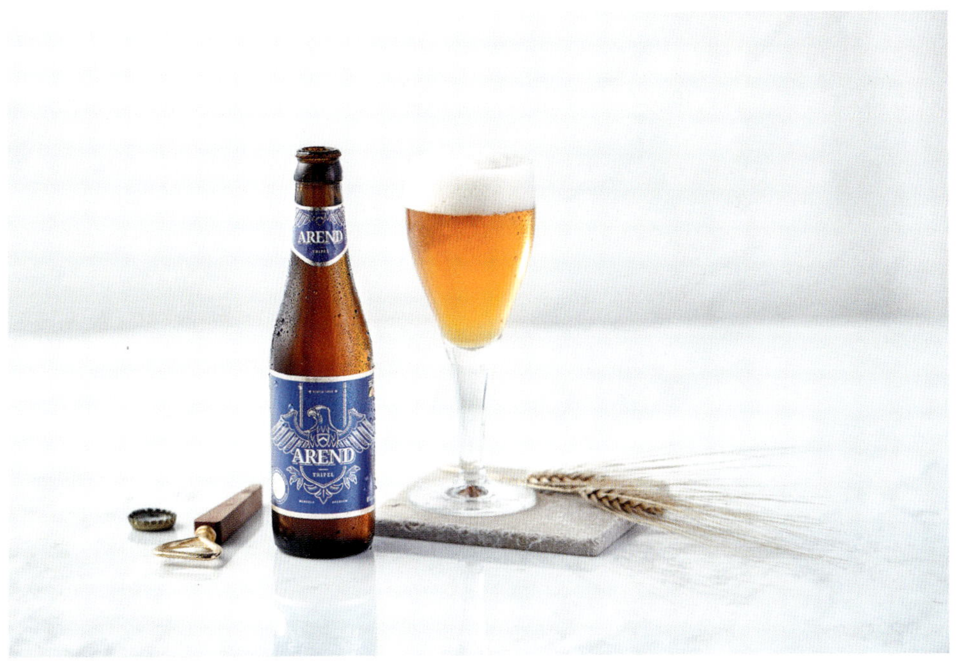

GARNISHES

You can go all out with garnishes. From half a slice of lemon to a pineapple slice, basil leaves, even a burning sprig of rosemary for that little bit of extra spectacle. Simplicity is often the best. For example, for a cocktail, prick a few berries onto a stick and place them horizontally onto the glass. Straws are best placed diagonally at the back of the glass, so that they don't stand out too much.

COLOUR

Drinks are a rewarding subject because of their colour. For smoothies, it's often a good idea to add berries for a pink or purple colour. You get green with spirulina powder. But for mocktails and cocktails also there's a whole range of syrups with fun colours. Syrup has the property of sinking, while alcohol has a lower specific weight and can therefore remain in a layer on top of it.

You can also experiment with the background colouring. Build a setting with similar colours to the drink. Or work with complementary colours for a statement effect. A background in neutral shades of white or black brings calm and focuses attention to the drink.

VANTAGE POINT

Depending on the type of drink, a front-on side view or a 45° angle are best. In side view, the focus is on the glass. This is therefore less interesting for, for example, a latte on which you've made beautiful 'latte art'. In this case, opt for a slightly higher position, so that you can see the shape of the cup but emphasize the top of the drink.

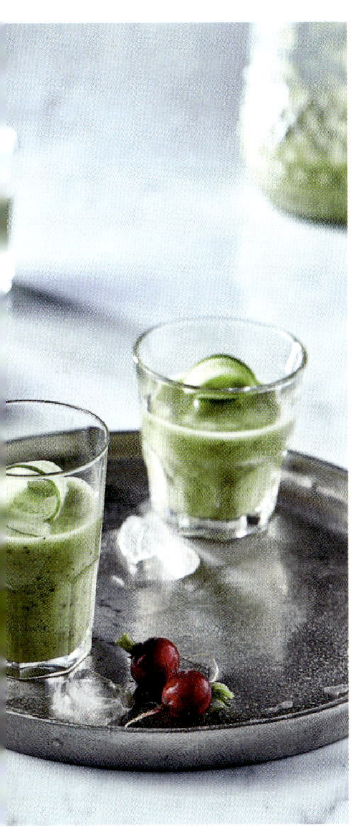

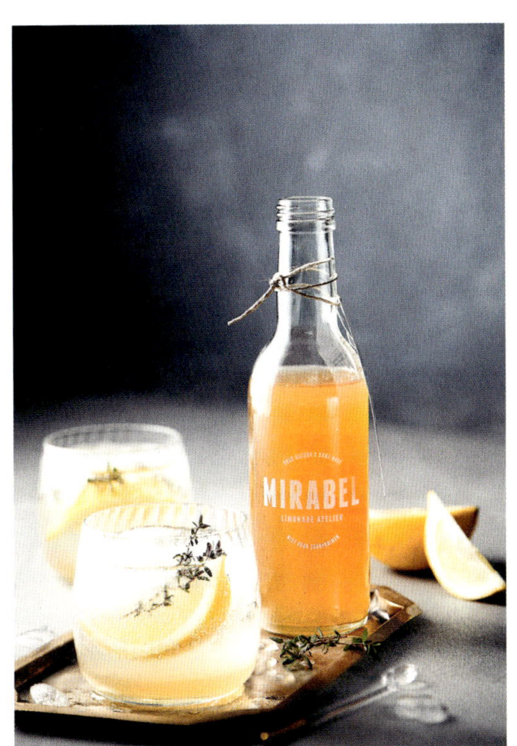
MIRABEL

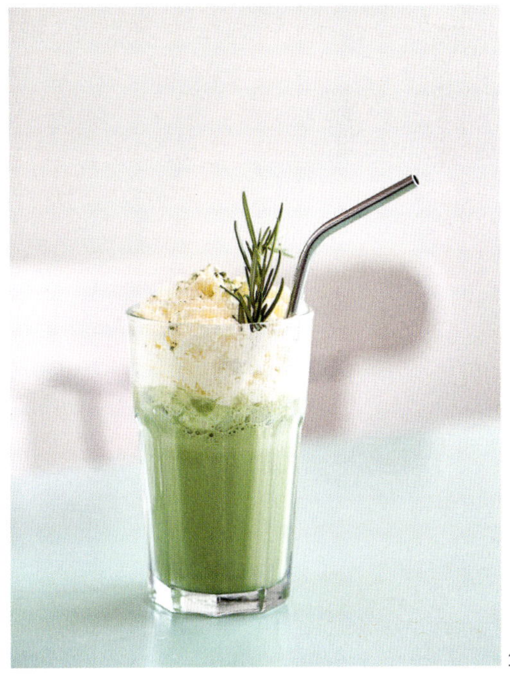

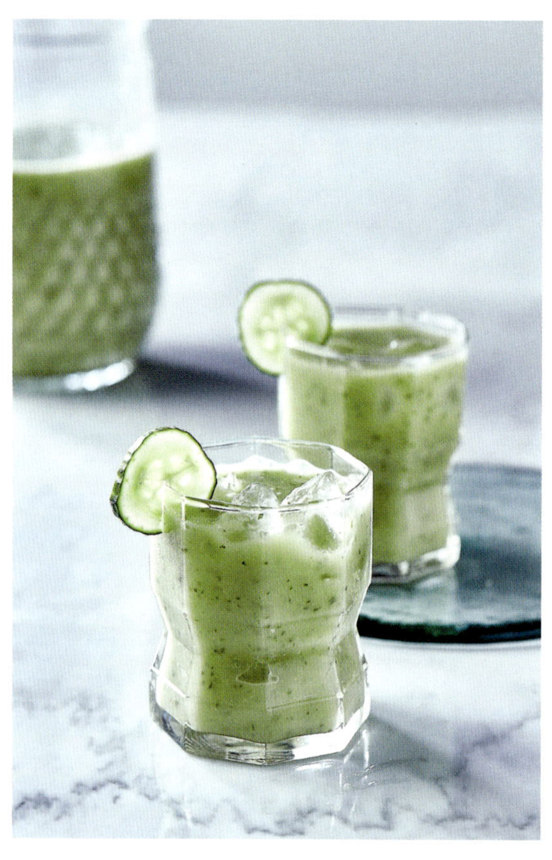

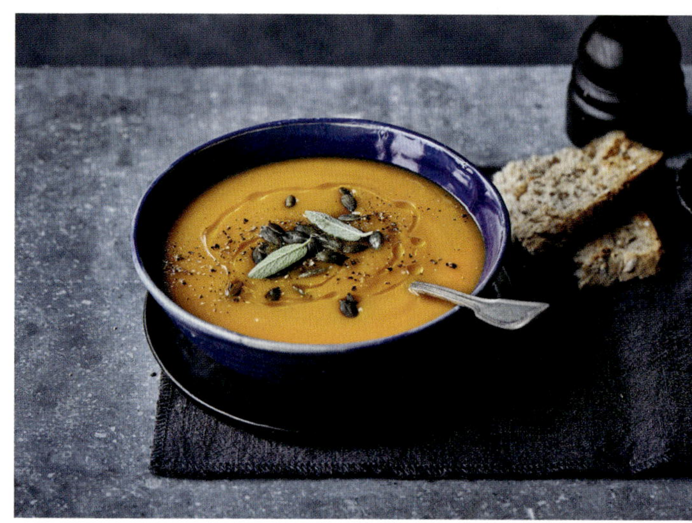

SOUP

Problem:
The colour. Unless you're making pumpkin or carrot soup, there are few vegetables that give your soup a nice colour. If you want toppings on your soup or an Insta-worthy cream swirl, then your soup should not be too thin. Otherwise the whole caboodle will quickly sink to the bottom of the bowl.

Solution:
Soups come in all types, colours and tastes. To quote three extremes: a wonderfully refreshing gazpacho on a balmy summer day, a heart-warming pumpkin soup on drizzly autumn days, or a hearty Japanese noodle soup to get through the rest of the day.

GAZPACHO
It's hot. Very hot. A fresh gazpacho does its job best when the sweat's running off your forehead. So you serve this soup ice cold. Cool colours can help with that. A glass that's been in the freezer for a while will produce a nice condensation when you pour the soup into it.

PUMPKIN SOUP
It's cold outside. And wet. And you've received 30 kilos of pumpkins from avid gardener friends. Time for a delicious steaming pumpkin soup. You guessed it, to create a warm atmosphere you can work with warm colours. But since pumpkin is orange, which is already a warm colour, you can work equally well with contrasting colours. Blue, that is. A dark background helps create the autumnal atmosphere. A toasted bun and some pumpkin seeds add to the story.

NOODLE SOUP
A noodle soup is a busy dish. All attention has to be on the soup itself. Start by placing noodles at the bottom of the bowl and add soup. Arrange the vegetables, possibly the meat and half eggs, on top. You can dress some noodles in an S-shape or pull some up with tweezers. Finish with some fresh green herbs, such as rings of spring onion and sesame seeds.

VANTAGE POINT
Also try to photograph a soup from a slightly tilted perspective. You can see the shape of the soup pot or the soup bowl better than if you photograph it in topshot.

SOUP DON'TS
Don't put a full pumpkin in the background of your photo. It's a clumsy object and its colour and size will draw all the attention, while the focus must be on the soup bowl. As far as I'm concerned, this applies to all types of vegetables. Personally, I don't like photos littered with ingredients to tell the viewer all that went into the dish. Pumpkin seeds, on the other hand, are small and link sufficiently with the main ingredient. More than that you don't need.

Floating blocks of vegetables on your soup. The specific weight of vegetables is generally higher than that of soup, and in a thin soup they will normally sink to the bottom. The old styling techniques remedied this by placing an upturned cup in a soup bowl on which to rest the vegetables, nuts, or whatever. It's the miracle of Christ walking on water: it feels unnatural. Parsley leaves and light herbs or seeds will float, especially if your soup is made with hearty vegetables, such as pumpkin or cauliflower.

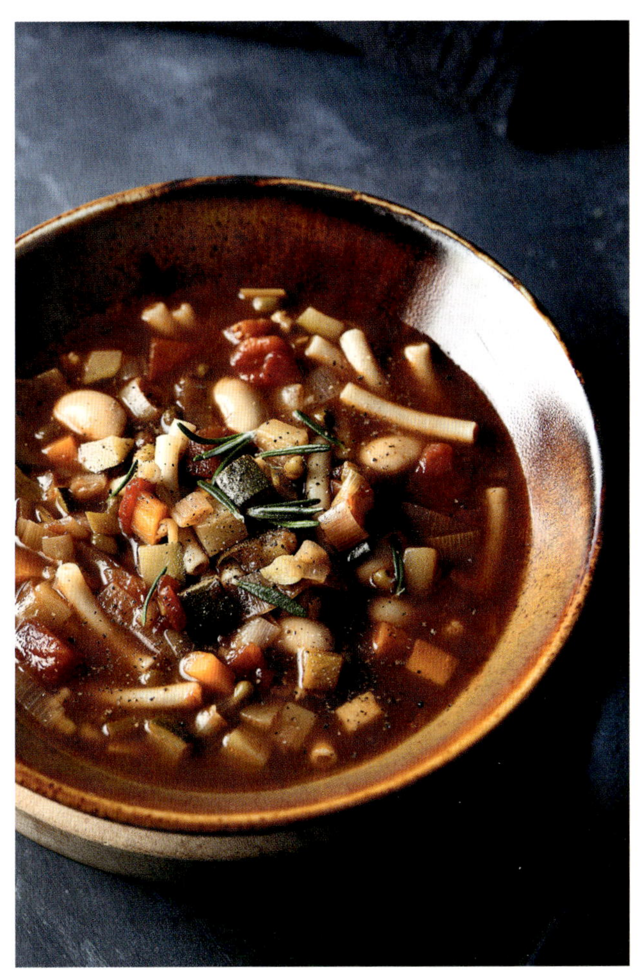

SIDENOTE:

Colours are extremely important in a dish like soup that lacks texture and shape. When shooting this noodle soup, something was missing. I started shooting on a background in the same shade as the bowl containing the soup. As beautifully as Ann, the food stylist who contributed to this book, prepared the soup, something was not right. I changed the surface to a dark colour, the same shade as the stone plank and everything suddenly seemed to fall into place.

AT THE RESTAURANT

Problem:

This is where few people can resist getting out their smart phones to take a picture of what they've been served. I too plead guilty here. But in a restaurant the lighting is never the best and standing on your chair to take a photo a bit out of the question.

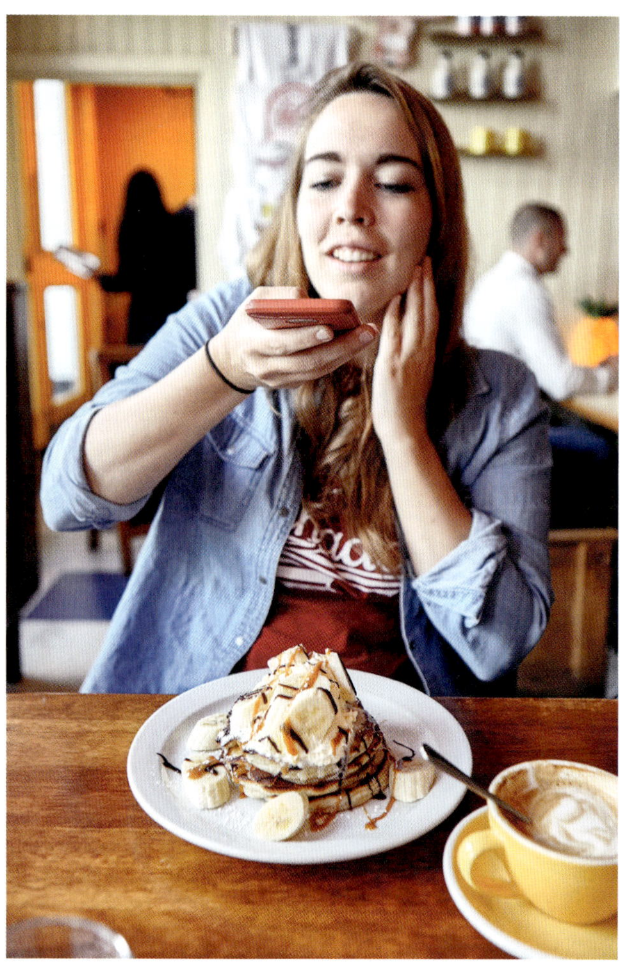

Solution:

1. If you're going for lunch, choose an indoor table next to the window. At noon you have the advantage of having already beautiful natural light. In the evening you can use a slow shutter speed and manual white balance to overcome the problem of too little and too yellow light.
2. Make sure that the shadow of your smart phone or a table companion doesn't fall on the dish. You'll need all the light there is, especially at night.
3. Choose a portable LED light to act as a fast source of light instead of your on-camera flash! Apart from throwing ugly shadows, flash also disturbs the other guests.
4. Remove all 'ugly' items from your framing. A dirty napkin, bunch of keys, a wallet and the like disrupt your composition.
5. Keep the composition simple. Often your plate at a restaurant is a picture that does not require many props. Maybe a small glass of water at most (a wine glass is tall and big and diverts a lot of attention) and a fork.
6. Ask your table companion to hold a plate for human presence.

SIDENOTE:

When I go out for dinner, I hardly ever take the time to take a nice picture of my plate. The result is therefore not great. This type of photo İ generally take just for myself, to share in a family circle or at most for Insta Stories. The light is lousy, no thought has been given to the composition, but the food was tasty, and as long as I know that, it's more than enough.

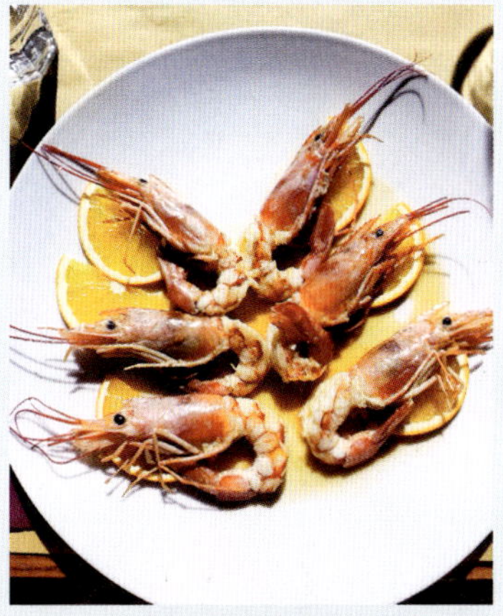

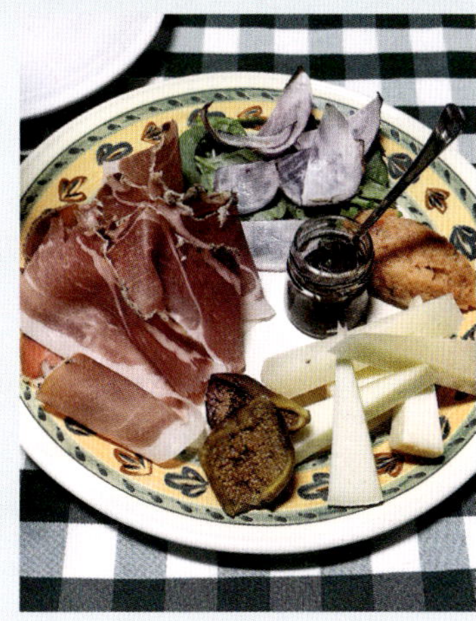

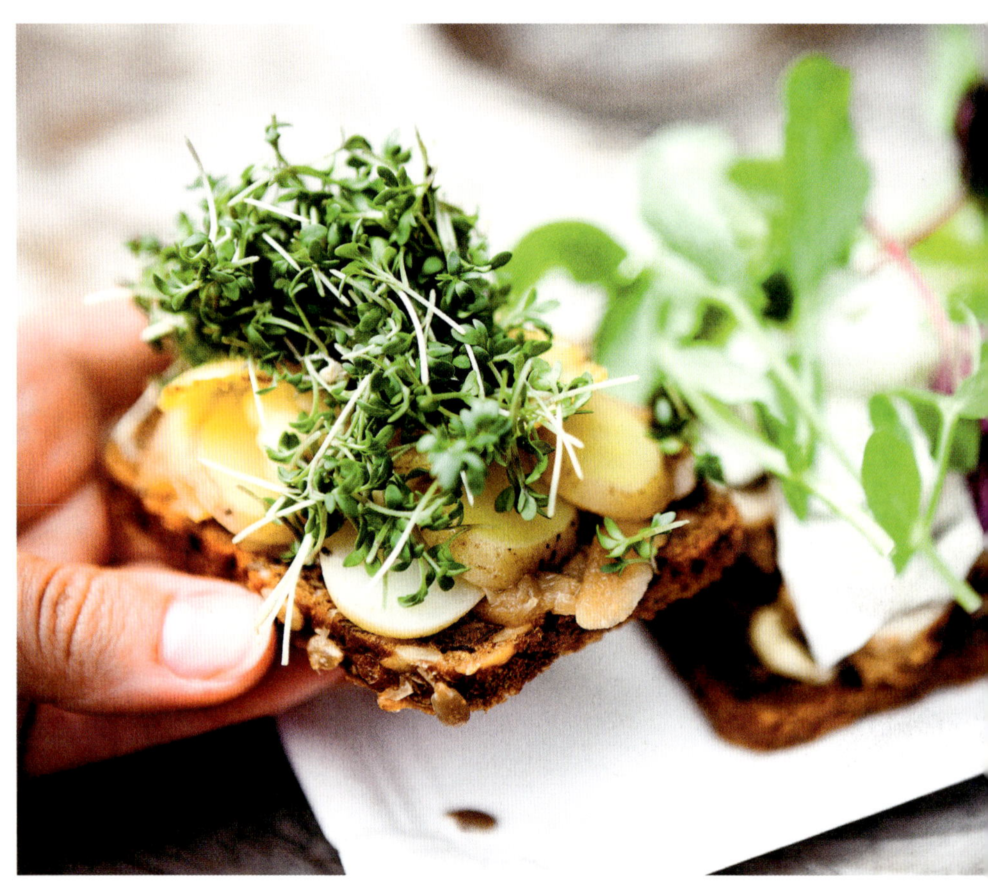

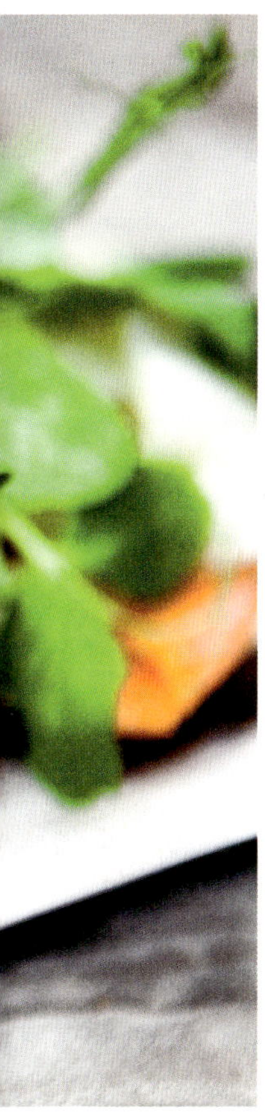

These are snapshots I took at a street food market. If the bystanders don't know that you are photographing them, be quick and have an answer ready when questions arise. With an assignment, on the other hand, the people portrayed are informed and you have less hesitation and more time to take a good picture.

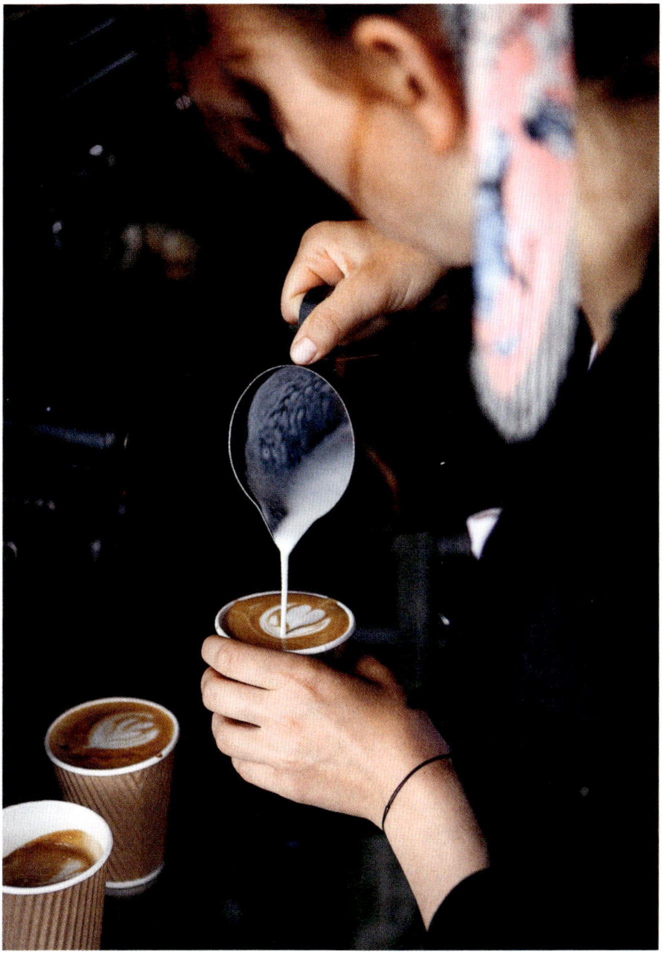

INGREDIENTS

It doesn't always have to be a full meal. Raw ingredients can be beautiful on their own. Look for colour, texture, structure. What nicer sight than red, round, home-grown tomatoes in the sun on your patio? Play with light and composition to bring out the beauty of ingredients.

RULE OF THUMB

Practice makes perfect. This phrase is applicable in so many areas. In food styling too: just try it! Not working like you thought it would? Try it differently next time. The third time you do something, you've already learned from the mistakes of your two previous attempts.

For food styling it makes no sense to impose all kinds of rules for every possible dish. Each dish has different but at the same time not very specific requirements. I give some tips for difficult cases, such as soup, burgers, casseroles, meat. But otherwise - hate to disappoint you! - there are no real rules or magic tricks for natural food styling.

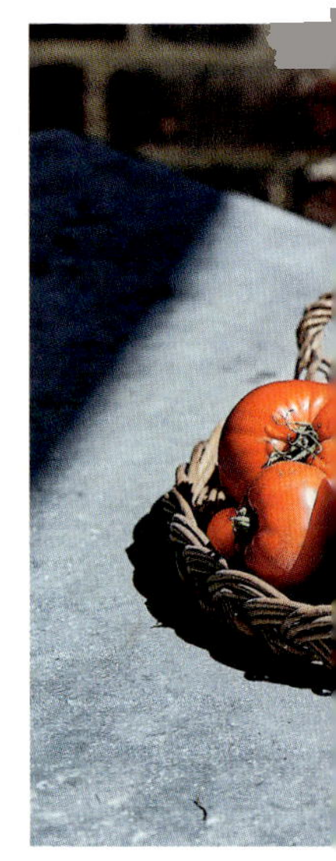

TIP:

Use the ingredients that go into your dish as props. Don't overdo it, less is more!

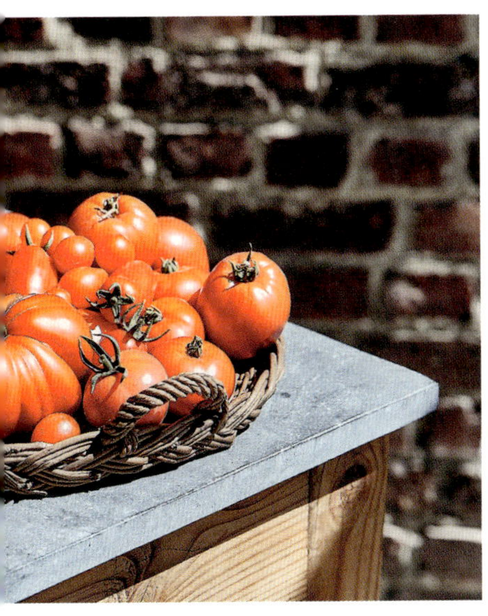

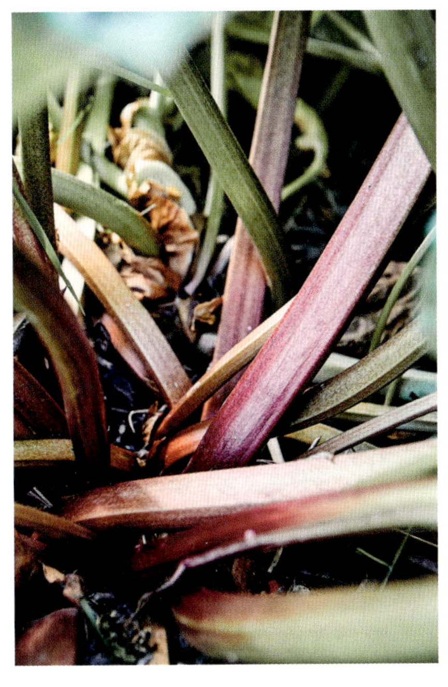

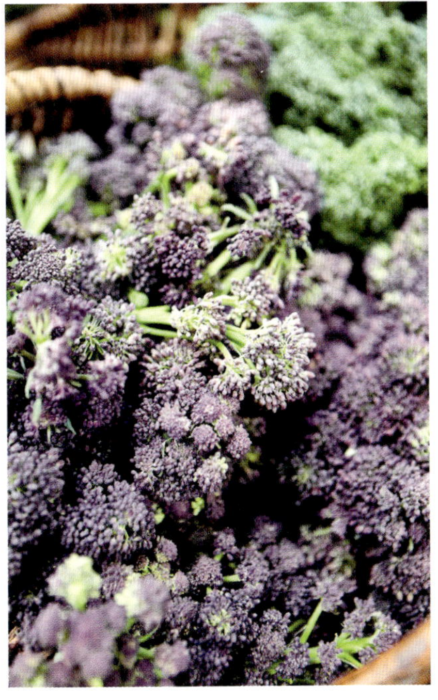

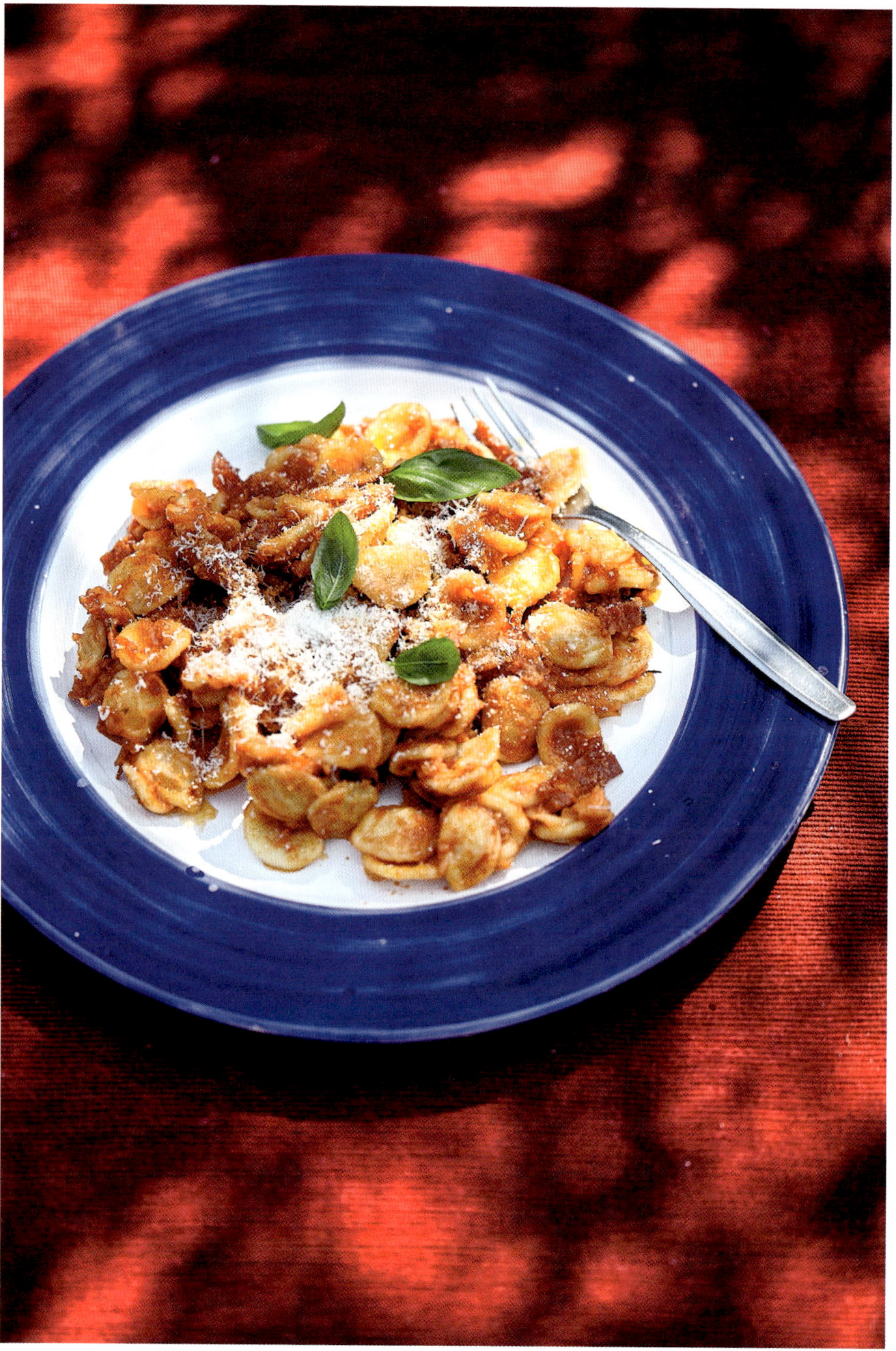

ON VACATION

My last trips were car holidays. Here you'll have the luxury of taking a few props along with you and photographing in your holiday home, I thought. Honest? I haven't used any prop from home on vacation yet. That's because I'm not in the mindset of staging everything when I'm on a relaxing vacation.

The moments I still want to capture on a photo are often beautiful as they are. There will always be a nice patio table, an attractive plate and a tablecloth. More than that you don't need.

So use what you can find at the location. That too is creativity. Accept that you don't have to take the same kind of photo as at home. Stand under an olive tree to evoke the southern atmosphere or photograph a game animal on a rock high up on a mountain peak. It's the environment in which you find yourself that makes your photo 'your very own'. This is how you tell the story of the type of holiday.

MOREOVER, TAKING LESS WITH YOU FROM HOME MEANS MORE SPACE TO BUY NICE THINGS ON HOLIDAY!

TIP:

Be sure to check out the Cases in this book. There I go deeper into photography in less controlled situations, such as at a restaurant and during a dinner party.

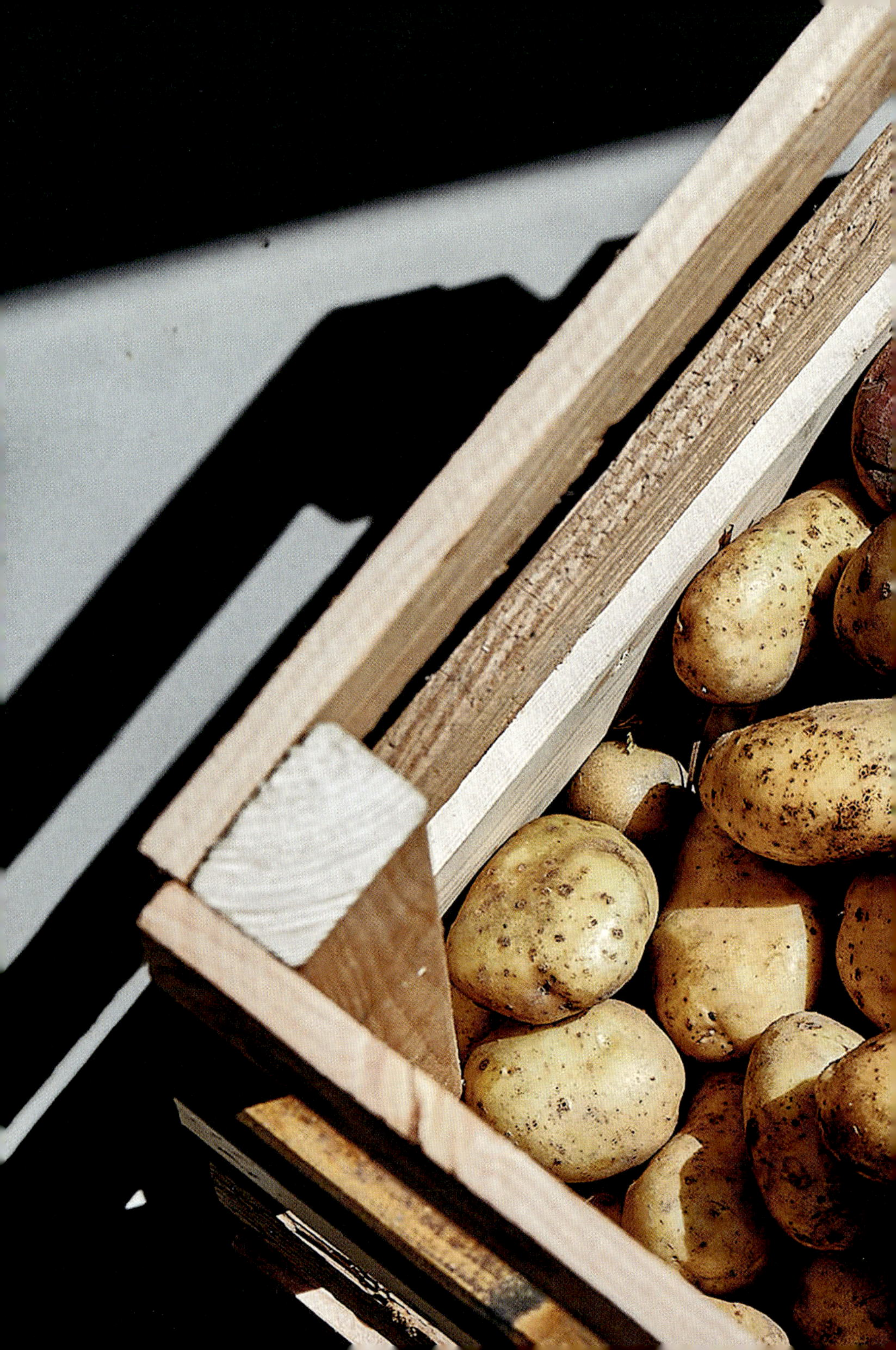

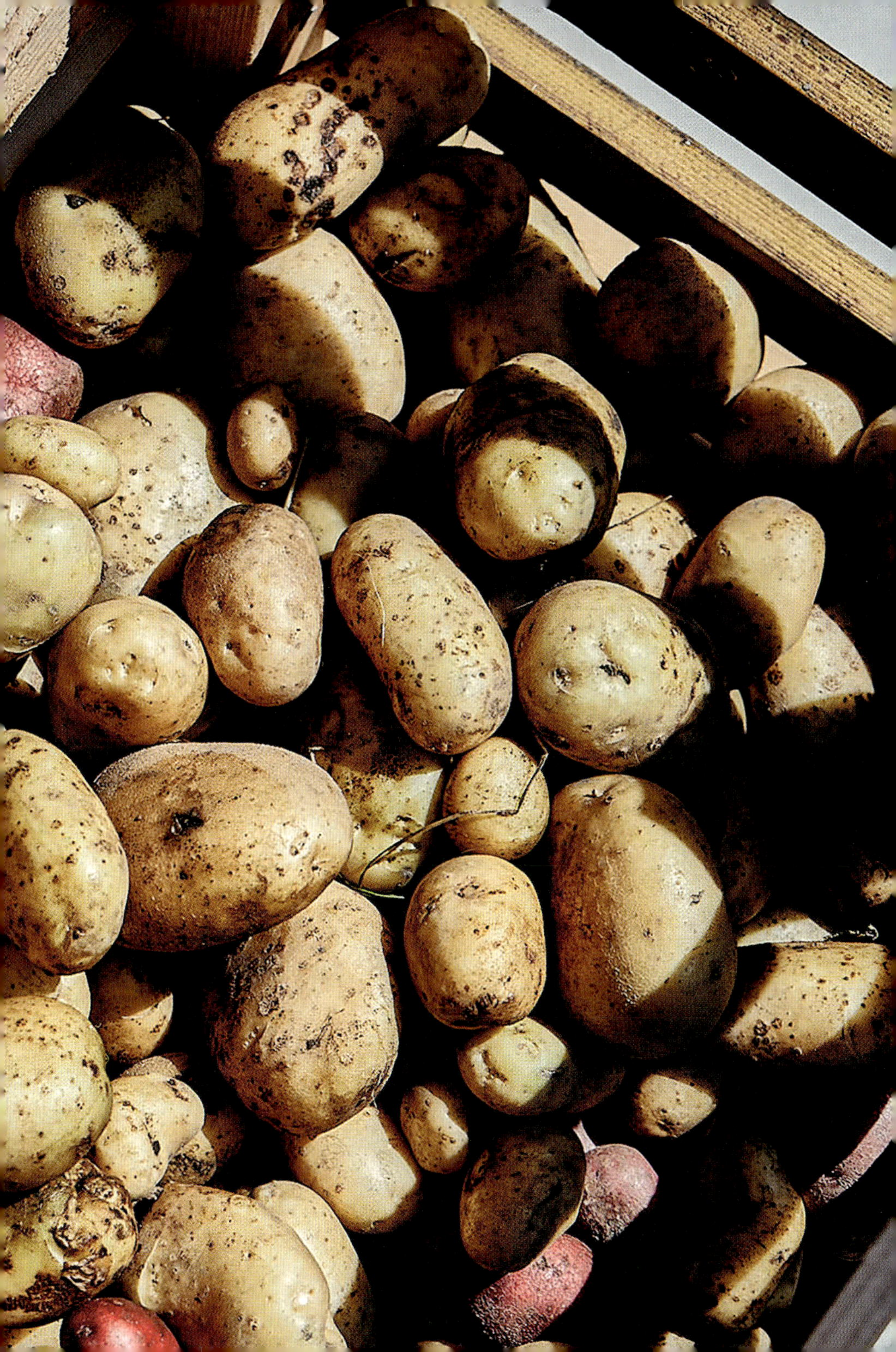

BY WAY OF CONCLUSION

Do you have any questions after reading this book? Have you browsed it 130 times and is it falling apart? Are the photos not working out as you'd like?

You can go to the *Foodfotografie & styling* Facebook group for questions and complaints. You can also ask for feedback on a photo you took. The community and myself will be happy to help you. I also give more exercises in addition to this book.

Keep a close watch on the website www.workshopfoodfotografie.be. New workshops in small groups and e-books are regularly published, on both general and specific topics in the field of food photography and food styling.

Thank you for purchasing this book, I hope it has already helped you!

Greetings,
Eveline Boone

THANK YOUS

I owe it to my parents that I am now a photographer and can earn my living with it. They left me free to choose to study photography and walk my own path. Although self-employment isn't part of our family tradition, they've continued to believe in me and are always ready to help me.

My love, my listening ear, great cook, nimble-fingered aid and IT masterbrain Leander; thank you for your unconditional support and help with so many things that I sometimes reluctantly admit I can't do on my own. I'm happy to be able to share crazy ideas and big plans with you.

It's nice to have family, friends and acquaintances who appreciate my work and give me a little push (or a kick in the butt) when necessary. Thank you to them too, for being ready to read my text for this book just before the deadline, tracking down remaining errors and for inspiring me.

Thank you Canon for the great collaboration on this book. A thank you to Delhaize Zottegem-Geraardsbergen for the wonderful ingredients for some of the dishes in this book.

Finally, thank you Lannoo, for giving me the opportunity to publish this book.

www.lannoo.com
Register on our website to receive a regular newsletter with information on new books and interesting, exclusive offers.

www.frenchbeans.be
Foodfotografie & styling
frenchbeans.be

Text and photography: Evelien Boone
Food styling: Ann De Roy, Evelien Boone
Photography portrait p. 11 and back cover: Wendy Huyghebaert
Photos commissioned by: Eveline Delnooz (p. 68, 70, 106, 109), Dripl (p. 20), EVA vzw (p. 57, 139), Karamel Branding (p. 64, 189), Den Eeuwigen Beenhouwer (94), Steunpunt Adoptie (p. 71, 111, 137, 164, 165, 168, 170, 180, 187), Mirabel (p. 159, 191)
Graphic design: Elke Treunen
Format: Android

If you have any comments or questions, please contact our editorial team at: redactielifestyle@lannoo.com

D/2021/45/187 - NUR 460-473
ISBN: 978 94 014 7097 1